Empires, Ruins + Networks

EMPIRES, RUINS + NETWORKS

—THE TRANSCULTURAL AGENDA IN ART—

EDITED BY

SCOTT McQUIRE & NIKOS PAPASTERGIADIS

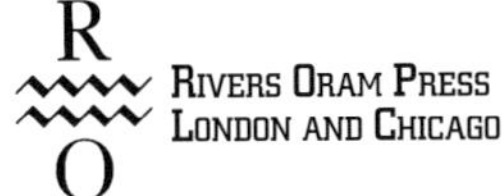

RIVERS ORAM PRESS
LONDON AND CHICAGO

Rivers Oram Publishers Ltd
144 Hemingford Road, London N1 1DE
www.riversoram.co.uk

First published in 2005

Distributed in the United States of America by
The Independent Publishers' Group
814 North Franklin Street
Chicago, Illinois 60610

Designed and typeset in Australia by Andrew Budge, Designland
Printed in Australia by BPA Print Group

A catalogue record for this book is available from the British Library

ISBN 1 85489 165 0 (hardback)
ISBN 1 85489 166 9 (paperback)

Contents

Acknowledgements

Empires Ruins + Networks: The Transcultural Agenda in Art belongs to an ongoing project that critically examines contemporary aesthetic and cultural transformations from the perspective of the South. The central aim of this book is to probe the frontiers of artistic practice in the age of ubiquitous digital technology and the post-9/11 'war on terror'. Such an undertaking is impossible without drawing on a network of diasporic intellectuals and artists who investigate the subtle liquidities and immutable resistances of contemporary cultural practices and their relation to identity. The editors extend their sincere gratitude to all the contributors from around the world who provided words, images and inspiration for this publication.

Parts of this book originated in presentations at the highly successful conference, *Empires Ruins + Networks: Art in Real Time Culture*, held at the Australian Centre for the Moving Image in Melbourne in April 2004 as a result of a partnership between the Australia Council, ACMI and the University of Melbourne. Thanks must go to Geert Lovink for his invaluable input to concept development for the conference, and to Helen Stuckey and Victoria Lynn from ACMI for their skill and grace under the pressure of staging such a complex event. The editors would also like to acknowledge the vision of the Australia Council Multicultural Advisory Committee in commissioning the conference, and particularly the ongoing support and enthusiasm of Cecelia Cmielewski and Lisa Colley for its realisation. We also gratefully acknowledge the Australia Council's contribution towards the publication of this book, which stands in dialogue with *Complex Entanglements* (2003), which was also supported by the Australia Council. The conceptual framework underlying our contribution to this book was refined in the course of a project on art and digital technology funded by the Australian Research Council.

Many people contributed to the book's production. In particular we would like to thank Meredith Martin and Vicky Mason for their tireless research, and Louise Adler at MUP and Liz Fidlon at Rivers Oram Press for their support.

Our thanks also to the following authors and publishers for permission to print extracts from their texts.

V. S. Naipaul, *The Enigma of Arrival,* © V. S. Naipaul 1987.

J. G. Ballard, *Drowned World,* © Victor Gallancz, a division of
Orion Publishing Group.

Robert Smithson, *Robert Smithson: The Collected Writings* (ed. Jack Flam),
© Nancy Holt.

Amitav Ghosh, *Dancing in Cambodia, At Large in Burma,*
© Ravi Dayal Publishers.

We would like to dedicate the book to Lachlan and Maya, whose smiles illuminated all stages of this project.

—*Scott McQuire and Nikos Papastergiadas*

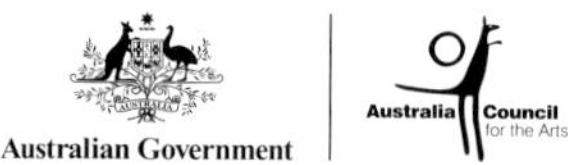

This project has been assisted by the Federal Government through the Australia Council, its arts funding and advisory body. It is an initiative of the Australia Council's Arts in a Multicultural Australia policy.

Contributors

EDDIE BERG founded Moviola (now known as the Foundation for Art & Creative Technology—FACT) in Liverpool in 1988. FACT is now one of Europe's leading arts organisations, specialising in the commissioning, presentation and support of film, video and new media art. He is an Executive Member of the Board of VAGA (Visual Arts & Galleries Association in Britain); a member of the Creative Industries Think Tank for the North West of England; and was part of the curatorial team that created and produced the International Exhibition of the 2002 Liverpool Biennial of Contemporary Art.

TONY BIRCH is a writer who has published widely in the areas of short fiction, poetry and creative non-fiction. He has also worked as a writer and curator in collaboration with photographers, film makers and artists. He was the senior curator on the 'Koori Voices' exhibition at Melbourne Museum's Bunjilaka Centre. He has a Master of Arts in creative writing from the University of Melbourne and a PhD in urban cultures and histories.

CARLOS CAPELÁN was born in Uruguay and has been living in Nordic countries since 1973. He is Professor at the Bergen Art School in Norway, and is currently based in Spain. Carlos is an installation-based artist who has exhibited all over the world, including Havanna, Johannesburg, Kwang-Ju, Bogata, Santa Fe and San Paulo. Carlos works in the area of intellectual performance about political diversity and cultural strategies dealing with issues of representation.

PAUL CARTER is an artist and writer whose books include *The Road to Botany Bay* (1987), *The Lie of the Land* (1996), *Repressed Spaces: The Poetics of Agoraphobia* (2002), *Material Thinking: The Theory and Practice of Creative Research* (2004) and *Mythform: The Making of Nearamnew at Federation Square* (Miegunyah Press, Melbourne University Publishing, 2005). This last is an account of the public artwork he made for Federation Square in collaboration with Lab architecture studio. Other public artworks and installations include: *Relay* (with Ruark Lewis) at Fig Grove, Homebush Bay (a commission of the Sydney 2000 Olympics) and *The Calling to Come* (Museum of Sydney). He is Professorial Research Fellow at the University of Melbourne.

SEAN CUBITT (seanc@waikato.ac.nz) is Professor of Screen and Media Studies at the University of Waikato, New Zealand. He has published widely on contemporary arts, media and culture. His most recent books are *Digital Aesthetics* (Sage, 1998), *Simulation and Social Theory* (Sage, 2001), *The Cinema Effect* (MIT 2004) and *EcoMedia* (Rodopi, 2005).

OKWUI ENWEZOR is an international scholar and historian who has pioneered curatorial practice on the themes of cultural difference and globalisation. He was the Artistic Director of DocumentaXI, in Kassel, Germany, 2002. He was the Artistic Director of the 2nd Johannesburg Biennale, 1997. Until recently, Enwezor held a position as the Adjunct Curator of Contemporary Art at the Art Institute of Chicago. He is currently Adjunct Professor at the University of Pittsburgh.

MARINA FOKIDIS is an independent curator and critic based in Athens, Greece. She is a founding member and Co-director of Oxymoron, a non-profit organisation founded in 2000, which dedicated to the promotion of contemporary visual art in Greece. Oxymoron has emerged as a springboard from which artistic and intellectual discourse develops into art productions for the public realm. Fokidis was the commissioner of the Greek pavilion at the 50th Venice Biennale, and project director of the public projects on the Monument to Now, for the Olympic Games cultural program. She is a frequent contributor to the arts sections of major newspapers in Greece and Flash Art International.

KENDELL GEERS was born in May 1968. He grew up in Johannesburg and it was there that he first began making art. Influenced by the immediate, highly charged political context, his art from that time was characterised by a strong political charge. He has participated in Documenta, the Biennials of Gothenburg, Valencia, Johannesburg, Istanbul, Pusan and Taiwan, and is in the process of setting up his own, called Videnial.

ROSS GIBSON is a teacher and writer who also makes films and multimedia systems. His most recent books include *Exchanges: Cross-Cultural Encounters in Australia and the Pacific* (edited, 1996) and *Seven Versions of an Australian Badland* (2002). He has written and directed award-winning films, including influential *Camera Natura* (1985) and *Wild* (1993). He has also curated several acclaimed exhibitions, including the '?Crime Scene?' installation at the Justice and Police Museum in Sydney in 1999 and 2000, and 'Remembrance + The Moving Image' at the Australian Centre for the Moving Image in 2003. Gibson was senior consultant producer at the Museum of Sydney between 1993 and 1996, and Creative Director at the Australian Centre for the Moving Image from 1999 to early 2002. He is currently Research Professor of New Media and Digital Culture at the University of Technology, Sydney.

SIMRYN GILL is a Singapore-born artist who presently divides her time between Sydney and Port Dickson, Malaysia. Some of her methods have involved object making, making collections, photography and the use of texts. Recent solo exhibitions include at Ikon Gallery, Birmingham in 2000, Petronas Gallery, Kuala Lumpur in 2001 and the Art Gallery of New South Wales in 2002. Gill exhibited a new project at Matrix, University of California Berkley Art Museum in February 2004.

GEERT LOVINK (1959, Amsterdam) is a Dutch/Australian media theorist, net critic and activist who studied political science at the University of Amsterdam (MA) and holds a PhD from the University of Melbourne. During 2003 he was a postdoctoral fellow at the University of Queensland in Brisbane. In 2004 he was appointed 'lector' (research professor) at the Hogeschool van Amsterdam (interactive media) and associate professor in new media at the University of Amsterdam. Recently his position was renamed the Institute of Network Cultures <www.networkcultures.org>.

VICTORIA LYNN is an independent curator and writer. She has held the posts of Australian Commissioner for the 50th Venice Biennale; Director, Creative Development at the Australian Centre for the Moving Image and Curator of Contemporary Art at the Art Gallery of New South Wales. The author of two books, ten exhibition catalogues and more than fifty chapters, reviews and articles, Victoria was also Chair, Visual Arts/Craft Board of the Australia Council from 2001 to 2004 and the Performance Space from 1998 to 2000.

SCOTT MCQUIRE teaches in the Media and Communication Program at the University of Melbourne. He is the author of a number of books including *Crossing the Digital Threshold* (1997), *Visions of Modernity: Representation, Memory, Time and Space in the Age of the Camera* (1998), *Maximum Vision* (1999), *The Media City* (forthcoming, 2006) and co-author with Peter Lyssiotis of the artist's book *The Look of Love* (1998).

MULTIPLICITY is a cross-disciplinary and collaborative team that includes artists, urbanists, architects, film makers and writers. They are based in Italy and have created projects that address the politics and history of migration in the Mediterranean (*Solid Sea*), as well as the appropriation of urban spaces for new aesthetic projects and the critique of the commercialisation of public spaces in Europe (*Uncertain States of Europe*).

KEVIN MURRAY is Executive Director of Craft Victoria, and maintains a creative engagement with craft through curating and writing. He has presented a number of keynote addresses, most recently at Red Deer College, Alberta in 2004 and 'Make The Common Precious' at the Ingenuity and Critique Conference at Harborfront Craft Centre, Toronto in 2004. Kevin is Director of the South Project, and has travelled to South Africa and South America to develop relationships and dialogues for this initiative. He holds a PhD in Narrative Psychology.

NIKOS PAPASTERGIADIS is Deputy Director of the Australian Centre, the University of Melbourne. He has contributed to many academic and public panels on contemporary art and the impact of migration. His own research and writing has focused on cultural theory and artistic practice in relation to place, migration and globalisation. His publications include *Modernity as Exile* (Manchester University Press, 1993), *Dialogues in the Diaspora* (Rivers Oram Press, 1998) and *The Turbulence of Migration* (Polity Press, 2000). Recently he edited *Complex Entanglements: Art, Globalization and Cultural Difference* (Rivers Oram Press, London, 2003).

VIRGINIA PÉREZ-RATTON is an artist, independent curator and cultural agent in Costa Rica. She is founding Director of TEOR/éTica, a private, non-profit project in San José for the research and dissemination of regional artistic practices and their relationship with the international context. The first General Director of the Contemporary Art and Design Museum of Costa Rica (MADC), she has also curated the São Paulo 1996, Venice 1997, Lima 1997 and 1999, and Cuenca 2001 Biennales, and was regional curator for Central America and the Caribbean for São Paulo 1998 and Cuenca 2004. She has published numerous articles and catalogue texts, both for individual artists and for institutions, locally and internationally.

LISA REIHANA works with a range of materials from video, photography, sculpture and fashion. She has an impressive exhibition record, both locally and internationally, representing New Zealand in the 2000 Sydney Biennale, the Noumea Biennale in 2002, and the Asia Pacific Triennial in 1996 and 2003. Her work is also included in the New Zealand Contemporary Art Exhibition 'Paradise Now?' at the Asia Society Museum in New York in February 2004. Recent residencies include the Institute for Modern Art in Brisbane and The Banff Center in Canada.

LORENZO ROMITO is a founding member of the group Stalker, initiated by a group of architecture students during an occupation of Rome University in 1990. Stalker is an interdisciplinary collective whose members and collaborators have included artists, art historians, theoreticians, an astro-physicist, a geologist and a dentist. The collective focuses its projects on interstitial urban spaces, migrations of non-European cultures, urban social mobility and living patterns, observation, mapping, site-specific interventions and new media.

GILANE TAWADROS is the founding Director of inIVA (Institute of International Visual Arts), a contemporary visual arts agency based in London. She has curated or co-curated numerous exhibitions including: Shen Yuan (Arnolfini, Bristol and Chisenhale Art Gallery, 2001); Veil (New Art Gallery, Walsall; Bluecoat Art Gallery & Open Eye Gallery, Liverpool, Modern Art, Oxford, 2003 and Kulturehuset, Stockholm, 2004) and Fault Lines: Contemporary African Art and Shifting Landscapes, 50th Venice Biennale (2003). As a writer and critic,

Gilane Tawadros has written extensively on contemporary art; most recently she edited *Changing States: Contemporary Art and Ideas in an Era of Globalisation* (inIVA, 2004).

NICK TSOUTAS is Executive Director of Artspace, Sydney. He has extensive curatorial experience in Australia and internationally, and was curator of the Australian Pavilion for the 2004 Sao Paulo Biennal. He was co-convenor of the major international conference *Art + Cultural Difference + Globalization* at Artspace in July 2001, which fed directly into *Empires, Ruins + Networks*.

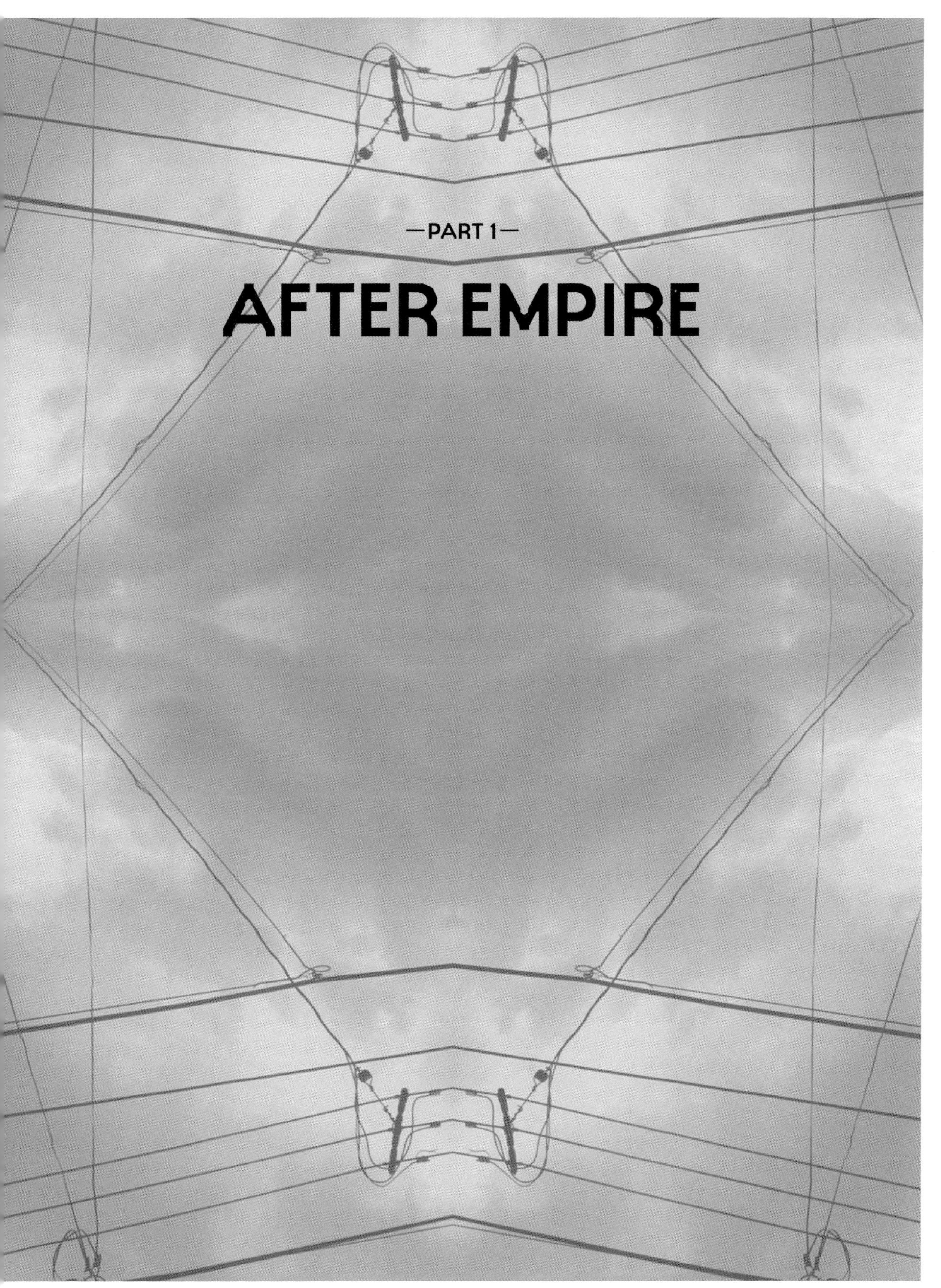

—PART 1—

AFTER EMPIRE

Introduction

SCOTT MCQUIRE AND NIKOS PAPASTERGIADIS

The title of this book reflects the field of tensions in which its debates about contemporary art and cultural difference are situated. The three terms—Empires, Ruins and Networks—should not be read as indicating a linear progression, as though history is simply moving from the ruins of empire towards the new society of networks. The following discussions map a trajectory that is far more complex, ambivalent and over-determined. Here, we begin by sketching a few coordinates of the particular historical conjuncture within which the essays that make up this book developed.

By the 1990s, with the fall of the Berlin Wall and the collapse of the former Soviet Union and its client states, the end of empire was being widely proclaimed. The ruins of the Soviet Empire were seen as the logical completion of a process that had begun with the de-colonisation of India, the Algerian war, Indonesian independence and so on. In this account, democracy— or rather, its substitute the free market—reigned supreme across most of the world.

Yet, even as the old colonial empires were crumbling, it had become clear that a new type of imperial power had emerged. What *Time* publisher Henry Luce famously declared 'the American Century' was founded less on direct territorial domination than interlocking forms of indirect economic, political and cultural control. The 'soft' missiles of Hollywood and Burbank were as much a part of the Cold War as the nuclear arsenals and military bases dotted around the world. The decisive shift towards the 'new economy' in the 1990s confirmed the rule of this new empire of information flows. The global market, consolidated on the back of new information and communication technologies, is an empire not in ruins but very much ascendant. The collapse of the older colonial empires suggested to some the collapse of political opposition to capitalism. As Guy Debord lamented before his suicide: 'One cannot go into exile in a unified world.'[1]

While economic globalisation is not solely directed by, nor uniformly of benefit to, the US economy, the laissez-faire agenda of deregulation, privatisation and submission to market imperatives is widely associated with the extension of Western domination. If the plan of extending the American century from the twentieth into the twenty-first has proved far more problematic than its proponents imagined, it is clear that the USA remains a critical measuring stick for both advocates and opponents of the global economic agenda.

The ruins of the World Trade Centre (WTC) towers in New York in 2001 marked a direct symbolic attack on this agenda. Such a reactionary tactic immediately produced an equally reactionary response: the transformation of globalisation into an explicitly military phase as the American empire initiated a series of military assaults on its perceived enemies.

The attacks on the WTC towers were designed to be seen around the world. The time lag between the first and second plane strikes ensured that news crews would be in place and that live coverage would generate maximum impact. In other words, the hijacking was not just of planes, but of screens; the terrorists occupying a fault line in the same media empires often charged with 'coca-colonisation'. The first global media event of the twenty-first century was the 'real time' image of the collapsing towers, their ruins radiating shock effects across the increasingly networked world.

Just a few years earlier, the centralised dominion of broadcast TV networks was itself thought to be in ruins as prophets such as MIT's Nicholas

Negroponte heralded 'new media' as the form of techno-liberation appropriate to the new millennium. 'Cyberspace' was the new frontier at which all the old baggage —for example, forms of embodied identity based on race, ethnicity and gender—would be left behind. A standard joke showed two dogs typing at a keyboard, with the tagline 'on the Internet no one has to know you're a dog'. The promise of social anonymity served to release many older imperatives. As the commercial stampede to stake out the virtual domain accelerated in the late 1990s, extending Moore's Law to dotcom start-up share prices, it seemed a new law of evolution—digital Darwinism—was being established. The old culture, the old economy, like the old notion of communities rooted in geographical territory, was declared defunct.

This inflated vision predictably encountered its own ruin. The 'tech wreck' of 2000 truncated the more extreme proclamations of cyber-libertarianism and scared a lot of venture capital out of the sector, leaving more space to see how others—particularly artists and activists who had been experimenting with new media forms for several decades prior to the 1990s—were actually using the new technologies. The importance of new media lies not only in the opening of new ways of making art, using digital techniques for manipulating images, text and sounds. It is also found in the potential to establish a new social context for cultural exchange. The virtue of decentralised horizontal networks is precisely their capacity to provide new ways of linking the heterogeneous communities and dispersed populations so characteristic of the twenty-first century. The political effects of this connectivity could be seen in the rolling global wave of protests opposing the invasion of Iraq in 2003, rapidly co-ordinated by Internet and mobile phone.

Yet, the potential for new media to sustain creative cross-cultural exchanges is riddled with contradictions and ambiguities. New media technologies, from digital cameras linked to pattern-recognition software surveying airports, shopping centres and streets, to 'cookies' tracking everyday patterns of Internet use, are directly implicated in new forms of surveillance and policing. Moreover, the political climate has changed markedly since the 1990s. The events of 2001, such as the turning back of the Tampa, which was carrying rescued asylum seekers in the context of the Federal election campaign in Australia, and the 'war on terror' following the attacks of September 11, have hardened political stances on border crossings (even as 'free trade' is still promoted). The positive value of cultural hybridity, which gained new legitimacy throughout the 1980s, has been clouded with new suspicion directed at strangers. Alongside the networks of political resistance to economic globalisation are the phantasmagoric images of the shadowy networks of people trafficking, arms smuggling and money laundering invoked by political parties waging 'law and order' election campaigns.

Two themes cut across many of these debates and are the twin axioms of this book:

1. the possibility of exploring a new network of global cultural dialogue— one that proceeded in horizontal southern spirals, linking South Africa, the Pacific and the USA, rather than repeating ad nauseam the well-worn colonial axes of the North–South
2. the significance of new information and screen technologies on the representation of cultural identity and the formation of new diasporic networks. In what sense has race politics been reconfigured by the codes and communication practices of the Internet?

The aim of this book is not to parade the diversity of new media, or to make another plea for the acknowledgement of multicultural perspectives. At this historical point we are seeking to interrelate and produce exciting new conjunctions between emergent forms of cultural practice and those critical voices that continue to exist, almost in the form of a tradition, at the edges of the dominant discourses.

The book unfolds and coils around a series of spirals. At the broadest level, there is the question of globalisation. The next ring is the southern regional circuit. Following down the loop is a re-thinking of national borders. Embedded within these rings is the transformation of the city to comply with the new global and civic cultural pressures. Finally, at ground level, are the emerging artistic practices that take root in local places but also splice into diasporic networks. These rings do not sit neatly inside each other; rather, they cut across each other in turbulent motion.

A key reference point for this complex pattern of cultural and historical interconnection was the exhibition and publication of Documenta XI, directed by Okwui Enwezor. The exhibition was informed by the interplay of two historical streams. First, there was a mapping of the cultural consequences of decolonisation that showed the dual but interconnected trajectories of the diasporic communities and the unending legacies of colonialism. Alongside and cutting into these trajectories was a survey of both the artistic expression of the utopian promises of modernism and the artistic responses to the dystopian ruins of post-industrial spaces. By splicing together these two narratives, post-colonial migration patterns and postmodern aporias, we gain a revealing insight into the criss-crossing traffic and mutating structures of contemporary culture and urban life.

In his introductory essay here, Enwezor extends his earlier thinking on the relationship between art and politics. The point of contact is not defined in terms of either the social activism of the artist or the contents of the artwork, but shifts to the production of new social and aesthetic relations that can in themselves transform the public sphere. He asks: 'How can we construct a global common?' The examples of the collectives serve as spurs to new ways of building connections between individual practices, civil society and international networks. This is both complemented and tempered by the contributions by Gilane Tawadros, who tracks the uneasy negotiations between African modernity and the West's claim to universalism, and Geert Lovink's blistering critique of the loss of faith in the creative potential in new media by mainstream institutions, as well as the failure of the techno-enthusiasts to seize the full responsibility of their times.

Re-thinking the global and local from the horizontal affiliations of the South is a new modality for imaginative and critical thinking. As Lisa Reihana noted 'travelling with those you love is home in motion', and in the collage of past and present that is transposed across various places under the Southern Cross there can be found surprising memories and future friend-ships. Carlos Capelán both affectionately recalled transnational links between his hometown Montevideo and stories from Australia and South Africa, while also ironically inviting Kendell Geers and others as future members of his gang without bloodlines; united not by ethnicity but by common desires. Geers's more abrasive declaration of the need for art to provoke shock was a direct response to the obliteration of dialogue that is also the ground swell of terrorism. Terror begins when the voice of the other is denied, displaced or disfigured.

To consider the place of art today is not a matter of imagining alternative places that exist outside capitalism or beyond the reaches of colonialism, for these structures have already claimed a space within us. There is no escape from these internal and external dimensions. A more rigorous strategy would include a practice that not only interrogates from within, seeking to reclaim the past and 'hijack' the present, but also develops collaborative practices that allow a space for ethical relations and the appropriate language that can make sense of specific situations. Joseph Grima explained the practices of the collective Multiplicity as an attempt to provide new kinds of mappings between cultural, technical and political agencies. Simryn Gill ruminated on the unintended rec-lamation of failed urban developments. From the futile ambitions in humid wastelands and the surveillance of traffic in the Gaza strip, to the choreo-graphed resistance by contemporary Aboriginal youth explored by Tony Birch, we witness the unexpected forms of energy and resistance that emerge from these 'negative' spaces. Maps, photographs and videos are in these instances not just representations but also tools for confronting an oppressive condition and transforming a pessimism of the will into an active responsibility.

City wars today are being fought along the front of competition for cultural tourism. Some of the most exaggerated efforts to capture attention, known as either the Acropolis complex or the Bilbao effect, have also produced an architecture of amnesia and gigantism. Paul Carter reflects on the curious transposition of rhetorical signs in the construction of urban meaning and its commodification of cultural differences, while Eddie Berg has shown that venture culturalism not only veers away from realistic capitalist development but also becomes a new form of 'cultural vulturalism', producing a kind of ruins in reverse that gives substance to the famous cartoon of a man and child peering over a horizon filled with the industrial wastelands of the north of England and the man declaring that: 'One day, son, all this will be an art gallery.' The ambivalence of place and history is consistently erased or sterilised by the very process of both 'inventing' heritage and 'creating' innovation precincts. In places such as Costa Rica, where the social polarities are even more extreme and the US hegemony at its sharpest, the cultural contradictions of globalisation are both a more distant fantasy and an even more bitter reality. The institutions of art are, in these places, not new cultural palaces, but reconfigurations of abandoned liquor factories, unused airport hangars and empty gaols. After September 11, people in Central America can shrug their shoulders in a blasé manner and say 'shit happens', and they must also brace themselves for even greater levels of political authoritarianism.

The models of artistic collaboration that were inspired by the need to involve different communities, access new technologies, disperse creative responsibility and stimulate heightened forms of feedback are now at the core of debates on contemporary practice. Marina Fokidis demonstrates through her collaboration with the collective Stalker that this is no longer an additional option but a necessary strategy for addressing the complex historical and political issues that are confronting artists on the edges of Europe. Ross Gibson reflects on the more subtle dynamics that are at play when teams of individuals come together. He focuses on the processes of attunement and agility that enable the communication between individuals to stretch prior conceptions and redirect possible energy lines. Nikos Papastergiadis argues that collaborative practice is one way in which the dominant discourses of globalisation might find new lines and networks of resistance.

In conclusion, Sean Cubitt examines the modes of identity sustained in contemporary societies characterised by dispersed empire and immanent sovereignty. If the consumer is the dominant figure of the present era, Cubitt argues that more critical stances are still possible, particularly those gleaned from the double-edged freedom of the exile and the migrant whose displacement means they cannot help but produce new cultural 'information'—in Bateson's terms 'the difference that makes a difference'. Cubitt poses questions about making a home in a world in which traditional forms of homeliness are increasingly problematic. These questions inform much contemporary art, not simply as 'content', but, as Bourriaud has noted, in the sense that the work of art itself takes on the role of generating relationships between people.

Modernity has long been haunted by the spectre of the loss of home. Not simply nostalgia for the absent home so often expressed by the coloniser or the tourist, but a more apocalyptic loss of all homes, of homeliness as such. This threat, which has a material basis in the wholesale dispossession of indigenous peoples, the exile of refugees and the mass migration of many peoples, is the other face of the modern desire to re-invent the home by transcending its previous limits. The ambiguity of electronic media is that they not only accentuate the migratory tendencies of modernity, but actively undermine the mode of inhabiting space and organising territory on which the industrial world was based. 'Access' is no longer a matter of passing beyond a wall, opening a gate or entering through a door, but demands the satisfaction of various forms of electronic scrutiny, which may or may not be connected to biological data. The relation of inside to outside—of home, of the city, of the nation, of the self—is no longer a matter of stable spatial dispositions with integral values which can be taken for granted, but has become subject to incessant modulation.

In this context, the role of art and the responsibility of the artist are of vital importance. However, critical art is no longer limited to its traditional role of reflecting existing social polarities, according to the metaphor of the mirror. Critical art must increasingly take an active role in constituting new social relationships, providing a matrix for new modes of inclusion and forms of collaboration that might counterpoint the extension of commodity production into the interstices of everyday life.

NOTE

1   Guy Debord, *Comments on the Society of the Spectacle*, Verso, London, 1998, p. 47.

The Artist as Producer
in Times of Crisis

OKWUI ENWEZOR

On 27 April 1934, Walter Benjamin delivered a lecture at the Institute for the Study of Fascism in Paris. In the lecture, 'The Author as Producer'[1], Benjamin addressed an important question which, since, has not ceased to pose itself: namely, to what degree does political awareness in a work of art serve as a tool for the deracination of the autonomy of the work and that of the author?

In addressing this vexing issue, Benjamin proposed, first, that any work of art that wishes to address political issues must by necessity avoid doing so dogmatically. But, most importantly, such work should show not just the political character of the work, but should also include its artistic quality. For Benjamin, political subject matter is not necessarily the primary problem for any artist hankering to underline a political conviction; rather, it is the competency of realisation of the work as artwork. Here is how he outlines the program of such a work: 'You can declare: a work that shows the correct political tendency need show no other quality. You can also declare: a work that exhibits the correct tendency must of necessity have every other quality.' For Benjamin, 'the tendency of a literary work can only be politically correct if it is also literarily correct'[2] is at the crux of how we can judge such work as successful. Contrary to the tendency by critics to abjure works that show a clear political tendency as empty of aesthetic integrity, Benjamin's formulation inscribes a much more rigorous test for any work aspiring to combine the qualities of the aesthetic and political in a single work. Rather than reject such work, he raised the critical stakes of what such a work must aspire to. This distinction is important for the issues I will take up throughout this text in relation to certain conceptions of artistic work by practitioners working beyond the standard aesthetic nomenclature of modern art, namely the autonomy of the work of art through its formal separation from politics or the sociocultural context.

I should also point out that Benjamin's point was made during a period of incredible pressure on artists and intellectuals, in a climate of increasing political repression under fascism and Nazism. This pressure on artists to prove their political commitment in an alliance with certain revolutionary programs during the 1930s bears on the relationship between artists and the public sphere. Therefore, his evaluation was to locate what a radical critical spirit in art could be in a time of such momentous, yet undecided, direction in the political consciousness of Europe: between the Bolshevik Revolution in Russia and the productivist model of artistic practice it instantiated and the storms of repression unleashed by fascism and Nazism across Europe. In a sense, Benjamin's lecture addressed the question of the artist's or writer's commitment under certain social conditions. This would lead him to bypass the question he raised, namely 'What is the attitude of a work to the relations of production of its time?' for a far more engaged investigation, which is what the work's position is in them.[3]

Georg Lukács posed a similar question in his 1932 essay 'Tendency or Partisanship?'[4] in which he identified a prevailing tension between the work of art and its time against an opposing point of view. What were the relations of production at the time Benjamin and Lukács were writing, and how do they compare with those of today? The situation in Europe in the 1930s was marked by a profound crisis in the international public sphere and therefore could be said to have generated a situation in which all art was produced under a climate of instability and political uncertainty. In the Soviet Union, the Bolshevik

Revolution, which attempted to dissolve the distinction between classes—whereby the so-called dictatorship of the proletariat would lead to the utopia of a classless society—became a victim of Stalinism, while the crisis of the Weimar Republic brought Hitler and the Nazis to power, and the Italian monarchy fell to Mussolini's Fascists. The global financial crisis of 1929, after the collapse of the stock market, brought about a profound and dangerous destabilisation in the international financial market, led to the Great Depression and further exacerbated the situation. These changes, beginning in the 1920s and intensifying in the 1930s, had a powerful effect on the work of the artistic avant-gardes, not least because a climate of partisanship was produced, bringing about a separation between opposing ideological forces and artistic tendencies, not just on the political front, but in the cultural and artistic spheres as well.

In the artistic sphere in Europe, the work of Dada artists is part of this legacy. Similarly, the change from the radical avant-garde project of Russian constructivism to socialist realism brought about not only abrupt change in artistic language, forms of expression and content, but also terminated the spirit of experimentation that accompanied advanced production of art. In the USA, artists of the Harlem Renaissance enacted a reverse form of modernism, one which embarked on a kind of representational art that sought to depict the nature of black life under the segregationist politics of US culture. In this reversed form, artists of the Harlem Renaissance self-consciously privileged figuration over abstraction, naturalism over illusionism, in an attempt to foreground concrete things and imagery rather than the purely speculative and theoretical conventions of avant-garde modernism. The same impulse could be seen in the context of Mexico, where artists attempted to merge the formal methods of the modernist avant-garde with the realism of socialist idealism. In Europe, the emergence of Négritude among expatriate African and Caribbean writers and artists (in alliance with Surrealism) is part of the critical spirit of artistic activism of this period. It is important to note the international dimension of this moment.

In outlining the nature of the artistic sphere during this period of political change around the world, I want to draw a comparison between then and today. I may not go so far as to identify the current situation within the global public sphere as similar to that of the 1930s, but they are comparable in two senses: first, in the deepening sense of crisis that overhangs the entire political sphere and, second, the feeling of insecurity and instability such crisis has produced within the cultural sphere. In the artistic context today, this is clear in the attempts by leading cultural institutions and critics in the media to de-legitimise artistic works that bear direct relation to the prevailing political climate. In museums, the recent return to canonical art and the historical recuperation of major careers is but a symptom of such attempts at closure that mirrors the one in the political sphere. The difference is that today, we are faced not with the machinery of state ideological forms, but a dispersed regime of political actions and increasingly vulnerable cultural platforms.

It would be unnecessary to enumerate here that from the forces of insecurity and instability (across all fields) have emerged a crisis of legitimisation that surrounds all cultural production. Today, artistic production is once again caught up in a line of separation between ideological forces: between the purveyors of beauty for beauty's sake in art and practices that insistently attempt to link form and content in the production of art works in the social realm. This link, evidenced in many cases as the connection between the social and cultural, political and artistic, constitutes a form of 'social aesthetics'[5] whereby artists attempt to go beyond the demands of conventional aesthetic norms to comment on the social crisis that pervades all relations of production and reception. However, in the present dispensation of social repression of the memory of past critical activism in the art world (most recently of the AIDS pandemic in the 1980s and 1990s), what we are instead confronted with in the distinction between artistic imperatives is not a climate of functioning, open public debate in the leading institutions and media. Rather, the opposite effect is taking root via a pervasive cultural amnesia and the brutal flattening of the artistic field into a market-sanctioned production of taste, discrete narratives and a curatorial disinclination to view artistic practice in a light not sanctioned by museological norms. The forms of contemporary art that are on offer in this realignment of aesthetic and critical forces, when viewed in the context of the changes occurring in the political and cultural field, appear either strategically ambiguous or obtusely opaque.

If we look back at the period of the early 1920s and 1930s and the conditions of production of that time, we identify them as the clearest moments at which to observe the struggle between capitalism and socialism as the driving forces behind attempts to define modern subjectivity. Today, the nature of globalisation, and its unleashing of forces of homogenisation and domination, confronts cultural producers of all stripes with a different environment within which to think knowledge in relation to subjectivity. It has been a mistake of the artistic sphere in the past decade to try to suppress the articulation of this dialectic by art and artists. As in the period of the 1930s, the complexity of the artistic field shows, more than ever, a need to make the site of artistic reception a space of vigorous, open contestation and engagement. The field of contemporary art, and practitioners within it, is broad and diverse enough to admit this necessity. Proscriptions of one form of art against another, however, limits the possibility of artists to truly function in a properly autonomous manner.

For the purposes of reviewing the positions of artistic practice in the current context, perhaps it would be worth our investigation to extend the questions raised by Benjamin and Lukács in their respective texts and apply them to the critical context of contemporary art. The insights to be gained from these two thinkers are not only relevant to understanding and decoding a visible turn that has become increasingly evident in the field of culture at large; that is, the extent to which a certain critical activism in contemporary art has become a way to restate the questions each of them raised seventy years ago. I do so by recourse to a mode of artistic activity known as collective practices.

My focus is not on activism per se, but on work driven by the spirit of activism otherwise aligned to the methods of art.

To that end, recent confrontations within the field of contemporary art have precipitated an awareness of the emergence in increasing numbers, within the past decade, of new critical, artistic formations that foreground and privilege the mode of collective and collaborative production. But the question to ask is whether this presages the return of the repressed; a bite out of the Proustian Madeleine in which memory of a social unconscious much in evidence in older collective practices from the 1950s to the 1980s—from the Letterist International, Situationist International, Laboratoire Agit Art and Art Workers Coalition to Group Material—reappears in the neon glow of a newly minted radicality. If this return could be linked to some of these earlier examples, is the collectivisation of artistic production really a critique of the poverty of the language of contemporary art in the face of large-scale commodifications of culture that have merged the identity of the artist with the corporate logo of global capitalism? Or is it just a retooling of the old avant-garde mode of dissent already disciplined by museum collections? These questions shadow the return of collectivity in contemporary artistic practice. Given its present insistence and the broad geographic area in which it has sprouted, it appears that something more than art-world fashion is the guiding principle behind this turn. Therefore, to ignore the consequences of the disaffection with contemporary artistic practice and the brutal positioning that takes place within the art world, by artists working within this mode, is to miss the vital power of dissonance that is part of its appeal to the contemporary thinkers and artists who propose collectivity as a course of artistic work. Of course, we need not be reminded that there is nothing novel about collectivity in art, as such. It's been a crucial strategy (and a 'tendency' in the sense deployed by Lukács) of the avant-garde throughout the twentieth century. How was this 'tendency' deployed? According to Lukács:

'Tendency'... is something very relative. In bourgeois literary theory...
a text is seen as displaying 'tendency' if its class basis and aim are
hostile (in class terms) to the prevailing orientation; one's own
'tendency', therefore, is not a 'tendency' at all, but only that of one's
opponent. The positions of struggle that the various literary factions
of the bourgeoisie took up against one another, in which connection,
of course, it was generally the more politically and socially progressive
trend that was particularly reproached for its 'tendency', rather than
the reactionary trend, were assumed with double vigour against the
first beginnings of proletarian literature.[6]

This reproach of 'politically and socially progressive' work for its 'tendency'
illuminates succinctly the key point of ideological struggle evident in
contemporary art. Of course, it would be naïve to speak of the key ideological
tussle today as being between bourgeois and proletarian cultures. Or that
social relations are fundamentally determined by class antagonism. Yet, a
persistent antagonism between two socially differentiated ideals of artistic
practice remains in the definitions and de-definitions of art; between
aesthetic and anti-aesthetic positions, much as Lukács addressed it in his
essay. This tension is particularly acute with work that takes an overtly
realistic approach to the representation of social life, whereby:

Any depiction of society, whether the society of the proletariat or that
of the bourgeoisie, and no matter whether this was presented from the
class standpoint of the proletarian itself or simply from one close to
it, was viewed as 'tendentious', and every possible argument as to its
'inartistic' and 'hostile-to-art' character was marshaled against it.[7]

While such antique terms as bourgeois and proletarian concept of society
have become intellectually inoperative as descriptors of the contestation of

values within contemporary art, the more antique notions of tradition and canon endure and remain powerful. Institutions of art and mainstream critics, in fact, insist on them. So what does the artist who is disenchanted and alienated from the limited and limiting options of working within a specified grid of modernist artistic conduct do? If not exactly an outright revolutionary, or having the belief that art can effect any kind of change, there is, minimally, a level of earnest belief (oftentimes treated derisively by cynical critics, especially in times of political repression such as is again current) in Marx's dictum that the intellectual's revolutionary role is not to interpret but to change the world. That artists readily subscribe to this dictum can be detected in a variety of forms of collective or collaborative work. Therefore, a proper understanding of collectivity would have to be traced through its affinities with past examples as a tendency of responses by artists to relations of production in its time. This story belongs to the history of modernism proper.

The position of the artist working within collective and collaborative processes subtends earlier manifestations of this type of activity throughout the twentieth century. Collectivity (a good example of its most intellectually stringent form is the work of Art & Language) performs an operation of irruption and transformation on traditional mechanisms and activities of artistic production that locate the sole figure of the individual artist at the centre of authorship. Under the historical conditions of modernist reification, collective or collaborative practices (that is, the making of an artwork by multiple authors across porous disciplinary lines) generate a radical critique of artistic ontology qua the artist and, as such, also question the enduring legacy of the artist as an autonomous individual within modernist art. This concerns the authenticity of the work of art and its link to a specific author. However, there is a level at which the immanence of this discourse is also evidenced in the critique of the author in postmodernism. On both levels, I would argue that the anxieties that circumscribe questions concerning the authenticity of either the work of art, or the supremacy of the artist as author, are symptomatic of a cyclical crisis in modernity about the relationship of art to its social context, and the status of the artist as more than an actor within the economic sphere within which art operates. This crisis has been exceptionally visible in all the decades of the twentieth century.

Historically, collectives tend to emerge during periods of crisis; in moments of social upheaval and political uncertainty within society. After the relative tranquillity of the 1950s—a period of coming to terms with the immense destruction as a result of World War II—the political and cultural climates of the 1960s evidenced by national liberation movements in the former European colonies, the discord of the Vietnam War, the Civil Rights movement in the USA, the rise of military dictatorships in Latin America, the women's movement, among many other changes, opened up the discursive space of culture to new articulations of cultural resistance and artistic critique. The crisis of the 1960s not only changed the rules of engagement in the critical spheres of culture, it also forced reappraisals of conditions of production, the re-evaluation of the nature and forms of artistic work, the transformation of artistic expression, content, material etc. and the reconfiguration of the position of the artist in relation to economic, social, cultural and political institutions.

If the evaluative context of collectivity flows from the contestatory demands of political, social and cultural formations, there are two types of collective and collaborative practices that are important for this discussion. The first type can be summarised as possessing a structured modus vivendi based on permanent, fixed groupings of practitioners working over a sustained period. In such collectives—for example, London-based groups such as Black Audio Film Collective, Sankofa Film Collective and New York-based collectives such as Group Material—authorship represents the expression of the group rather than that of the individual artist, regardless of the level of contribution by a member. The second type of collective tends to emphasise a flexible, non-permanent course of affiliation—here, the Situationist International is the best paradigm—privileging collaboration on a project basis rather than on a permanent alliance between its members. This type of collective formation can be designated as networked collectives, working across affinities of interest, whether artistic, discursive or ideological. Such networks are far more prevalent today due to radical advances in communication technologies in the age of globalisation, whereby a group can engage in a sustained collaborative work with multiple individuals and organisations, as RAQS Media Collective, Multiplicity, Le Groupe Amos, and Huit Facettes do in New Delhi, Milan, Kinshasa and Dakar, respectively.

However, if we shall trace the emergence of the artist as producer in times of crisis we do so by first linking up with modernism. Consequently, in collective work we witness immediately the complication of modernism's idealisation of the artwork as the unique object of individual creativity. For in collective work what is forcefully delineated is the simultaneous aporia of artwork and artist. In the immediate sense, this delineation tends to lend collective work a social or political, rather than artistic, character, thereby radically vitiating the normative rules of modernist formalism and its insistence on the primacy of the artistic object. Consequently, the collective imaginary has often been understood as essentially political in orientation with minimal artistic instrumentality. In other instances shared labour, collaborative practice and the collective conceptualisation of artistic work have been understood as the critique of the reification of art and the commodification of the artist. Though collaborative or collective work has long been accepted as normal in the kind of artistic production that requires ensemble work, such as in music and architecture, for example; in the context of visual art under which the individual artistic talent reigns such loss of singularity of the artist is much less the norm, particularly under the operative conditions of capitalism.

Over the centuries there have been different kinds of groupings of artists in guilds, associations, unions, workshops, schools and movements. However, each of these instances always recognised the individual artist as the sine qua non of such associational belonging. In fact, the idea of ensemble or collective work for the visual artist under capitalism is anathema to the traditional ideal of the artist as author whose work purportedly exhibits the marks of her unique artistry, such that the very positivistic identification of the artist as author leads to a crucial differentiation, one that represents the historical dialectic under which modern art and artists have long functioned: the former on the basis of originality, qua authenticity, of the work of art and the latter on the authority and singularity of the artist as an individual talent and genius. To designate a work as the product of a collective practice in a world that privileges and worships individuality raises a number of vexing issues concerning the nature and practice of art and the status of the work that emerges from such collaboration, especially in networked versions of collectivity, whereby a method of open work delays or defers any attempt to come to the conclusion of a work as a product.

To the extent the discourse of collectivity has been circumscribed by the above issues, debates on collective artistic formations and collaborative practices tend to be much less concerned with the question of 'who is an artist?'[8] and 'what is an author?'[9] However, in certain segments of collective work that have recently emerged, there is a pervasive sense of the loss of this critical distance. One may say that this critical loss of distance is at once by design, in which case it is a strategic move or simply a function of the broader loss of interest in the past. The current positive reception of such collective activity— much prevalent in positions that are more driven by pop-cultural simulations in the work of groups such as Dearraindrop and *assume vivid astro focus*—in fact, their very ability to be fashionable may have something to do with the historical amnesia under which its recent revival operates. While collectivity portends a welcome expansion of the critical regimes of the current contemporary art context which has been under the pernicious sway of money, speculative art market and conservative politics, to make common cause with its counter-intuitive positioning and therefore avoid participation in the co-option and appropriation of its critical nature, it is important to connect collectivity today with its historical genealogy. This may mean going as far back as the Paris

Communes of the 1860s, the socialist collectives of the Russian Revolution in the early 1920s, the subversive developments of Dada, the radical interventions of 'neo-avant-garde' movements, such as the Situationist International, and activist-based practices connected to issues of class, gender and race. The nature of collectivity extends also into the political horizon constructed by the emancipatory projects of the liberation movements of the mid twentieth century. They are registered today within the strategies of anti-globalisation movements.

How do we then place the history of collectivity within the history of modernism? Nearly a century has passed since that fateful turning point in the epic march towards the redefinition of the concept of the work of art. Though we could all chuckle today in self-satisfied bemusement at the provincialism of the then-British minister of culture Kim Howells' castigation of the work of four artists short listed for the Turner Prize, for the poor quality of their work[10] which he reduced to nothing more than so much *conceptual bullshit*. In 1914 such *bullshit* was received as nothing short of heretic. Marcel Duchamp's insertion of the ready-made into the discursive frame of art has acquired its own impressive inventory of epithets and dumbstruck admiration. In fact, its legacy has been called upon in the defence of so much more than the legitimacy of a number of discursive strategies that insist on the idea that they are works of art fashioned by the autonomous creative entity 'the artist'. Having profaned both the concept of art and artist in order to bring modernism back to a zero degree of its task of legitimation, Duchamp's ready-made in a sense could be viewed as the founding philosophy of what is today designated as contemporary art. The genealogy of such strategies (which consistently attempt an improvement of our understanding of the nature of the artistic object or statement) is fundamental to the historical discourse of modern art. It also furnishes the fundamental dialectic between modernist art and contemporary art, not least because the distinction between them remains at once porous and tendentious. Modernist art is said to have its roots in the myth of originality[11]; in the idolatry of images and objects whose very physical existence was

dependent on the reified nature of their objectivity. Or, if we speak specifically about images, we tend to relate to their iconicity and uniqueness on the
basis of aura as one would religious images or objects.[12]

Moreover, modernist art was said to function with an internalised awareness of the hierarchy that structures the relationship between its constitutive
parts, such as how the relationship between works of art came to be conceived
as distinctions across genres, forms and media (a heritage, no doubt, of clas-
sicism) evident, for example, in a line that separates fine and applied art, or
the relationship between media such as the one between painting and drawing. On the other hand, contemporary art is understood to proceed from
the evisceration of the idea of the authority of originality and the aura of the
image. Rather, through its heterogeneity and the structure of simultaneity, it
has overseen the remarkable dispersal of the legacy of modernism.

One legacy of the expansion of the idea of contemporary art is the degree to
which it abjures and has remained largely ambivalent to the dialectic of modernist art (between originality and aura), having taken aboard the idea that art is
neither defined by its specific medium nor by the form through which it declares the very purpose of art, but simply by the context of art. Of course, the
two models for this cultural turn in the understanding of art in the twentieth
century remain cogent, the first being the radical termination of the idea of
originality that Duchamp first inaugurated through his ready-mades and
critique of painterly modernism ('retinal art', as he famously referred to it)
which culminated in the *Large Glass*. The implications and consequences of
Duchamp's intervention are already well known, even if they have developed
their own cargo cult of epistemological reification, sedimentation and certainty
as art history. However, Duchamp's mutilation of the perceptive order in which
the work of art is embedded is more than the transition between the meaning
of an object, whether technologically fabricated, as many of his ready-mades
were, or the *artistically* fabricated work in which originality rests on the fact that
the work is singular and not repeatable by any technology of standardisation.

It is in the discursive domain of art's definition that Duchamp's proposition is said to generate that moment when the *history* of contemporary art is said to begin. Similarly, Walter Benjamin's conclusions in his essay 'The Work of Art in the Age of Mechanical Reproduction' have been equally deployed as the watershed theory that defines the tension between modernist art and contemporary art; between the artistically fabricated object and the technologically generated image.

If we take Duchamp's intervention and Benjamin's theory as the immediate ancestors for the proposition of what Thierry de Duve identifies in Duchamp's gesture as the shift from *here is art* to *this is art*[13] we would, nonetheless, still remain very much preoccupied with what the object of art is, as such, after the re-elaboration of its plasticity. There is, of course, a second horizon through which we can read some of the conclusions that, since the 1960s, have continuously questioned both the nature and status of the work of art. The struggle, as such, is not so much about how art generates its meanings through its many objects, forms and media that can now be extended to activities or non-activities, be they technologically fabricated, digitally serialised, structured by index, or programmatically schematised. But can art now go beyond embedding itself in *specific objects* of minimalism's phenomenological posture, or can it move to a truly radical position that is its complete reduction into nothing more than a linguistic description?

The severe deretinalisation that such a reduction proposes is part of the legacy of *conceptual art* in which recourse to language carries the seed of Duchamp's original idea, except now the model of *this is art if I say so* has produced a moment of deep fecundation in which its social ramification has tended to open up the space of contemplation to that of speech, or just simply the exchanges that inhere from a range of social relations (this is fundamentally the place opened up by collectivity), thereby transporting the experience of art into sites of the multiple activities that today generate art as idea, discourse, activity or whatever as an extended field of many types of transaction. Part of this synthesis or fusion of the contemplative and the linguistic, the formal and the social, at any rate, led *conceptual* art to attempt also to abduct the traditional role of the historian and critic for its cause. Again, the work of Art & Language, and such artists as Joseph Kosuth and Dan Graham, are significant here. *Conceptual* art was not simply content with destabilising the traditional categories within which art functioned; it also sought to inaugurate and propagate a philosophy for such destabilisation as the basis for an ontology of advanced contemporary art. Kosuth especially made this part of his credo, as witnessed in his *Art after Philosophy* model.[14]

If contemporary art, as inaugurated by Duchamp in his casual still-lives of quotidian objects refashioned as ready-mades in 1914, was already impatient with modernist claims of the uniqueness of vision, skilful finish, and such as the prerequisite for judging correctly what a work of art is, modernist critics were no less dismissive of the claims of certain contemporary styles, seeing them either as fraudulent or ideologically compromised. From Cubism onwards, and throughout the twentieth century, modernist art has had to grapple with the constant pluralisation of the concept of art and its forms and media (for example, the Cubist collage and film montage) and the hybridisation of the art object (for example, the ready-made and Dada). At every turn in the shift to-wards pluralisation and hybridisation, modernist art has tried to prove its own staying power and is not devoid of its own spectacular weapons against the impudent assaults of Duchampian contemporary art, as witnessed in its at-tempt every decade since the first ready-made to storm the barricades and seize back the space of representation that painting and sculpture represent for classical art. In a sense, the historical debate between modernist art and con-temporary art rests on a single philosophical tension, namely the issue of the authenticity of the work of art. For example Benjamin observed that, 'The revol-utionary strength of Dadaism consisted in testing art for its authenticity'.[15]

The issue of the authenticity of the work of art, and by extension that of the artist (who in typical postmodernist fashion became the author), has a sociocultural basis beyond the art historical questions it generates, especially as the basis for conceptual art become more and more dissociated from the polemics of statements about art to the politics of that statement and, finally, the politics of representation. The legacy of Duchamp in the formulation of the theory of *conceptual* art produced consequences beyond his original intent, to the extent that, at a certain juncture, Duchamp ceased to be a useful avatar for the range of heterogeneous strategies and statements that have devoted themselves to being expressions of artistic intention outside the framework of objects and images.

Benjamin Buchloh has rightly observed that in 'confronting the full range of the implications of Duchamp's legacy … conceptual practices … reflected upon the construction and role (or death) of the author just as much as they redefined the conditions of receivership and the role of the spectator'.[16] Though Buchloh's statement is quite correct, in relation to the spectator the historians of *conceptual* art have not gone far enough in theorising the funda-mental political nature of spectatorship. What I mean is that in the postwar transformation of the global public sphere, the traditional construction of the spectator within both Western and modernist understanding had experienced a radical rupture with the emergence of post-colonial discourse. Post-colonial and civil rights discourses put under the spotlight a new kind of spectator. This spectator would construct, during the postwar period, new subjective relations to institutions of Western democracy and economics. For example, in the USA, desegregated institutions needed also to rearticulate the philosophy informing their work as public spaces. The appearance of the subject within the framework of the experience of art was a new phenomenon that hitherto was unacknowledged, insofar as the concept of the institutions of art experi-enced pressures to be more attentive to the publics towards which they directed their undertakings. It was not just the primacy of the art object that demanded new consideration, but the primacy of the social exclusions that purportedly were built into the way in which institutions of art mediated the history of those objects. The postwar democratic public sphere repositioned the spectator in ways that would only become much more clear with the emergence of certain politically centred interpretations of subjectivity; models of subjectivisation that were dependent on a number of socially bounded identifications (gender, sexuality, race, ethnicity, etc.), of which multiculturalism today functions as the dark spectre of the politics of the subject. While conceptualist paradigms may have opened a space for the considerations of some of these shifts, surprisingly the operation of conceptualism still predicates itself on the hinge of the modernist dialectic of the object and the gaze. As such, the shift in the role of the traditional spectator within the structures of hegemonic institutions of power such as museums and Western gallery systems was not substantially articulated in the operations of *conceptual* art. Already in 1952, a decade before *conceptual* art purportedly began the redefinition of the role of the spectator, Frantz Fanon had called this homogeneous spectator into question in his classic psychoanalytic study, *Black Skin, White Masks*. Fanon's study of subjectivity drew from the master/slave relationship of the self and other in colonial discourse, in which he foregrounds the importance of language whereby 'to speak is to absolutely exist for the other'.[17] Therefore, the fact of *conceptual* art's interpellation of language into the field of artistic vision cannot simply be adopted, in toto, as the radical critique of language, for its own action of critique is called into question with regard to the self-sufficiency of its own language games.

THE PRODUCTION OF SOCIAL SPACE AS ARTWORK: PROTOCOLS OF COMMUNITY IN THE WORK OF LE GROUPE AMOS AND HUIT FACETTES

So far I have focused on the historical and intellectual trajectory necessary to understand collective practice within the field of contemporary art. While artists across a broad global arena have adopted this method with great creative and stimulating vigour, I will focus here on two key groups: Le Groupe Amos from Kinshasa and Huit Facettes from Dakar, which have emerged in Africa in the past two decades. My focus owes much to the fact that the two groups operate from within a specific cultural and historical context to which modernism, and sometimes contemporary art, have been antagonistic. If the dialectic between modernist and contemporary art has been caught in attempts at elucidating, within each field, what the authenticity of the work of art and artist (author) is, the unexplored political consequences of this question take us now to the important question of identity formation, the politics and crisis of the subject, and the processes of homogenisation and assimilation of non-Western cultural sites into the framework of late capitalism. Because most non-Western artistic contexts lack power (in the neo-liberal sense of market capitalism in which modern and contemporary art objects function), it is often easy to either dismiss their importance or ignore them as unimportant contributors in the changing discourse of art. The history of modernism in relation to African art is well known in this regard. Africa fulfils a role in which it could be absorbed as an astonishing example of a certain ethnographic turn towards which modernism's fascination with otherness has always tended, or, in the very worst case, as embarrassing cases of an impossible mimesis in the resemblance of modern African art to the 'superior' Western paradigm. In this way modern African art is treated as either exotic or strange, corrupted by colonial mimicry and devoid of authenticity.

In whatever epistemological mode African art, or artists, is grounded, in the larger discussions of modernism or contemporary art it is first on the basis of a pure disavowal, what the critic Hal Foster calls a process of dis-identification; that is, both African art and artist resemble the least what modern art is about. This is an old argument. Yet, another way this dis-identification occurs is through appropriation and assimilation of Africa as an effect of certain tropes of authenticity and cultural purity invested with the power of ethno- graphic realism. Most notably, for the African artist authenticity has become a congenital condition. Authenticity, because it partially hosts in its ambiguous carapace the kernel of the stereotype, is a burden unsupportable by the practical, conceptual and historical forms through which it is transmitted in contemporary cultural discourse. Authenticity, rather than affirming the continuities of a cultural past (based on certain nineteenth-century Western romanticism[18] as a general signifier for an African tradition) in fact comes off more as the antithesis of such continuities. Authenticity's primary structure thus is the fiction that reproduces it as the figure of a unitary, homogeneous belief in the particularism of an African essence.

Authenticity as an idea toward the standardisation, hence making banal the complexity of contemporary African identity, appeals to certain romantic notions of African uniqueness that have been promoted for so long. Authenticity, therefore, must be understood as the handmaiden of an ethnocentric discourse blind to the complexity of the modern map of African social reality, and doubly blind to the multiplicity of identities forged in the crucible of colonisation, globalisation, diaspora and the post-colonial social transformation of insular cultural worlds. Authenticity is not only a vague notion with ambiguous features that no one can possibly identify, let alone describe, its practicability in the context of African artistic procedures, but also is a code for fixity, absolutism, atrophy. Writers such as Wole Soyinka and artists such as Issa Samb and the members of Laboratoire AGIT Art in Dakar were correct in questioning the efficacy of the ethnocentric model of Négritude in the 1960s.[19] In the same manner in which their critique of Négritude as a universal of the African world functioned, so did their rejection of the false claims of Eurocentric universalism over the territory of other cultures. To say this much is not to be beholden to the relativism that governs what passes today as cultural exchange, but to point to the difficulties that reproduce dichotomies that ground themselves in the discourse of power.

In its attempt to arrest the African social imaginary one could impute that the denotative idea behind the construct of authenticity is its primordialism;

that is, as an a priori concept that determines and structures the bonds of the self to the other; the other as always unchanging, arrested, bound to tradition, tethered to the supernatural forces of nature; the other whose social temporality is governed by an innate world and its systems of kinship, beliefs and symbols, all of which remain beyond the reach of any structural or material transformation of reason and progress, except in superficial circumstances, after which he/she returns to an original state. Therefore, authenticity as primordialism conceives of the other in a vacuum of history, locates him/her in the twilight of origin, fixed in the constancy of the unchanging same. Or, on the other hand, it conceives of the other as an excess and spectacle of history, as a cycle of repetition, mimicry, demonstration, performance, habitation, expression and practice.

This latter idea of authenticity as primordialism in Michael Taussig's terms could be called part of its mimetic faculties[20]; that is, in its tendency to quote, copy and imitate that which is believed to be the original. So, in a paradoxical sense, the authentic is always false. According to such a logic, the mimetic faculty allows for the inexhaustible permutations of quoting, copying and imitating an idea of African authenticity: for example, real Africa is traditional rather than modern; rural rather than urban; tribal and collective rather than individual and subjective; black rather than hybrid; timeless rather than contingent.[21] With every process of affirmation and disavowal we participate in the game of ceaseless mimeticism and reproduction of the authentic. Taken to its most absurd level these binarisms and conjectures take on a facticity and truth, which should then govern and aid all relations of production in art, literature, film, music and other spheres of modern knowledge production. Yet, in the same logic we witness the contingency of the destiny of the African artist in the face of various instruments of modern subjectivity, one of which concerns his/her liberation from the determinism of race. We may pause here to pay attention to the full emergence of a crisis: the crisis of the African subject.[22] In the game of authenticity, the politics of the subject is an important one in relation to how this crisis is critically engaged. For the African subject, this crisis is paradoxically engaged through the instrumental rationalisation of the idea of free will. Achille Mbembe captures this succinctly. He writes that:

> The triumph of the principle of free will (in the sense of the right to criticize and the right to accept as valid only what appears justified), as well as the individual's acquired capacity to self-refer, to block any attempt at absolutism and to achieve self-realization through art are seen as key attributes of modern consciousness.[23]

For those Africans who disavow the *fiction of authenticity*—the mimetic excess par excellence—what choice do they have beyond the violence of the dichotomy between the fake and real[24]; authentic and inauthentic; primordialism (backwardness) and modernity (progress); the universal and the particular? If we are to hypothesise authenticity, what else could it mean beyond its interpretation as an act of constant self-repetition, self-mimicry and self-abasement in the stew of origin? Shouldn't we begin the quest for the authentic in African cultural discourse, first by ridding ourselves of all illusions that it can be conjured by a simple appeal to the past and tradition? Second, should we not be insisting that the most meaningful place to seek the figure of the authentic is not in the swamp of fantasies in which Africa has been caught as the true historical opposition between reason and unreason; between the West and the rest, but elsewhere: in the very politics of the subject? The quest for the authentic, it seems to me, is in the search to locate the African subject, not simply as African (for that is already a given), but as a universal subject endowed with capacities far beyond the lure of authenticity. Such a subject is neither a mere fantasy of over-determined cultural theory nor a fanciful postmodern caricature. Pace Mbembe, we can therefore present the case of the African subject in the following manner:

> … the constitution of the African self as a reflexive subject … involves doing, seeing, hearing, tasting, feeling, and touching. In the eyes of all involved in the production of that self and subject, these practices constitute what might be called *meaningful human expressions* [author's emphasis]. Thus the African subject is like any other human being: he or she engages in *meaningful acts* [author's emphasis] … the African subject does not exist apart from the acts that produce social reality, or apart from the process by which those practices, are so to speak, *imbued with meaning* [author's emphasis].[25]

If the speech of the African subject is *imbued with meaning* at the moment he/she speaks (whether as an artist or not) cultural subjectivity for the modern African artist opposes itself to the binary violence of either/or; universalism/particularism. The complexity of such a speech extrudes from the dynamism of multiple traditions and is transformed in aleatory patterns of cultural production and reception, as well as in the juxtaposition, mixing and creolisations that define the contact zone of culture, especially after colonialism.

As I have tried to show above, the discourse of crisis[26] is not only endemic to the political and social formation in Africa; it also concerns the crisis evident in the processes of subjectivisation, by which I mean not only the ability to constitute a speech not marked by the failure of intelligibility and communicability but the very act of creative transformation of African reality. Thus the process of subjectivisation is the ability for a given subject to articulate an autonomous position, to acquire the tools and power of speech (be it in art, writing or other expressive and reflexive actions) is connected to the idea of sovereignty. This sovereignty operates around the ethical–juridical territory of power relations, namely between the recognition of the given fact of natural rights and that right regulated and legitimised by the law: here, the individual is 'subjectified in a power relationship'[27], whether in relation to the state, or to nationality or ethnicity.

The idea of the sovereign subject as it concerns Africa is important if we are to rethink questions of authenticity in cultural practice. I want to do so by turning to the position of the artist as producer in a time of crisis.[28] This crisis points first to the crisis of the post-colonial state[29] and to the general climate of uncertainty unleashed by globalisation. For Africa in particular, there is also the crisis of development discourse that has been the bedrock of the democratisation and liberalisation of the post-colonial state and economies since the 1960s. Here it is important to note that the post-colonial state has been exacerbated in the past two decades by the brutal macro-economic Structural Adjustment Program (SAP) policies of the World Bank and International Monetary Fund (IMF) during the 1980s and 1990s. Though there are disputes among experts about the actual causes of the kind of congenital underdevelopment we see in Africa today, it is generally agreed that SAP deepened it and weakened the capacity of the state to manage and respond effectively to its effects. SAP put into place the inability of a host of African subjects to properly conceptualise and formulate their own futures; that is, to speak as true social subjects. All through Africa, institutions and citizens are vulnerable to the rapacious calumny of the industrial forces of economic rationalisation and political coercion. Rather than reform and economic growth as promised, the shock of the experiment of liberalisation produced stagnation, structural atrophy, collapsed economies, deep poverty, failed institutions and loss of state autonomy from donor institutions and markets. Liberal reform of the economy (devaluation of currencies, imposition of austerity measures, privatisation of state assets) all set in motion a deepening crisis, leading to further underdevelopment and dependency across institutions. Of these, cultural and educational institutions were the most vulnerable. Consequently, artists and intellectuals were placed on very precarious ground in society. Only recently have liberal economists, the World Bank and IMF begun to acknowledge the failure of the economic shock therapies[30] that have affected institutions across the continent. As a test case the neo-liberal ideology of free-market capitalism not only failed in Africa, it also produced a wave of disenchantment, instability and erosion of social networks.

If, as Foucault claims, 'the theory of sovereignty assumes from the outset the existence of a multiplicity of powers ... [imagined as] capacities, possibilities, potentials'[31], the grim assessment of the post-colonial state and the post-colonial subject within the development discourse of neo-liberal market ideology introduces a series of illiberal effects. But here we need to fashion a proper critique of crisis as not always the logical outcome of the neo-liberal transformation of the modern African state. Yet, its effects cannot be discounted, especially when the state fails, as we can witness in the context of what is known as Democratic Republic of the Congo (DRC). Seen from this example, crisis not only situates the subject, it mortifies the subject. The chief and primary effect of this is traumatic. This trauma compels a complete rethinking, if not necessarily the overhaul, of the forms, strategies and techniques of everyday existence as well as the devices through which cultural production occurs and in the places in which it is grounded. Because this crisis influences the effectiveness of institutions, conditions of production and the visibility and quality of discursive formations, the position of the artist and intellectual within the African public sphere is constantly called into question. Furthermore, the coercive power of the state to force artists and intellectuals to adapt their practices according to an official dictum of the state apparatus, forces attempts to disclose the autonomy of the artist and intellectual under such force.[32] Many intellectuals, researchers and non-government organisations (NGOs) working in the area of African political and cultural sectors in recent years have focused on different strategies to strengthen civil society, governance, democracy and informal economies as a way to boost the sovereignty of the subject in the time of crisis.

This has given rise to a number of responses. Though much of the focus has been concentrated around the work of NGOs, community associations, social science think tanks and multilateral global institutions, very little attention has been paid to the dimension of culture. I do so here by examining the work of two distinctly different collective groups of practitioners who have made the analysis of the conditions of production under this crisis the sine qua non of their reflexive activities since 1989 and 1996, respectively. The two groups, Le Groupe Amos in Kinshasa and Huit Facettes in Dakar, were each formed as specific responses to (a) the crisis of the public sphere under the long dictatorship of Mobutu Sese Seko in the former Zaire and its further deterioration under the late Laurent Kabila, who overthrew the regime of Mobutu in 1997; (b) the erosion of the link between the state and formal institutions of culture; (c) the collapse and disappearance of the public sphere; and (d) the crisis and alienation of the labour of the artist working within the forced bifurcation of social space between the urban and rural contexts of Senegal. All of these responses, the first in the DRC (formerly Zaire) and the other in Senegal, are positions specifically articulated toward the production of a common social space and the development of protocols of community as the first condition for the recognition of the sovereign subject.

It is by this insight that we can situate the work of Le Groupe Amos and Huit Facettes, especially in light of their direct engagement with the politics of crisis in African social, political and cultural discourse in order to produce new networks that link them to local communities. Each, in its conception of the social and community, calls for evaluative procedures in the construction of a reflexive practice within their given context.

Le Groupe Amos was founded in 1989 by a group of writers, intellectuals, activists and artists in Kinshasa. It emerged out of the political and economic crisis of the past decade of Mobutu's corrupt, dictatorial misrule as Congolese civil society began a process of realignment and finally disintegrated into civil war. Taking its name from the biblical prophet Amos who, in the Old Testament is identified with the struggle for social justice, the grassroots activist movement initiated by members of Le Groupe Amos use classic means of social aesthetics to communicate their work to the community at large.

The collective evolved in the context of the changing realities in Zaire during the Mobutu regime and afterwards under the autocratic government of Kabila in the DRC. The activities and work of the group take up methods of cultural activism that can be best considered an extension of the tactics found in Latin American liberation theology, infusing their activism with the ethics of civil disobedience and 'creative non-violent action'.[33] As a collective, one of their principal quests was to find out how to deal with the crisis of legitimation which faced millions of disempowered Congolese silenced by the venality of two brutal regimes. In a way, there was an idealism surrounding this quest, especially concerning the choice to offer a different critical option to the Congolese public beyond the armed rebellion being waged against Mobutu and Kabila in order to free the subjective force of their repressed society by means of direct action. Four points are important in the work and conception of Le Groupe Amos: the first is its identification with the political, social and cultural aspirations of the ordinary Congolese. This means that all its work is produced to intervene directly in the sphere of political and social formations seeking to affect its reality. These interventions often take a didactic format and are produced both in French—the official lingua franca of the state—and in the vernacular, Lingala, the language of everyday discourse among ordinary people in Kinshasa. The second aspect of the group is its relationship to the sphere of institutional power, not only that represented by the state but also that of the church; in this case the Catholic church. Here, the group foregrounds a critical, discursive activist relationship to the res publica in the conception and organisation of its projects. In order to do so, it translates its intellectual ideals into a series of programmatic activities (via theatre, art instruction, pamphleteering, sex education etc.) broadening its network among neighbour-hood associations in order to organise and harness those aspirations operative in the field of power. Third, the field of its actions and techniques of dissemi-nation, production and media (often accessible and direct, such as a play using the organisation of power in a family unit to explore the underlying production of inequity within democratic systems) are carefully fused whereby, as part of the social production of the public sphere, the site of reception is also constituted as a democratic civil forum. And fourth, is its definition of its relationship to the public sphere in the manner which Antonio Gramsci defined the role of the intellectual in the context of culture. For Le Groupe Amos, this is principally formulated on the ethics of self-governance. Here, the work of the intellectual is both in the activity of particular forms of praxis and in the functions that require a certain minimum intellectual dispensation 'within the general complex of social relations'.[34] In the field of social relations in which Le Groupe Amos has positioned its work, the targets of its actions are the state and those institutions and organisations: the church (especially the Catholic church), political parties, rebel movements and multinational global institutions linked to powerful economic interests. These groupings are generally regarded as complicit in suppressing the subjectivity of the Congolese people.

Working with a variety of grassroots organisations, Le Groupe Amos employs a number of devices, such as pedagogy, for its projects on literacy and non-violence. With regard to politics, it uses public interventions in various media to transmit its message within the urban neighbourhoods of Kinshasa and more broadly beyond the immediate locus of the city. These interventions manifest as forms of direct action targeting specific deficits within the political, social and cultural economy. The actions can be in the form of a theatrical production organised with local actors (housewives, workers, young students). Other activities of the group involve didactic teaching material, essays, commentaries and cartoons published in newspapers, pamphlets, posters and magazines. Along with these, it publishes books, teaches clinics and organises workshops on democracy and democratisation, governance and citizenship, tolerance, civil disobedience and gender equality. The group also produces radio broadcasts, audio and video documentaries, taking advantage of the endless reproducibility of the media as a way to reach communities in other parts of the vast country. Since there is no gallery system to speak of in Kinshasa, where the group is based, this form of direct intervention into public discourse is unique and in many ways novel within its context. It is important to note that the concept of art to which the group adheres is broader than the narrowly defined aesthetic sense of art. For them, the tools of art are a means rather than ends in themselves. Questions raised, positions taken, debates engaged in are of greater significance than final outcomes. The work then is part of a longer, durational process of acculturation and procedural inscription. One could rightly say that there is a proselytising dimension in the way Le Groupe Amos employs dominant media strategies to reach a wide variety of publics in its work. The effectiveness of its practices and the level of critical respect it has received could be observed in the most recent work it is involved in, which focuses on the work of reconciliation among the warring factions of different Congolese rebel movements. In this capacity, Le Groupe Amos was invited as a participant/observer at one of the privileged forums of the Congolese civil society organisations to the peace conference on the Congolese civil war, hosted by the South African government in 2002 in Sun City, South Africa.

Previously, I pointed out the degree to which language plays a role in the activities of the group. With a large segment of the population being illiterate, Le Groupe Amos is aware that for its work to have a direct consequence within the field into which it intervenes, it would need to be conscious of the language of its discourse. In this case, its work maintains a critical awareness of the social and class divisions perpetuated through the mastery of the colonial language. Le Groupe Amos's tactic is not to disavow French, which is the language of official discourse, but rather to empower the vernacular languages (for example, Lingala and Swahili) as a tool for popular discourse. In so doing, the group seeks to decapitate the class distinctions between those who occupy the space of power and therefore are perceived to possess discursive authority, and those on the margins of power who lack a voice. Of the latter class, women are the most vulnerable to the distortion of power relationships that define the chaotic and impoverished character of the Congolese public sphere. Thierry

N'Landu, a professor of US literature at the University of Kinshasa and a founding member of Le Groupe Amos, describes some of its projects, stating that:

> Groupe Amos's commitment to changing Congolese society through nonviolent strategies is evidenced by numerous inspirational and informative projects. In particular, Amos has focused on the plight of women in short video documentaries such *Congo aux deux visages; L'Espérance têtue d'un peuple*, 1997; *Femme Congolaise: Femmes aux mille bras*, 1997; *Au Nom de ma foi*, 1997. *Et ta violence me scul ta Femme*, 1997, is a video in Lingala, a vernacular language from Kinshasa, which celebrates the power of Congolese women who struggle for rights in a context where traditions, customs, religion, and even existing laws do not facilitate equality.[35]

Two things are noteworthy in N'Landu's statement. The first concerns the form through which Le Groupe Amos undertakes its work as a sociocultural activity rather than specifically as a visual art activity. This would lead one to consider the group's work in the broader context of knowledge production, rather than that of artistic or visual production. The effectiveness of direct communication to its audiences leads the group to pursue its work through the discursive utility of linguistic identification with each of its specific and general audiences. The second point concerns the relationship of power to the social reproduction of agency and sovereignty, particularly with regard to women. Here, specific critiques of the patriarchal structure of Congolese society are directed at the customs, traditions and existing laws that place women in subservient positions. Again, the serviceability of the figure of the authentic has a far more limited purchase than the idea of the subject, insofar as the status of women is concerned in the Congolese context. This, again, is articulated as one of the stated intentions of the role of citizenship in the development of new forms of social discourse of civil society in the DRC. José Mpundu, another member of Le Groupe Amos, in an essay on the future of democracy in the DRC, writes:

> Civil society in the situation of this crisis and in view of the resolution of the conflict will have to reconnect with its primary vocation: to educate the people in order for them to be able to take charge of themselves on all levels. Civic, political as well as moral education will make of our people the authors of their history and the masters of their destiny. Civil society is asked to play a role of primary importance in the process of liberation of the people ... Political liberation, economic liberation, cultural liberation, social liberation: that is the true struggle of civil society. In order to do so, it will have to help the people organize in an efficient manner and to elaborate strategies of social struggle.[36]

Having elaborated this quasi Marxist view of class struggle, Mpundu, a few sentences later, makes clear the idea that the liberation imagined by Le Groupe Amos was not just a liberation from the despotism of the state and its rulers (including the surrogates of Rwanda and Uganda who occupy the eastern part of the country), but the hegemonic power identified with European and American interests. Throughout the discourse of the crisis in Africa, the identification of the mendacity of forces of production with external powers has become deeply entrenched and not without foundation. These forces, in the name of a number of abstract concepts connected to the great liberal trinity of democracy, free market and human rights, are often believed to be a kind of third force that has to be fought before the sovereign African subject can emerge.

Huit Facettes was formed by a group of eight individual artists—hence its name, 'eight facets'—in 1996, in Dakar, Senegal. Huit Facettes is different from Le Groupe Amos in that it is self-identified as an artistic collective, using the means of art and its corollary, creativity, to probe the relationship between the aesthetic and the ethical; the social and cultural. However, the task Huit Facettes set out for itself was first a confrontation with the impotency, immobility and disempowerment the artists in the collective perceived in the artistic context of Senegal. The second question that concerned members of Huit Facettes was the increasing social stratification that defined the relationship between the elite and the poor in the city; a stratification that also had impoverished the relationship of their individual work to the society in which it was produced, leading it inexorably toward becoming a code for its own alienation. This stratification and alienation is even more acute in the lines that separate rural and urban communities in Senegal. In the city, the terms of dwelling and perceptions of social agency are often aleatory. While the urban economy is governed by a tendency toward informality and improvisation within the capitalist economy, the rural community is entirely tethered to a pre-industrial, agrarian past. In the city, social networks that bind one community to another have not only exploded, producing scattered trajectories, they have also become implacable, diffuse and difficult to organise. The urban material consistency, having succumbed to obsolescence, is now shaped by growing spatial distortions that collapse into fleeting temporalities.

On the vast outskirts of the urban rim, forgotten communities in the villages that are the historical link between the past and the present, the local and global, live on the edge of official amnesia; on the dark side of a politics of invisibility.[37] Though massive in population and visible through the meagre, deracinated social amenities that can barely cope with their demands, the poor in Africa have become the disappeared of globalisation. In broad daylight Africans are short-circuited between development and underdevelopment; between the *third world* and the *first world*. The poor are invisible because official discourse long ago stopped seeing them. Instead, they have become a blind spot in the neo-liberal catechism of the move toward market economy. They have become ghosts in the political machine[38] of late modernity. Deracinated by structural adjustment policies, the rural and urban contexts in Africa have become manifestations that produce their own structure of fecundation, a fertile soil for new possibilities of being. Urban and rural inhabitants have increasingly begun working with new kinds of experimentation contra to the logic of development modernity. They are involved in inventing new subjective identities and protocols of community.

All these issues coalesce in the activities of Huit Facettes. Its principal project since its formation is the Hamdallaye project, an extended collaboration with the inhabitants of the village of Hamdallaye, some 500 kilometres from Dakar in the Haute Cassamance region, near the Gambian border. Huit Facettes perceives its work exactly as the inverse of the logic of development strategies through the utility of art. In so doing, its central mission has been to 'disentangle modernism's historical contradiction between art's claim to aesthetic autonomy and its ambitions for social relevance'.[39] The sustained, continuing project at Hamdallaye attempts, through collaboration between the members of the group and the villagers, to concentrate on the circulation of not only the symbolic goods of artistic skills, but also on the strategic transfer of vital skills from the artists to the village community. However, this transfer of skills is directed to ensure that the villagers retain creative control of their artistic labour. To empower the isolated villagers and thereby increase their economic capacity through artistic skills not only profits the villagers, it also helps them bridge the social distance between Huit Facettes as artists and the villagers, who perceive artists from the point of view of being a privileged urban elite identified with elements of the state. According to Kan-Si, one of the founding members:

> Huit Facettes in rural Senegal is much more the story of a procedure or process which, as it unfolds, has given us (contemporary Senegalese artists living in the city) a point of anchorage or reconciliation with the part of society that feeds us and from which we were cut off. One particular elite rejoins its roots in the same sociocultural (Senegalese) context.[40]

Since 1996, each year in Hamdallaye the project with the villagers begins with a series of public discussions that then move into the phase of art workshops dedicated to specific areas of popular artistic idioms. Each workshop is designed to transform basic skills into professional skills—for example, in under-glass painting, ceramics, batik dyeing, carving, weaving, embroidery and mural painting. Depending on the level of work needed to accomplish the training at hand, the workshops are normally conducted over a period of one to two weeks. The concentration on specific kinds of skills is arrived at based on their utility and creativity, as well as on dialogue with members of the community. Women are especially targeted as a group which can profit from the link with the artists. For Huit Facettes, the arrival at what to do in each workshop is connected to utility of certain creative systems (they have to be accessible, inexpensive, skilful, sustainable over a long period and draw from the exchange of knowledge between the two groups). What the artists offer, in addition, is access to materials, advertisement of the results and access to the urban market. Above all, the autonomy of the Hamdallaye residents in deciding what is most useful for them in the collaboration is important for the critical discourse of Huit Facettes. The group tries to avoid the hierarchical structure of NGO development work. This is partly to stimulate the agency and subjective capacity of each participant in the workshop, to help them establish an individual expression. But above all, it is to avoid at all cost the possibility of dependency. By paying critical attention to the idea of subjectivity, Huit Facettes works in the interstices of development and empowerment, whereby 'in the end the participants are able to set up self-sustaining practices as non-dependent citizens'.[41]

This approach is attempted as a subtle contradiction of the development discourse, which recently has been the dominant vehicle by means of which many African crises are addressed. The top-down, donor–client model of NGOs and development agencies from wealthy Western countries has been perceived as undermining Africa's ability to be non-dependent. Oftentimes, development organisations, through donor institutions, operate on the assumption of economic and sociopolitical templates that can be domesticated within an African context; transforming the templates, as it were, into substrates of an authentically African ideal. As such there is the preponderance of support for an aesthetic of recycling, the make-do, makeshift and bricolage, rather than invention, sophistication and technologically sound transfer of knowledge.[42] In short, development has given rise to the spectacle and excess of *Tokunbo*[43] culture, whereby discarded and semi-functional technological objects and detritus of the West are recalibrated for the African market. From used cars to electronics, from biotechnology to hazardous waste, Africa has become the dumping and testing ground for both extinct Western technology and its waste.[44] All of these issues come up in the analysis of the political-social-cultural economy of Senegal by Huit Facettes.

On a certain level, this approach may in certain quarters be perceived as naïve. However, Huit Facettes is under no illusion that its work makes any difference beyond its ability to establish a particular type of social context for communication between itself and different communities in Senegal. One example is its work in health, particularly the campaign to raise public awareness on the AIDS pandemic, for which the work they produced included a hip-hop concert they organised on the subject. Different members of the group have also been involved as participants, as individual artists, in the multidisciplinary urban renewal project called *Set Setal* during the early 1990s in Dakar. The conception of art on the basis of activism is one in which its statements have been soundly equivocal. There is no overdetermined claim for the emancipatory capacity of art. Like Le Groupe Amos, art of the kind that Huit Facettes proposes in the name of actualising a community is a means in the process of coming together in a discursive as well as cultural recognition, rather than an end towards consecration as an artistic talent alone. According to Kan-Si, in the view of Huit Facettes:

> Artistic work that aspires to engage with social issues … contributes in one way or another to the development of the 'real world', only much will depend on the nature of that work. Such contribution will have to be perceived differently and in a wider sense, just as the notion of a work of art can be understood more in terms of process than as finished cultural object, to be instantly consumed (seen, appreciated or indeed judged). Society's concerns become the medium for an intervention, if only suggestively, for a formula through which we may engage with and seek solutions to problems encountered in everyday life.[45]

This statement demonstrates the group's inclination to treat sceptically any notion that art of the kind they are involved in ought to supply surplus value as cultural products that can be consumed, collected and classified.

By forcing themselves to confront the incommensurable in the relationship between the ethical and the aesthetics, between the subject and the state, Huit Facettes and Le Groupe Amos operate in the vanguard position of a new type of debate within the contemporary African public sphere. As we know, all activities, events and practices of art are grounded in specific paradigm formations; that is, all activities, events and practices of art are determined by a history and the structure of the formation of that history. It is also important not to analyse the complex manifestation of this practice from the perspective of an aesthetics of political action that today is not only problematic, but has increased the dialectical tension between notions of ethics and aesthetics. Whether it is possible to address ethical questions through the vehicle of aesthetics seems, for now, not only overdetermined but also subject to deep ideological appropriation by both liberal and conservative forces. In fact, the combination of the political and the poetic, the aesthetic and the ethical, have often led to an unhappy conflation of power and morality.

Consequently, the conjunction of ethics and aesthetics in certain forms of institutional critique have tended to view artistic practice through the lens of a simplistic analysis of the politics (between good and bad, proper and improper, virtuous and cynical) rather than the more critical notion of the political, which to my mind grounds all relations of power and discourses between artists, activists and institutions. Ethics today has a high currency in the field of contemporary art, all the more so because of the kinds of surprising prohibition placed on the political in relation to art.[46] Contemporary discourses in many areas, be it in the conduct of war (the adherence to or violation of the Geneva Convention); medicine (euthanasia and abortion being two examples); biotechnology (the recent debates around the ethics of cloning); law (capital punishment); or human rights (child labour, slavery, racism) have engaged further explorations of the ethical as that which sutures certain complex conducts in the political, scientific and cultural spheres. And here artists have been at the forefront of an interdisciplinary response to the debates that have grown out of them. However, the relation between the ethical and the aesthetic, the aesthetic and the political, the poetic and the social, have increasingly brought the philosophical discourse and moral force of ethics before us in an unresolved form. This is where I believe that the discourse of authenticity as the force that gives positive content to the work of the African artist is not only misguided, but deeply problematic. Therefore, to understand that which animates the worldview of the African artist, we must do well to invent a new politics of the subject.

NOTES

1   Walter Benjamin, 'The Author as Producer' in Peter Demetz (ed.), *Reflections: Essays, Aphorisms, Autobiographical Writings*, New York, Schocken Books, 1978.

2   Ibid., p. 221.

3   Ibid., p. 222.

4   Georg Lukács, 'Tendency or Partisanship?' in Rodney Livingstone (ed.), David Fernbach (trans.) *Essays on Realism*, Cambridge, MA, MIT Press, 1980.

5   I borrow this term from the perceptive essay 'Social Aesthetics' by David Deitcher. See David Deitcher, 'Social Aesthetics' in Brian Wallis (ed.), *Democracy: A Project by Group Material*, Seattle, Bay Press, 1990, pp. 12–43.

6   Lukács, p. 35.

7   Ibid., p. 35.

8   In a famous statement, Joseph Beuys provocatively proclaimed the point of view that everyone is an artist and therefore we are all artists. Such judgement no doubt can equally be conceived as part of the hubristic simplification with which some critics often associate Beuys.

9   In an essay written after World War II, Jean Paul Sartre asked this question in 'What is Literature?'; see Sartre *'What is Literature?' and Other Essays*, Cambridge, Mass., Harvard University Press, 1988.

10 In an interview in *The Guardian* of 31 October 2002, Mr Howells described the work of the artists thus: 'If this is the best British artists can produce then British art is lost. It is cold, mechanical, conceptual bullshit'. The artist Martin Creed, who presented an installation of lights going on and off in one of the galleries of Tate Modern, London, as part of his presentation for the Turner Prize, was especially marked out for excoriation. Suffice it to say that the minister's reaction was not so much about the work as much as it was about a prestigious award being conferred on something that displays a minimum of artistic originality or labour.

11 Rosalind Krauss, *The Originality of the Avant-garde and Other Modernist Myths*, Cambridge, MIT Press, 1985.

12 Walter Benjamin, 'The Work of Art in the Age of Mechanical Production' in Hannah Arendt (ed.) *Illuminations: Walter Benjamin Essays and Reflections*, New York, Schocken Books, 1969. This essay has remained a classic and the most penetrating analysis of the contingency of the nature of aura as what

determines the uniqueness in the work of art. The transfer from uniqueness to reproduction inherently marks the end of the idea of aura insofar as the question of the nature of art was concerned.

13   Thierry de Duve, *Kant After Duchamp*, Cambridge, MIT Press, 1996.

14   See Joseph Kosuth, in Gabriele Guercio (ed.) *Art After Philosophy and After: Collected Writings, 1966–1990*, Cambridge, MIT Press, 1991.

15   Walter Benjamin, 'The Author as Producer' in Peter Demetz (ed.), Edmund Jephcott (trans.) *Reflections: Essays, Aphorism, Autobiographical Writings*, New York, Schocken, 1989, p. 229.

16   Benjamin Buchloh, 'Conceptual Art 1962–1969: From the Aesthetic of Administration to the Critique of Institutions' in Rosalind Krauss, Annette Michelson, Hal Foster, Benjamin Buchloh, and Silvia Kowbolski (eds), *October: The Second Decade*, Cambridge, MIT Press, 1996, p. 119.

17   Frantz Fanon, *Black Skin, White Masks*, transl. Charles Lam Markham, New York, Grove Press, 1967, p. 17.

18   See Sydney Kasfir, 'African Art and Authenticity: A Text with a Shadow' in Okwui Enwezor and Olu Oguibe (eds), *Reading the Contemporary: African Art from Theory to the Marketplace*, London, Institute for International Visual Arts and Cambridge, MIT Press, 1999, pp. 88–113.

19   See, for example, Soyinka's critique of Négritude in *Myth, Literature, and the African World*, Cambridge, Cambridge University Press, 1976.

20   See Michael Taussig, *Mimesis and Alterity: A Particular History of the Senses*, London and New York, Routledge, 1993.

21   Yinka Shonibare and Chris Ofili are but two of the most well-known African artists who have made the critique of authenticity central to their work. In the case of Shonibare, he has used the idea of excess as a strategy to undercut the power of the authentic as a marker of cheapness and lack of sophistication.

22   See Achille Mbembe and Janet Roitman, 'Figures of the Subject in Times of Crisis', *Public Culture* 7: 2, 1995, pp. 323–52.

23   Achille Mbembe, *On the Postcolony*, Berkeley, University of California Press, 2001, p. 10.

24   Sydney Kasfir has made the important observation on the fact that questions of authenticity of African art were first a value of connoisseurship of the Western collector for whom the importance of authenticity depended on the establishment of what is valued as fake and what is not valued as a copy or

a fake. Therefore, the science of authentication is not more than a fantasy of projection through the construction of 'tribal style' whereby 'Authenticity as an ideology of collection and display creates an aura of cultural truth around certain types of African art (mainly precolonial and sculptural)'.

25   Mbembe, p. 6.

26   Throughout, I have pivoted my idea of crisis around Achille Mbembe and Janet Roitman's exceedingly important text: 'Figures of the Subject in Times of Crisis'.

27   Michel Foucault, '21 January 1976', in Mauro Bertani and Alessandro Fontana (eds), *Society Must Be Defended: Lectures at Collège de France, 1975–1976*, transl. David Macey, New York, Picador, 2003, p. 43.

28   In 1934, during an address to the Institute for the Study of Fascism in Paris, Benjamin raised the issue of the 'Author as Producer'. His insights made nearly seventy years ago remain remarkably prescient even today. Under the threat of the looming political crisis in Europe at the dawn of fascism, Benjamin averred that the context of production—here he was speaking specifically about literature—must be set in a 'living social context', namely the social context of production. Conversely he observed that, 'Social conditions are … determined by conditions of production. And when a work was criticized from a materialist point of view, it was customary to ask how this work stood vis-à-vis the social relations of production of its time'. The second point made by Benjamin in this direction was that 'Rather than ask "what is the *attitude* [author's emphasis] of a work to the relations of production of its time?" [one] should… ask "What is its *position* [author's emphasis] in them?" This question directly concerns the function the work has within the literary [artistic] relations of production of its time'.

29   See also Frantz Fanon, 'On National Culture' in *The Wretched of the Earth*, (transl. Constance Farrington), New York, Grove Press, Paris, Présence Africaine, 1963. On the role of intellectuals in the post-colonial emancipatory project, see also Sekou Touré, 'The Political Leader as a Representative of his Culture' in *Expérience Guinéenne Unité*, Paris, Présence Africaine, 1962.

30   See Joseph Stiglitz, *Globalization and its Discontents*, New York, W. W. Norton and Company, 2002; one of the more prominent critics of the World Bank and IMF.

31   Foucault, p. 43.

32   A typical response throughout the onset of the crisis, are attempts at de-legitimising the artist and intellectual, forcing many into prison, dissendency or exile, as in the case of Nigeria during the period of political repression by

the Abacha regime. When artists and intellectuals are forced to go to exile, many experience an anxiety of the *authenticity* of their work.

33   Thierry N'Landu, 'Le Groupe Amos' in *Documenta 11—Platform 5: Ausstellung/ Exhibition, Kurzführer/Short Guide*, Stuttgart, Hatje Cantz, 2002, p. 102.

34   David Forgacs (ed.), *An Antonio Gramsci Reader: Selected Writings*, 1916–1935, New York, Schocken Books, 1988, p. 304.

35   See the introduction of 'Le Groupe Amos: Reader', a compilation of writings of the group presented as part of a reading/media room dedicated to its work in *Documenta II—Platform 5*, Kassel, Germany, June–September 2002, p. 116, trans. (French to English) by Muna El Fituri-Enwezor.

36   José Mpundu, 'What Future for the Democratic Republic of Congo?' in *Documenta II—Platform 5*, p. 148.

37   AbdouMaliq Simone, 'The Visible and Invisible: Remaking African Cities' in Okwui Enwezor, Carlos Basualdo, Ute Meta Bauer, Susanne Ghez, Sarat Maharaj, Mark Nash and Octavio Zaya (eds), *Under Siege: Four African Cities; Freetown, Johannesburg, Kinshasa, Lagos*, Stuttgart, Hatje Cantz, 2002.

38   Ibid.

39   Nadja Rottner, 'Huit Facettes' in *Documenta 11—Platform 5*, p. 114.

40   Kan-Si, 'Dimensons Variable: Reply from Kan-Si' in *Metronome*, 4–5–6, 1999, p. 126.

41   Exhibition statement, *Documenta 11*, Kassel, Germany, 2002.

42   Artists such as Georges Adeagbo, Kay Hassan, Antonio Olé, Romauld Hazoumé and Pascale Marthine Tayou have thoroughly dismantled the randomness and poverty of the bricollage aesthetic by elaborating new sculptural and pictorial devises with recycled materials: Olé with his painterly and monumental refabrications of urban architectural fragments; Adeagbo with his mnemonic recontextualisations of archives of colonial and post-colonial history in his sculptural and sign painting appropriations; and Hassan with his arresting collages of masks, portraits and crowds fabricated out of torn surplus billboard advertising prints that manifest an unusually raw, festishistic power. Hazoumé's plastic masks, fashioned out of cut-out plastic jerry cans, on the other hand, reside uneasily between genuine sculptural experiments and afro-kitsch. The larger and more critical question is why has the bricolage aesthetic persisted for so long all across Africa, and in fact seems to be acquiring an even greater acceptance in the work of even younger artists? The upshot is that for some reason recycling as an aesthetic option strangely continues to be

seen by many artists as a proper artistic choice for making art. This perhaps owes to the erroneous notion that using recycled, impoverished materials in clever ways somehow transforms and elevates the assembled oddities into innovative, albeit uncanny artistic products that raise local curiosity and please benevolent development workers.

43   *Tokunbo* is a Yoruba term which literally means 'second child', but in the typical wry humour that accompanies responses to bleak socioeconomic conditions in most African countries, the term has come to stand for the vast secondhand market in objects of Western technological products such as cars, computers, electronics, and assorted machines that have been *reconditioned* and made *suitable* for export to Africa. The scale of the *Tokunbo* trade far outstrips that of new technological products and increasingly has come under state scrutiny for the effects on the environment, productivity and safety.

44   In fact, it seems unimaginable that there could be any other reason for this response to secondhand, recycled commodity–fetish products of the developed world beyond the survivalist strategies of people caught in the grips of brutal global economic restructuring. It is also to such survivalist strategies that artists and intellectuals have turned in order to protect their autonomy as critical producers of culture.

45   Kan-Si, op. cit., p. 122.

46   A number of the critiques that accompanied the reception of *Documenta 11*, which devoted a strong part of the exhibition to exploring the relationship between representation and the domain of social life, were based on abjuring the political and ethical in the conception of the work of art. Typical of such responses were criticisms from neo-conservative writers such as Michael Kimmelman of the *New York Times*, Blake Gopnik of the *Washington Post* and Christopher Knight of the *Los Angeles Times*.

The Revolution Stripped Bare …

GILANE TAWADROS

In geological terms, fault lines reveal themselves as fractures in the earth's surface, but they also mark a break in the continuity of the strata. Fault lines may be signs of significant shifts, or even of impending disaster, but they also create new landscapes. This chapter focuses on the work of a small number of contemporary artists from Africa and the African diaspora whose works trace the outlines of fault lines that are shaping contemporary experience locally and globally. These fault lines have been etched into the physical fabric of our world through the effects of colonialism and post-colonialism, of migration and globalisation and their reverberations which echo through contemporary lived experience and in the work of these artists, who are working across a range of media, from painting and sculpture through to architecture, photography and installation.

The nationalist struggles of the first decades of the twentieth century gave rise in the second half of the century to post-colonial independence and a new self-determination in Africa and beyond that articulated itself in a heightened political consciousness but also in new forms of visual and architectural practices. These new practices sought to negotiate the difficult and, as yet, unexplored terrain between tradition and modernity, between formal concerns and political contingencies. Modernism and modernity is too often defined in Western terms as a decisive break or rupture with the past, and yet it is almost always experienced as an uneven negotiation between past and future that can remain unresolved. The artists and artworks discussed here explore the ambivalent space in which tradition and modernity, past histories and future possibilities are mapped out. This is a space that is continuously 'under negotiation', shaped by the uneven flows of cultural and economic exchanges between the so-called developing and developed worlds. This is not to say that this is an insubstantial or inconclusive zone, but rather that the push and pull of tradition and modernity, past and future, exert differing pressures and are negotiated differently in various geographical locations and at different historical conjunctures. In specific instances, artists and architects have developed what I term a 'vernacular modernity'; that is to say, they navigate between a national and international consciousness that gives rise to distinctly new forms of cultural production. Rooted in the conditions of a specific location, vernacular modernity is a term that can be applied to the innovative forms of artistic and architectural practice that push the epistemological and formal envelope of traditional forms of modernism. In the case of the Egyptian architect Hassan Fathy, vernacular modernity moved Fathy to challenge the limited internationalism of international modernism, while the Guyanese-born painter Frank Bowling peels away the apolitical gloss of abstract expressionist painting, placing it in a wider global framework.

Globalisation and its impact is a theme that underpins this assemblage of art works, but globalisation here is understood not purely in terms of the exchange of global commodities and the erosion of nation states in favour of corporate multinationals. Rather, the patterns of globalisation are traced through the experiences of political exiles, disenfranchised citizens, immigrants and refugees, among others. This essay proposes new ways of considering the work of artists from Africa and the African diaspora that resist the construction of an imagined and essentialist construction of Africa, undisturbed by the effects of globalisation and migration. Such a worldview inevitably follows the linguistic and political fault lines inscribed into the global landscape by colonialism, setting clear demarcation lines between Africa and the African diaspora, between sub-Saharan Africa to the south and Arab Africa to the north. The fault lines of our contemporary world manifest in the contradictions of everyday life which daily present us with both the closure of opportunity and the possibility of change, at one and the same time. This chapter proposes a space in which we can engage with these complexities of lived experience through the work of artists who have embraced the ambiguities and inconsistencies of the contemporary world through artworks that are by turns witty and serious, monumental and understated.

A COMMON STRUGGLE

On a hot July night in Egypt in 1952, at the stroke of midnight, 3000 troops and some 200 officers took control of the key army headquarters barracks in Abbasiyya, Cairo, precipitating a military coup by the Free Officers Movement. Troops commanded by Free Officers and their supporters occupied the headquarters of the Frontier Force, all airports, the broadcasting station headquarters and its relaying facilities at Abu Za'bal, the Cairo telecommunications centre and all major roads and bridges in the city. At 7am on 23 July, the first announcement was made to the public over Cairo radio by Anwar al-Sadat. The military coup would swiftly lead to the forced abdication and exile of King Farouk and the eventual overthrow of the monarchy in 1953, and the appointment of Gamal Abdel-Nasser as the first indigenous leader of Egypt for centuries. This was the final chapter in the colonial struggle against the British that culminated in the Suez crisis. Together with the Algerian War of Independence of 1954–62, the Suez crisis of 1956 marked the last attempts of Britain and France to reassert their position in North Africa, and gave rise to powerful articulations of a new post-colonial, pan-Africanist and non-aligned world order that would arise phoenix-like from the ashes of colonial struggles throughout the continent.

> Since the region is one and the same with the same conditions, the same problems, the same future and the same enemy, no matter how different the masks he might wear in an endeavour to conceal his identity, why should our efforts be dissipated? The experiences we have gone through after July 23 have manifestly demonstrated the pressing need for a common struggle.[1]

President Nasser's rallying cry for a new nationalism and independence, not only in the Arab world but throughout the African continent and the developing world, galvanised a post-colonial movement that aspired towards independence from the superpowers, and social reforms in the direction of greater equality and greater union between Arab, African and Islamic countries. Nasser characterised them as three circles—the Arab Circle, the African Continent Circle and the Circle of 'our Bretheren-in-Islam'—as though they were concentric circles, radiating from the hub of a shared battle for independence. The call for unity and the invocation to a common struggle, expressed so compellingly by leaders such as Nasser and Kwame Nkrumah (Ghana), emerged directly from the shared experience of shedding the mantle of colonialism. It propelled the idea of Africa as a unified geographical and political entity that eventually took institutional form as the Organisation for African Unity, which was founded in 1963.

> The movement for independence in Africa, which gained momentum after the Second World War, has spread like a prairie fire throughout the length and breadth of Africa … The 'wind of change' has become a raging hurricane, sweeping away the old colonialist Africa. The year 1960 was Africa's year. In that year alone, seventeen African States

emerged as proud and independent sovereign nations. Now the ultimate freedom of the whole of Africa can no more be in doubt.[2]

But what role was culture to play in this new world order? Could one speak of a single African cultural identity in the same way as a unified political identity? Would a spectrum of new national cultures emerge in the wake of these new nations throughout the African continent? How could the native intellectual and artist free themselves of the intellectual and cultural lens of colonialism that had consistently distorted and misrepresented indigenous experiences? Speaking of the experience of Morocco in the post-colonial aftermath and the struggle to write the Maghreb's history in its own terms, Abdullah Laroui asks, 'What each one of us wants to know today is how to get out of ourselves, how to escape from our mountains and sand-dunes, how to define ourselves in terms of ourselves and not of someone else, how to stop being exiles in spirit.'[3]

First published in France in 1961, *The Wretched of the Earth* was a thorough and prescient study of the national liberation struggle as witnessed in the Algerian War of Independence. The work of Martiniquan psychiatrist and writer Frantz Fanon, who had been assigned to a hospital in Algeria during the rise against the French, *The Wretched of the Earth* became a manifesto for decolonisation and the liberation struggles taking place throughout the continent. For Fanon, there could be no separation between the struggle for liberation from colonial rule and the formation of a national culture. The two were inextricably linked, creating the essential conditions not only for national cultural expression, but also for the cultural expression of the entire continent.

> To fight for national culture means, in the first place, to fight for the liberation of the nation; that material keystone which makes the building of a culture possible. There is no other fight for culture that can develop apart from the popular struggle. To take an example: all those men and women

who are fighting with their bare hands against French colonialism in Algeria are not by any means strangers to the national culture of Algeria. The national Algerian culture is taking on form and content as the battles are being fought out, in prison, under the guillotine and in every French outpost which is captured or destroyed ... It is around the peoples' struggles that African-Negro culture takes on substance, and not around songs, poems or folklore. Adherence to African-Negro culture and to the cultural unity of Africa is arrived at in the first instance by upholding unconditionally the peoples' struggle for freedom. No one can truly wish for the spread of African culture if he/she does not give practical support to the creation of the conditions necessary to the existence of that culture; in other words, to the liberation of the entire continent.[4]

Fanon was not calling for a Soviet-style agitprop or social realist art that would uncritically celebrate and eulogise the triumphs of the revolution. Nor was he making the case for a romantic return to traditional artistic practices. 'A national culture is not a folklore,' wrote Fanon, 'nor an abstract populism that believes it can discover the people's true nature.' On the contrary, Fanon emphasised the futility of looking back to outmoded customs for artistic inspiration. More often than not, these traditions, he argued, are taken up as 'mummified fragments', static and out-of-date traces of a dynamic culture which has in fact moved on as a result of the struggle for independence from colonial rule. Most importantly, perhaps, Fanon made it clear that he is not advocating nationalism or nationalist culture but rather 'national consciousness' which, he concludes, is the most elaborate form of culture. The responsibility of the artist or intellectual, according to Fanon, 'is not a responsibility vis-à-vis his national culture', but rather, 'a global responsibility with regard to the totality of the nation', of which culture is only one aspect.[5] While Fanon rejected the notion of an essentialist African culture or cultural identity, he recognised that it was colonialism and the struggle for liberation from colonial rule that connected different African nations. This struggle was, by its very nature, internationalist in its form and it was this interplay between the national and the international or, the local and the global as we might say now, that created the pre-conditions for the making of culture.

> National consciousness, which is not nationalism, is the only thing that will give us an international dimension. The problem of national consciousness and of national culture takes on in Africa a special dimension. The birth of national consciousness in Africa has a strictly contemporaneous connexion with the African consciousness … Far from keeping aloof from other nations, therefore, it is national liberation which leads the nation to play its part on the stage of history. It is at the heart of national consciousness that international consciousness lives and grows. And this two-fold emerging is ultimately the source of all culture.[6]

A VERNACULAR MODERNITY

It is precisely this negotiation between a national and an international consciousness that emerges from the life and work of the Egyptian architect Hassan Fathy. As Nasser Rabbat points out, Fathy's career 'more or less mirrored what was happening in Egypt, a country undertaking the long and torturous journey from colonialism to independence to development and its aftermath entangled with grand dreams of regional supremacy during the same period'.[7] The son of wealthy landowners from Upper Egypt, Fathy was well schooled in European ideas and, as a young architect, he had learnt the language of contemporary European architecture, experimenting with various different architectural styles before defining what I would term the vernacular modernity for which he subsequently became famous with his New Gourna project (1948–61). An ambitious scheme to rebuild an entire rural village in Upper Egypt, New Gourna provided Fathy with the opportunity

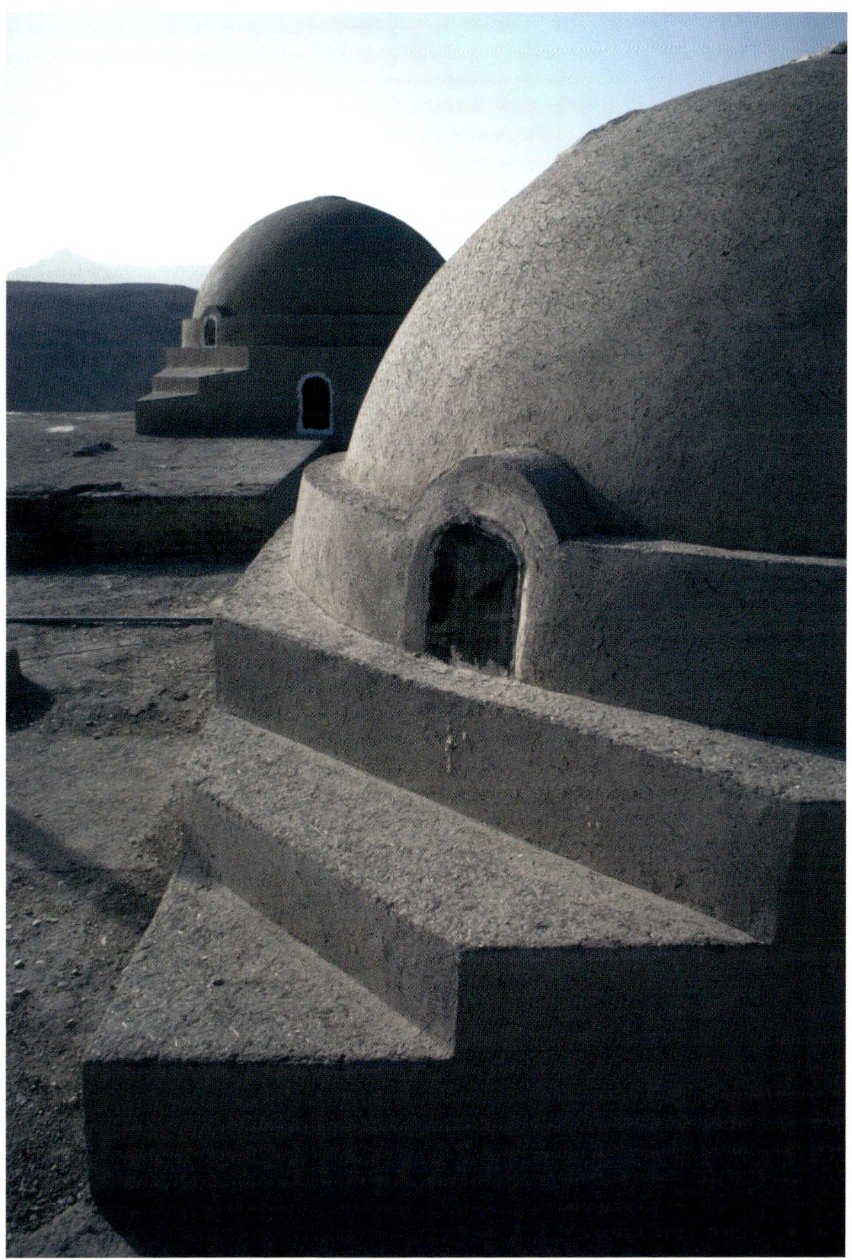

Hassan Fathy, *Stopplaere House* (1950), Luxor, Egypt;
© Aga Khan Trust for Culture.

to establish a cost-effective and modern solution to the problem of mass housing for the rural poor in Egypt while also staying true to indigenous materials and methods of construction. Working with highly skilled Nubian master builders from Aswan, Fathy built a village of domed and vaulted adobe courtyard houses that were, as Rabat points out, 'a mixture of rural traditional and modern, utopian principles'.[8]

Fathy's brand of vernacular modernity, which he defined in his treatise 'Architecture for the Poor'[9], was indeed utopian and idealistic, but it was also a radical rebuttal of the universalising tendencies of Western modernism. Rejecting the claims of Europe's modernists to have discovered universal solutions to contemporary living, Fathy's architectural response was an attempt to forge local, indigenous traditions of architecture with contemporary ideas and technologies. He refracted the lessons learnt from modern architecture through the lens of national consciousness, traditional building methods and the particular context of the Egyptian *fellaheen,* or rural poor. Fathy believed passionately in the importance of articulating a distinctive 'Egyptian accent' to national architecture through a 'living'—as opposed to stagnant—tradition of indigenous architecture. Tradition and modernity could co-exist, insisted Fathy, each modulating the other, but neither should be adopted as a stylistic device or architectural orthodoxy.

If, in the first decades of the twentieth century, modernism professed to speak universally from the privileged bastion of Western metropolises, then the vernacular modernity that emerged so vociferously in Egypt and throughout Africa in the middle of the twentieth century responded with an equally emphatic insistence on national and local specificities that were nonetheless in constant dialogue with an 'international consciousness'. Rather than replacing one brand of universalism with another, the artists, architects and intellectuals constructed these vernacular modernities as responses to the popular, national fight for liberation from colonialism and they emerged as an integral part of the struggle for national and continental self-determination.

Fathy's subsequent career saw him departing from his version of vernacular modernity, and his architectural ideas evolved in parallel to the changing ideology of Egypt 'from 1920s and 1930s Egyptianism, to Nasserist Pan-Arabism in the 1960s, to Islamism in the 1980s'.[10] These political and ideological shifts would be mirrored in different ways throughout the continent in the latter half of the twentieth century and were brought about, to a great extent, by the failure to realise fully the aspirations and dreams of the liberation struggles in Africa.

MAPPING SPACE

Just as Hassan Fathy sought to negotiate the intellectual and technical concerns of architectural modernism and Egypt's shifting political and cultural contingencies, other artists and intellectuals in Africa and the African diaspora in the second half of the twentieth century were also seeking to depart from modernism's universalising agenda in order to re-articulate contemporary art and literature through their own ideas and experiences. One of the most important artists of his generation, Frank Bowling created map paintings in the late 1960s and early 1970s that combine his investigations into the formal properties of picture making with his political preoccupations. Bowling not only put the political into pop art but also put post-colonial concerns into contemporary art, thereby creating a sublime tension between form and content, and laying the ground for subsequent generations of artists for whom aesthetic and political concerns are never mutually exclusive.

Bowling began making map paintings in 1967, at a time when maps were not uncommon in the work of cutting-edge artists of the 1960s and, as Kobena Mercer identifies, the motif of the globe attracted artists who were responding to the social and political turmoil of the time.

In the same way that Fathy found a way to reconcile the demands of tradition and modernity, Bowling did not distinguish a hierarchy of form over content, or content over form. The edges of Bowling's canvases frequently spill over across the frame that fails to rein in or constrain the rich, accumulated brush strokes, creating visual spaces that extend, like a horizon line, beyond our immediate field of vision. It is as though Bowling's brush is probing beyond the surface of the visible world to elicit a hidden reality that threatens to slip out of reach. In the sumptuous deep reds, pinks and purples of Bowling's epic work *Marcia H. Travels* (1970), the artist constructs out of pure colour a vast, three-dimensional oceanic space in which the outlines of the continental land masses recede and protrude like the ebb and flow of waves on the surface of the sea. The distinctive colourings of imperial possession that characterised the maps of colonial textbooks throughout Africa and the Caribbean become submerged beneath the thick, layered strokes of the artist's brush. The clearly delineated outlines of *South America Squared* (1967) had yielded by the end of the decade to the richly textured abstraction of *Who's Afraid of Barney Newman?* (1968), in which a radically new cartography could be glimpsed enlarging and receding into the depths of the paint. As Mercer puts it, these canvases represent nothing less than 'a painterly act of postcolonial re-vision':

> In the darkening vertical stains that threaten to engulf the outlines of Europe and the Americas in *Marcia H. Travels*, it is possible to suggest that the world picture imprinted by the Empire project was being placed 'under erasure'. By virtue of the ways in which they tackle the subject of postcolonial history, the map paintings were critically rewriting the Eurocentric projection of the globe.[11]

The ink drawings of Clifford Charles represent a very different kind of postcolonial revisioning, and yet they share with Bowling's canvases the search through painterly abstraction for a new visual and physical space that reflects a profoundly altered social and political reality. They are, in Bheki Peterson's

words, 'a provocatively ingenious response to South Africa's "altered states"…
of governance and consciousness'.[12] Charles's works are preoccupied with
the same double consciousness of 'blackness and abstraction' that Mercer
locates in Bowling's paintings, evoked through the motif of an endlessly
repeated journey, moving from the past to the present and back again. Sitting
tangentially to Clifford Charles's series of ink drawings is a documentary
journey 'We've Also Been to Soweto', a fictional text by Prince Massingham
that recounts a sightseeing tour of Soweto. Written in a kind of South African
esperanto that interweaves English, Sotho, slang, Afrikaans, Zulu, Tswana
and Tsonga, Massingham's text effects a parallel movement to the ink

Clifford Charles, *Rhythm and Blues* (2001), from the series
Painting on Water, ink on paper, 123.5 × 153cm; courtesy
of the artist.

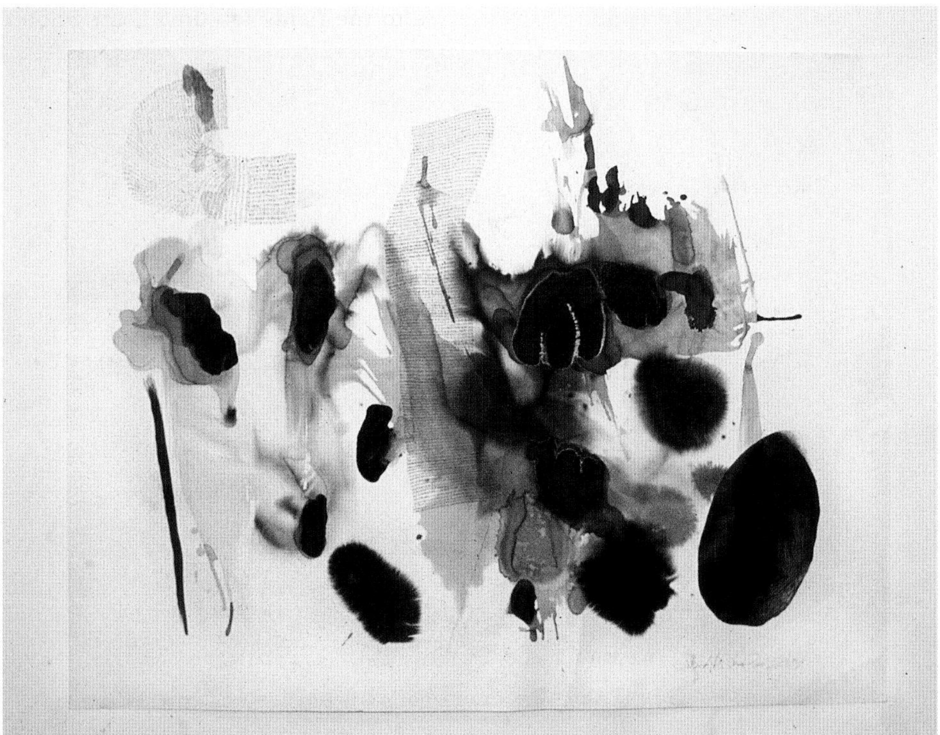

drawings, moving backwards and forwards between the city's apartheid past and its post-apartheid present.

Charting the passage of both space and time, Charles' drawings and Massingham's text unmask the illusion of arbitrary dividing lines that demarcate one distinct historical moment from another, from slavery to freedom, from colonialism to post-colonialism, from apartheid to post-apartheid. The reality of lived experience is somewhat different, bearing witness to incompleteness, slippage, multiple layers, forgetfulness and erasure. Charles's series of drawings that has the generic title *Painting on Water* (2002–03) evokes the uneven and slippery ground that the present occupies, balancing precariously on the past. The black ink flows unevenly across the surface of the white paper, dense and impenetrable in some areas, in other areas staining the paper only lightly, at times almost transparent. In *Interaction/Haiku* (2001), an inky mass spreads across the centre of the paper; while in *Looking Glass* (2001), the ink is contained in a tight oval, rock-like shape. In other drawings, the ink spills in fluid, unconstrained movements across the paper. As Peterson points out, this new series of works recalls an earlier body of work, a series of oil paintings under the composite title of *Metamorphosis* in which Charles made physical incisions on the canvas that were then layered with ink upon ink, resonating with the 'incisions upon the body as it was literally scarred, tortured and reconfigured under the violence of apartheid'. But here Peterson discerns a witty displacement that is contained in the very materiality of Charles's drawings 'of whiteness with the intricacies of blackness':

> They recall the black marks (usually blocks) that apartheid censors used to hide faces and material that was considered subversive … Let us not forget the sardonic humour of apartheid that euphemistically called areas populated by black people outside of the homeland reserves, as 'black spots' that needed to be removed from South Africa.[13]

Through their investigations of the material qualities of paint on canvas and ink on paper, Bowling and Charles make tangible, in different ways, particular political and social spaces in transition. In the case of Bowling, this is the post-colonial reconfiguration of political and cultural geographies in the aftermath of the independence movements of formerly colonised nations. In the case of Charles, it is the articulation of a more recently won post-apartheid space that is resolutely unsentimental or unromantic. In both instances, these spaces do not constitute a neat and uncomplicated break with the past, but rather are continual, forced reminders. In Charles's case, they are engagements with what has historically taken place, 'another necessary archival project', whereas in Bowling's works it is more a question of the unenunciated difference which hardens on the surface of his canvases, 'intervening in the codes of culture to delay and postpone the closure of the signifying chain'. As Mercer writes, 'Frank Bowling's map paintings activate an awareness of the agency of something that is not there anymore.'[14]

THE ALGEBRA OF DIFFERENCE

The echoes of 'something that is not there anymore' haunt the works of Zarina Bhimji. Her triptych of large-scale light boxes is an altarpiece, appropriate to a secular, postmodern age. Whereas the main protagonists and narratives of the traditional Christian altarpiece would have been familiar to their audience of worshippers, the narrative of Bhimji's irreligious triptych is enigmatic and difficult to pin down. The work provokes an overwhelming sense of absence and loss, an immediate emotional response in the first instance and, only after an interval, an intellectual response. Epic in scale, Bhimji's works reflect on the minutiae of people's lives, abandoned in the haste of sudden, enforced exile. A collection of fans has been felled from the ceiling, and lies abandoned on the floor of a large empty space. Another room is occupied by only a shaft of light spilling through an open door. A pair of shoes, hanging forlornly on the wall, is the last remaining evidence of human presence in an uninhabited room. Enlarged and illuminated, these minute residues are the only clues to what has taken place, and they evoke a disturbing sense of cataclysmic events that have shaken the everyday patterns of human activity, giving 'a sense of unspeakable horrors … but also a sense of long-term decay'.[15]

Bhimji has described the works as being concerned with 'learning to listen to "difference", the difference in shadows, microcosms and sensitivity to difference in its various forms. Listening with the eyes, listening to changes in tone, difference of colour … it is about making sense through the medium of aesthetics.' Far removed from the realm of factual history or documentary photography, Bhimji's approach proposes a new way of mapping the tragic and seismic events that have characterised a period of history riven by ethnic and racial conflicts, not only in Africa but throughout the globe. How does one begin to picture the devastating effects of elimination, extermination and erasure on a vast scale? If, as Stalin once chillingly observed, the death of one man is a tragedy and the death of millions a statistic, how is it possible for us to engage with the scale of mass trauma on an intimate, and even poetic, level? Bhimji extrapolates from the historically and geographically specific situation, distancing it and thereby transcending it; from the particular and personal residues of human activity, her work extracts a deafeningly quiet question: whether in Paris or Rwanda, London or Kosovo, why does it seem impossible for us to live creatively with difference?

It is the indexing of difference from the 'multicultural managerialism' of art circuits and the cultural industry in the 1990s through to the rigid, compartmentalising logic of apartheid that Sarat Maharaj exposes in 'Fatal Natalities'.[16] The fields of representation and cultural authority, according to Maharaj, are not so far removed from the exigencies of political power and conflict in their expression of incommensurate difference. Presented in opposition to this process of differentiation—of measuring, scanning and classifying difference—but ultimately bound up with it, are the 'natalising' tendencies that Maharaj discerns in the articulation of post-apartheid South Africa's Rainbow Nation but which have emerged at various junctures in different parts of the continent. Maharaj identifies the search for the 'authentically native place' as a reaction to apartheid's 'fraudulent natalities' and its 'map of homelands, racial areas, Bantustans'. Ultimately, the search for authentic, fixed identities is born from the negative space cast by the dismantling of apartheid, or by the failure of liberation movements to realise the aspirations of their peoples, or by the disempowering effects of globalisation. Caught in that sphere of negativity, of reaction to something outside of itself, a space is opened up for ideological polarities, intransigent orthodoxies and fundamental opposites that brings in its wake religious and ethnic conflict, political uncertainty and civil war.

Salem Mekuria's *RUPTURES: A Many Sided Story* (2003) is explicitly rooted in the recent political and social history of Ethiopia. Mirroring the tripartite structure of traditional Ethiopian Orthodox religious art, Mekuria's triptych video installation examines the turbulent events, from within and without, that have erupted periodically in the lives of Ethiopian people in recent decades. Visually referencing the Trinity—Father, Son and the Holy Spirit—in Ethiopian Orthodox faith, Mekuria's installation explores the chronological synchronicity which characterises contemporary Ethiopian life, namely the co-existence of past, present and future experienced simultaneously in the present. 'Time is circular,' observes Mekuria, 'one is never too far from encounters with the prehistoric, the pre-modern, the modern and the post-modern in the course of a few moments.' As new images emerge on the three-screen video projection, the old presences linger, never far from the surface. The co-existence of more than one temporal space and multiple perspectives lies at the heart of Mekuria's intervention that contests the dominance of a single, unifying narrative of Ethiopian experience. As Elsabet Giorgis writes, 'her work acknowledges the varieties and complexities of

Ethiopian culture and questions the ability of any single philosophical rationalisation to be the primal context of conventional value'.[17]

Whether within the religious context of Ethiopian Orthodoxy or the ideological framework of Marxism, Mekuria's fractured narrative of Ethiopian contemporary experience resists yielding to a single authoritative voice, replacing this instead with a palimpsest of images and voices that constitute the complex layers of Ethiopian lived experience. Her work speaks, more generally, to the contradictions and tensions that lie beneath the surface of contemporary societies in the so-called developed as well as 'developing' world; contradictions expressed through the push and pull of the totalising narratives of ideological or religious unity, on the one hand, and the centrifugal forces of migration, exile and diaspora, on the other.

Defying the political violence that has marked Algeria from the colonial struggle to present-day conflicts, Samta Benyahia's architectural installation (a tribute to the great Algerian writer Kateb Yacine) creates a utopian space in which the past and present are no longer in conflict with one another; here, a multiplicity of viewpoints becomes possible at one and the same time. Benyahia's wooden structure is a *circular* construction in three dimensions, built with sharp exterior angles in the form of a star-shaped polygon. As Benyahia describes it, the interior of the polygon is 'a space one enters like a cocoon, made up of seven recesses through which the spectator or the visitor discovers seven different stained glass windows ... and on which the key motif is the blue rosace, a form carrying the name of a woman: Fatima in the Arab–Andalucian repertoire'. Yacine's poetic concept of the 'starry polygon' (*le polygone étoilé*) stands as a metaphor for a utopian political and social space in which ideological and cultural polarities are negated. In direct dialogue with the rosace motif, the starry polygon is a structure without a defined beginning or end, but is experienced as a kind of vortex that eradicates everything in its orbit, thereby holding out the possibility of a fresh beginning, a new start.

Ali La Pointe and all those condemned to death are children of the polygon. They live a violent death, just as I write in an impasse. And the obsessive star that haunts prisons is a night star. For the condemned man walking to his death, this sleepless, sputtering night wipes out everything, begins everything afresh, to infinity. This is the inextricable completeness of the polygon, the empty interior of which is extinguished like a campfire, all forms abolished ... Peace to its ashes. But we may also inhabit the scaffold, holding our heads under our arms. This is the lot of the poet. Then we sing of the 'black sun of melancholy' and wander the Orient like Gérard de Nerval! We may also haunt a castle, like [Franz] Kafka, or pace the paths of a labyrinth. Or again, like [Henri] Michaux, we may send this 'inside space' for which we have lost the keys flying into pieces. Then there is no more East, no more West. The polygon reasserts its rights. And if the streets of Dublin find echoes in Algiers, it is because the creative artist does not inhabit, but is inhabited by a sort of starry vertigo, which is even starrier for those of us whose starting point is the darkest point in the darkest corner of an alleyway.[18]

The circular movement that takes us (the viewers) around Benyahia's starry polygon evokes the movement of Muslim pilgrims around the Ka'ba, the rectangular building that Muhammad had purged of idols and made the centre of Muslim devotion. But the circle also assumes a particular structural and symbolic significance in the literature of Kateb Yacine as a symbol of freedom that straddles both the spatial and the temporal. According to Yacine, the image of the circle is 'the reality of the revolutionary world, the freedom of men who are always on the move, freedom in both space and time'. Benyahia has created an ideal space, tinged with a deep, azure blue that underscores the notion of an ideal existence in complete contrast to the context of conflict and chaos that has scarred Algeria's recent history.

Entering Benyahia's utopian structure provides a space for reflection and memory; respite, if only for a short time, from the conflict and chaos that exists beyond its idyllic confines.

SIGNS AND MEANINGS

The possibility of reconciling different world views underpins the work of Rotimi Fani-Kayode, who creates a photographic world in which 'the body is the focal point for an exploration of the relationship between erotic fantasy and ancestral spiritual values'.[19] Situated at the vanguard of work that explored the politics of identity, Fani-Kayode's images insist upon the sensuality of the photographic image and its ability to elicit both an emotional and an intellectual response. Politics and aesthetics were not mutually exclusive terms in Fani-Kayode's visual vocabulary, nor were the different facets of his identity and artistic practice.

> In my case, my identity has been constructed from my own sense of otherness, whether cultural, racial or sexual. The three aspects are not separate within me. Photography is the tool by which I feel most confident in expressing myself. It is photography, therefore—Black, African, homosexual photography—which I must use not just as an instrument, but as a weapon if I am to resist attacks on my integrity and indeed, my existence on my own terms.[20]

Far from being a self-indulgent practice that meditated on personal experience and identity as the self-contained subject and object of his artworks, Fani-Kayode located his images within wider political, historical and cultural contexts. A committed activist on issues of race and sexuality, Fani-Kayode saw his political engagement as bound up with his own creative practice and that of others. He saw parallels between his own

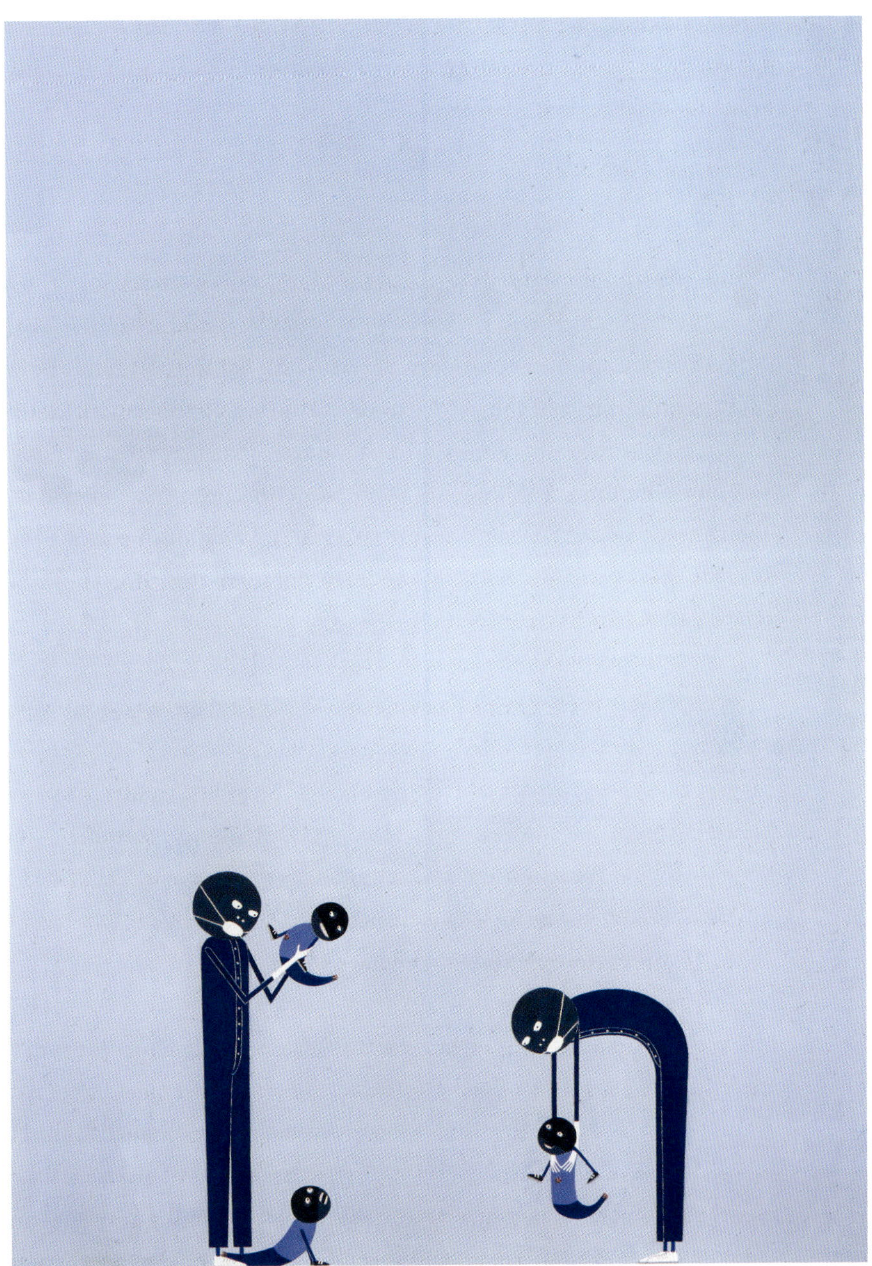

Laylah Ali, *Untitled* (2001), goauche on paper, 69 × 46cm;
courtesy 303 Gallery, New York.

work and that of the Osogbo artists in Yorubaland who 'themselves have resisted the cultural subversions of neo-colonialism and who celebrate the rich, secret world of our ancestors'.[21] The rich saturated colours of Fani-Kayode's photographs, his use of chiaroscuro and mise-en-scène, contribute to the construction of what Mark Sealy describes as a 'twilight cross-cultural zone' in which Fani-Kayode erodes the lines 'between black and white, gay and straight, acceptance and taboo'.[22] Ultimately, Fani-Kayode's images contest the idea of a settled world view dominated by an established canon of ideas and iconography; he disturbs fixed notions of African-ness, blackness and homosexuality that rely too heavily on an essentialist and uncomplicated view of the world and human experience.

While Fani-Kayode and Benyahia offer up alternative constructions of the world, which insist on the coexistence of different world views and the possibility of multiple interpretations, Laylah Ali paints an altogether darker, dystopian realm.

Evoked through her ongoing series of brightly coloured gouache paintings, Ali's cartoon-like images are deeply disturbing and ambiguous narratives that suggest repeated episodes of violence and conflict underpinned by the dynamics of race and power. Inspired by the graphic style of comic strips, Ali constructs a world in which the identities of her varied Greenhead characters are difficult to pin down and their behaviour is both ambivalent and contradictory. The apparent simplicity of Ali's work masks a sophisticated aesthetic strategy that, as Lisa Fischman points out, implicates the viewer in the process of decoding and interpreting the works, making the viewer responsible for the meaning they elicit from the images.[23] At first glance, the hard-edged contours of Ali's characters suggest that the content of the paintings might be as unequivocal and clear-cut as traditional comic strips in which the dividing lines between 'goodie' and 'baddie' are clearly drawn and the narrative conclusion foregone. But Ali's world is unsettlingly equivocal. Her strange, wide-eyed creatures—part human, part alien—with gigantic heads play their parts in a series of narrative fragments without a clear beginning or end and, as Fischman notes, explode 'simplistic binary categorisations—human/alien, male/female, good/evil, black/white— forcing their re-examination ... allowing them, as [Laylah Ali] puts it, to "act like a question mark"'.[24] The moral ambiguity of Ali's characters and their actions make the viewer's active role as interpreter and participant in these bizarre tales all the more uncomfortable. It is as though Ali is making us aware of our own position as both spectator and protagonist in the 'real' world, and the ethical choices that we make on a daily basis to watch or participate, or maybe even our mute culpability as spectators whose very inaction allows unspeakable things to happen.

Underpinning Ali's work is an acknowledgement of the social and political violence that consistently subverts human relations and erodes the will to effect political change. Ali's work signals a disillusion with the redemptive narratives of radical politics and liberation struggles but also a desire to re-engage without the benefit of rose-tinted spectacles.

Pitso Chinzima and Veliswa Gwintsa's installation *At Least One Person Was Killed* addresses the cumulative effects of relentless social violence as a global phenomenon that militates against the efforts of ordinary people to realise a full and meaningful existence. Rejecting the notion that social violence is a peculiarly South African experience, Chinzima and Gwintsa suggest that violence is one of the more troubling effects of globalisation and its discontents. Chinzima and Gwintsa describe their installation of children's furniture and toys covered with newspaper clippings of the dead as a 'visual monument for the dead'. Critical of the media representation of death as a daily spectacle, their work appears particularly resonant in the context of the recently waged war against Iraq and the saturation of media coverage. Does the media's representation of death bring us any closer to its reality? ask Chinzima and Gwintsa. Or does the incessant repetition and proliferation of the iconography of death simply distance us from its devastating impact on people's lives? By picturing death, do we take steps to avert it, or do we simply fuel a dehumanising abstraction of individual lives? This questioning assumes even greater significance in the context of South Africa's recent history, where the murder of ordinary black people, whether in the townships of South Africa or in the camps of exiled South Africans in the countries bordering South Africa, was a daily occurrence under the former apartheid regime. But, as Prince Mbusi Dube underlines in his essay[25], while Chinzima and Gwintsa's work emerges from their lived experience as black South Africans, it is not a reflection on death within a South African context; rather, it demands a recognition of the common threads that bind us in a shared humanity that transcends specific geographical context or unique individual experience.

It is the increasingly widening gap between two discommensurate worlds that informs the work of Sabah Naim: namely, that of the international arena of the media and global politics, on the one hand, and the everyday world of Egyptians and their daily effort to survive, on the other. Naim's images are frequently populated by ordinary Cairenes going about their daily business: two policemen sit on a bench; a group of people wait for a bus; a crowd of people cross a busy street. Naim's works represent an artistic intervention into the arena of media representation, offering alternative images which are characterised by their ordinariness, documents of the banality of everyday life that stand in stark contrast to the exaggerated depictions of Middle Eastern life that proliferate in the global media. But Naim's images are also a comment upon the process of mediation itself. The surfaces of her photographic images have been physically disturbed. Drawn upon, painted, scratched, inked, decorated, the images are irrevocably altered by the artist's hand. The act of marking and revising the photographs draws attention to the ways in which our experiences have become subject to greater and greater mediation. Paired with Naim's photographs are three-dimensional sculptures, moulded from newspapers and magazines (selected by the artist from both Egyptian and foreign print media), which are meticulously rolled and shaped by the artist.

In their form, these bifurcated installations—half-photograph, half-sculpture—physically reflect a divided public realm in which the words and images of the global media are rendered as abstractions and the 'real' documentary evidence of Cairene street life is 'tampered with', assuming a peculiarly heightened realism.

As Yasmeen Siddiqui points out, together with other Cairo-based artists, Naim is concerned with 'how the city is organised and how public space is occupied and territorialised'.[26] Perhaps this is not surprising given the history of Cairo, whose Arabic name 'the victorious' evokes what was once a global metropolis at the centre of an Islamic empire that has since waned and given way to new empires and global formations. But Naim is less concerned with

Sabah Naim, *Untitled* (2003), mixed media, photograph
by Muhammad Saif; courtesy of the artist.

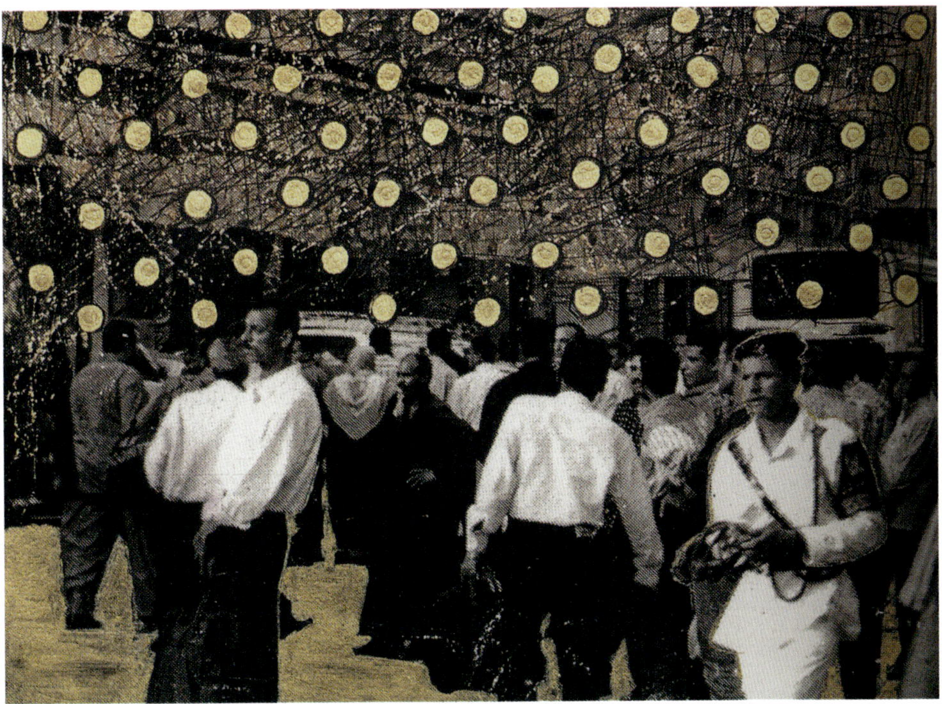

Cairo's glorious past as with its dynamic present. With her adoption of the moving image and sound, Naim's video work takes not one image but hundreds of individual frames that are manipulated and worked upon like her photographs. It is the city that assumes the role of chief protagonist in Naim's urban tale and 'the street', notes Naim, 'becomes the stage. All those who walk through it actors, a microcosmic glance at the larger Egyptian society. Each of the players walks through the scene [enclosed/isolated] in their own world, carrying a mixed bag of emotions and concerns, unaware of that which surrounds them.'[27] Her technique of manipulating the photographic image which, by turns, obscures or highlights particular details of the scene, removes individual characters from their environment, isolating them and alienating them from their everyday surroundings. It is difficult not to read Naim's work as a poetic critique of the alienation of thousands of people from the new political and economic global order and the re-inscription of other experiences and ways of living on to the international stage.

CITIES UNDER CONSTRUCTION

> The culture from which I am descended (my Algerian roots) has nothing in common with the culture from which I come … In contrast to the ancient culture of the bled, the culture of these [housing] estates is still under construction (through grafitti, street gear, rap, break dancing etc.).[28]

Contradicting claims that a settled political, economic and cultural regime has been established worldwide as a result of a 'new world order' that materialised after the crumbling of the communist regimes in Eastern Europe, the work of Kader Attia paints a picture of an assymetrical globalisation and of cities (and cultures) in the heart of Europe that are still under construction. Continuously monitoring the world for signs of shifts and changes (while also longing romantically for the developing world to remain frozen in an idealised past), the European metropolises, which were once the centres of Empire, recoil from the cultural transformations that are taking place in their midst. Globalisation, in this sense, has come home to roost in the figure of migrants, refugees and asylum seekers who, together with the second- and third-generation children of earlier migrants, are transfiguring indigenous European cultures irrevocably. It is these signs of cultural difference and dissonant experience that Attia marks in his photographs and installations.

In his slide installation piece *La Piste d'Atterisage* (*The Landing Strip*, 1998–2000), Attia depicts the lives of Algerian transvestites and transsexuals in Paris. Intimate and domestic, Attia's portraits evoke the lives of people who are on the margins of both Algerian and French society. Attia likens the protagonists of *La Piste d'Atterissage,* exiled from Algeria and living illegally (*sans papiers*) in Paris, to medieval saints, describing them as 'people who take everything upon themselves, who are persecuted, abused, ridiculed and finally adulated'.[29] Excluded from both Algeria and France, the figures which populate Attia's work represent the lived experience of globalisation and its disaffected and disenfranchised 'non-citizens'. But, for Attia, they also paradoxically represent the triumph of personal freedom over conformity and of difference over assimilation. In this sense, Attia's protagonists might be seen as the vanguard of an alternative world order that is still 'under construction'.

Like Chaucer's *Canterbury Tales,* which evokes the daily lives and experiences of a group of medieval pilgrims, Attia's work also carries a warning. In *La Machine à Rêves* (*Dream Machine,* 2002–03), Attia critiques the hegemonising effects of consumer society whose brands, labels and logos recall the rigid laws of medieval heraldry. A designer-clad young *beurre* (French-born Algerian youth) stands in front of an automatic vending machine that distributes an assortment of desirable objects that reflect sardonically on life in France's cross-cultural housing estates. Dispensing syringes, kosher salami, Mecca Cola, condoms and *hijabs* (veils), Attia's vending machine stands as a metaphor for the widening net of globalisation and consumer society, which absorbs and appropriates difference, transforming it into yet another consumable object with only the outer wrapping of difference.

Like Attia, Wael Shawky interrogates the uneven, discontinuous effects of globalisation and mass migration. Constructing his own massive cityscape in the centre of the exhibition space, Shawky's city is a hybrid metropolis, part rural, part urban. Encircled by perimeter walls, Shawky's *Asphalt Quarter* (2003) evokes the popular, urban districts of downtown Cairo and, yet, it lacks any distinguishing features that fix it as any city *in particular*. Drenched in asphalt and liquid tar, the buildings rise up, some separated by narrow alleyways, some topped on their rooftops by plasma screens, reminiscent of the billboards that litter today's cityscapes. A series of images alternate randomly on these screens, each the length of a standard TV commercial: a group of Arab Bedouins build cement houses and cover them with liquid tar against the backdrop of a desertscape close to the sea; Bedouin children create a runway from liquid tar; a nomad leaves his mud shelter, pulling a water buffalo behind him.

The convergence of incongruous elements is a frequent motif in Shawky's work. In an earlier video and installation piece entitled *Sidi el Asphalt's Mulid* (2001), Shawky set the rhythmic, hypnotic movements of a Sufi religious trance to the sounds of hip-hop group Cypress Hill.[30] The unlikely melding of the two results in a disquieting convergence between US hip-hop and a traditional Egyptian religious festival that points to the wider contradictions and incongruities of contemporary life effected by the dual processes of migration and globalisation. As Niru Ratnam comments: 'Can you get perfect fits between constituencies that know little and care to know little about the other? ... Or is the act of fitting them together the site of productivity and questioning?'[31]

Sidi el Asphalt's Mulid reflects upon the effects of modernisation on contemporary Egyptian culture and the dramatic shifts that have taken place in the country in recent decades, from the economic transformations of the 1970s, through the waves of immigration to the Gulf in the 1980s, leading up to the impact of globalisation from the 1990s to the present. In this context, the *mulid* is, according to Shawky, 'a stereotypical image of Egyptian society that encompasses all its coexisting contradictions without allowing any of its poles to affect the other negatively or positively'. In the same way that Attia points to the surprising convergence between the conformity demanded by consumer society and that defined by new forms of religious orthodoxy, Shawky suggests that these opposite poles of cultural experience coexist and come together to create a hybrid social and cultural reality which has many equivalences:

> Via its nomadic nature, the Bedouin community becomes a metaphor for globalisation: borders and space are broken, and the tribal tendencies of nomads find an equivalent in the notion of shared interests raised by the owners of capital—the driving force behind globalisation. The mutated water buffalo represents an amalgamation of the agricultural with the nomadic; its artificial hump comes to epitomise the nomadic. At issue here are the poetics of modernisation, where the primitive becomes urban, the nomadic agricultural, the bourgeois aristocratic, the popular bourgeois, and the sacred consumer.[32]

NOTES ON THE POST-COLONY

> The notion 'postcolony' identifies specifically a given historical trajectory—that of societies recently emerging from the experience of colonisation and the violence which the colonial relationship, *par excellence*, involves … The postcolony is characterised by a distinctive style of political improvisation, by a tendency to excess and a lack of proportion as well as by distinctive ways in which identities are multiplied, transformed and put into circulation.[33]

Fifty years after the revolution that dispensed with colonial rule, Moataz Nasr's mesmerising video installation presents a powerful critique of the cynicism of politicians and the indifference of their electorate in post-revolutionary, postcolonial Egypt. But while Nasr's work emerges from a specific historical and cultural context, it transcends that context. As Bheki Peterson writes of Charles's work, Nasr's artistic practice is 'deeply inscribed with historical specificity', yet 'stubbornly refuses to be reduced to, solely defined by, or more correctly, confined to the exigencies of time and place'.[34] Simon Njami accurately locates Nasr's work in the context of a generation of post-colonial artists who are raising questions about the nature of the post-colony and its regimes of power. Born of historical upheavals, as Njami points out, these artists are 'more or less the same age as the independent states of Africa' and they expose the 'illusion of pan-Africanism which never came to pass or the illusion of independence movements which happened to become nothing but failures and disappointments'. At a historical juncture at which the autonomy of the nation state has yielded power to corporate multinationals whose GDP often exceeds that of smaller nations, these questions assume a universal poignancy that extends beyond Egypt, Africa, or the so-called developing world, to encompass the entire globe.

We are all in the post-colony now

At the far end of an enclosed space, a man is playing a *tabla* (drum). His legs are wrapped around the curves of its finely crafted clay base, inlaid with mother-of-pearl and ivory. Remaining out of sight, the man's face and body extend beyond the edge of the large video screen. He plays out a repertoire of traditional Arab compositions, invoking a spectrum of emotions by his music, which ranges from nationalistic cries of war to melancholic love ballads. Extending across the floor of the space, Nasr creates a river of 400 hollow clay drums of various sizes. Raw and unpolished, these drums map

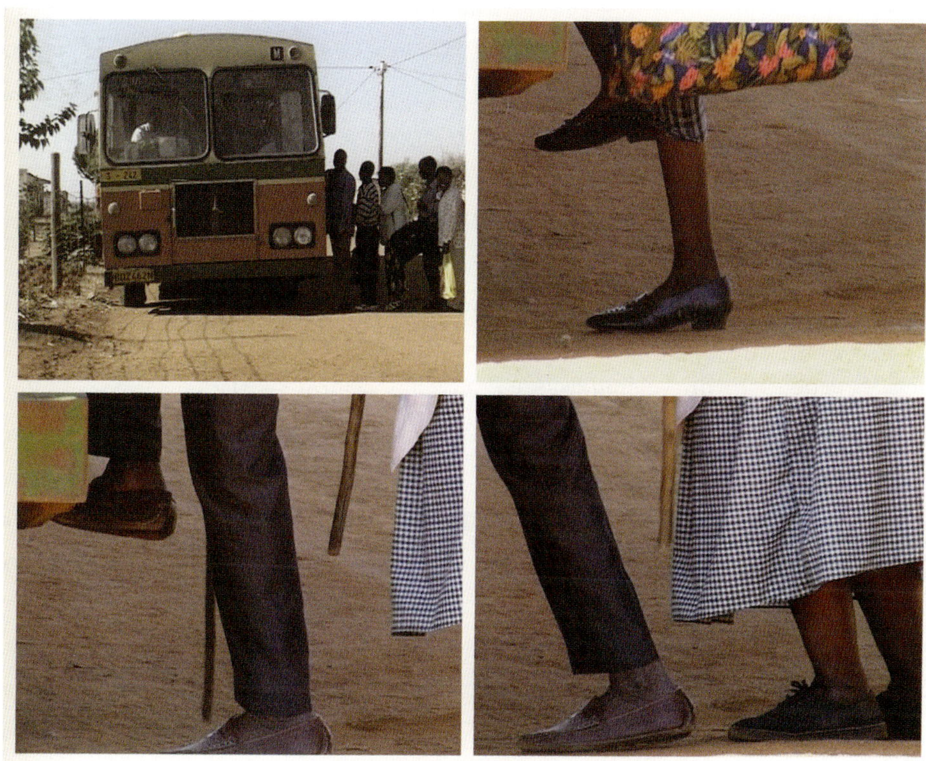

Moshekwa Langa, *Where Do I Begin?* (2001), from the *Waiting*
series, video stills 4 min 20 sec; courtesy of the artist.

the demographic structure of the Nile delta, densely concentrated at the
centre and gradually dispersing across the space. Nasr's work resists what
Mbembe calls the 'binary categories used in standard interpretations of
power—resistance vs passivity, autonomy vs subjection, state vs civil
society'. Nasr articulates instead the contingency of rulers and ruled and
the intricate web into which both are locked together. Describing the
condition of the post-colony, Nasr's work raises questions equally about the
conditions that exist in the urban metropolises of Europe and elsewhere
whose political and economic configurations are increasingly converging to
those of the post-colony.

If everyday struggles have taken the place of nationalist struggles in this new post-colonial world order, then waiting has displaced action. Moshekwa Langa's collages and installations reflect upon the continuous displacements and shifts, not only in linguistic and visual representation, but equally in the physical landscape of contemporary Africa. In this installation of large-scale drawings and video works, he presents a story in twelve parts: a 'non-story' in three acts in which people are waiting to get on a bus, waiting in doorways, passing the time or just smoking and waiting, waiting, waiting ... As Langa writes, 'The whole presentation really is like a drama without actors ... It is a fluid, essay-like thing with footnotes and so on so that the main text and the subtext and the offpaths are never quite differentiated ... I have always enjoyed and preferred the interwoven structure of spoken language and actual physicality or physical presentation over cleanliness and demarcation when it comes to art making.'[35] Made up of a series of collages and drawings that relate tangentially to a series of video pieces mounted on rough-hewn crates and dispersed across the exhibition space, Langa's work avoids any clear beginning, middle or end, but rather constructs a number of sequences or acts which have no linear narrative structure but yet are interrelated. The twelve elements of Langa's work could be read as the stories of nation states dispersed across the map of Africa, or of individuals connected and yet disconnected from each other in spite of their experiences in common.

The title of Langa's installation *Waiting* (2003) evokes Samuel Beckett's *Waiting for Godot*, in which two homeless tramps wander from place to place, always returning to the same location. They are of no fixed abode and no fixed identity. Their names—Vladimir and Estragon—are indeterminate and they could almost be refugees from another place. Like recent migrants grappling with a second language, they frequently muddle colloquial expressions. The existential question for Vladimir and Estragon, 'Why are we here?' has been answered. They are waiting for Godot. But Vladimir and Estragon have been asking the wrong question. Continually returning to the same place and repeating the same task, Beckett's tramps have neither a history nor a memory. But for Langa, as for so many of us from the post-colony, we cannot escape from the exigencies of history and memory. Emerging from what Okwui Enwezor defines as the 'post-colonial constellation' are a host of artists and artistic practices that are 'expanding the definition of what constitutes contemporary culture and its affilations in other domains of practice; the intersection of historical forces aligned against the hegemonic imperatives of imperial discourse'. In this context, the artist, like the poet, has a critical role to play; a role which is radical and revolutionary but which nonetheless should never be in the service of politicians or regimes of power. Reflecting divergent views, artists, according to Kateb Yacine, should 'create their own revolution within the political revolution', operating at the heart of trouble as 'perpetual troublemakers'. For the artist, like the poet, 'is the revolution stripped bare, the very movement of life in an unending explosion'.[36]

NOTES

1   Gamal Abdel-Nasser, 'Need for Unity', in Gamal Abdel Nasser, *Egypt's Liberation: The Philosophy of the Revolution*, Cairo, General Organisation for Government Printing Offices, 1958, pp. 63–70.

2   Kwame Nkrumah, 'I Speak of Freedom: A Statement of African Ideology', in Nkrumah, *I Speak of Freedom: A State of African Ideology*, London, William Heinemann Ltd, 1961, pp. xi–iv.

3   A. Laroui, *L'Histoire du Maghreb: un essai de synthèse*, Paris, 1970 (English translation *The History of the Magreb*, Princeton, 1977), cited in Albert Hourani, *A History of the Arab Peoples*, London, Faber and Faber, 1991, p. 394.

4   Frantz Fanon, 'On National Culture', in Fanon, *The Wretched of the Earth*, Harmondsworth, Penguin, 1990, 3rd edn, pp. 187–8, first published in France as *Les Damnés de la terre* by François Maspéro, éditeur, 1961.

5   Ibid., p. 187.

6   Ibid., p. 199.

7   Nasser Rabbat, 'Hassan Fathy and the Identity Debate', in Gilane Tawadros
     and Sarah Campbell (eds), *Fault Lines: Contemporary African Art and
     Shifting Landscapes,* London, Institute of International Visual Art (inIVA)
     in collaboration with Forum for African Arts and Prince Claus Fund, 2003,
     196–203, p. 202.

8   Ibid., p. 198.

9   Hassan Fathy, 'Architecture for the Poor', in *Fault Lines*, pp. 187–95.

10   Rabbat, p. 202.

11   Kobena Mercer, 'Frank Bowling's Map Paintings', in *Fault Lines*, p. 147.

12   Bheki Peterson, 'Clifford Charles and the Pleasures of Contemplative
     Insurgency', in *Fault Lines*, p. 156.

13   Ibid., p. 158.

14   Mercer, 'Frank Bowling's Map Paintings', p. 149.

15   Deepali Dewan, 'Tender Metaphor: The Art of Zarina Bhimji', in *Fault Lines*,
     p. 134.

16   Sarat Maharaj, 'Fatal Natalities: The Algebra of Diaspora and Difference after
     Apartheid', in *Fault Lines*, pp. 79–89.

17   Elsabet Giorgis, 'Salem Mekuria', in *Fault Lines*, p. 220.

18   Kateb Yacine, *Afrique Action*, Tunis, 26 June 1961.

19   Kobena Mercer, 'Eros & Diaspora', in *Rotimi Fani-Kayode & Alex Hirst*, Paris and
     London, Revue Noire and Autograph, 1996, p. 108.

20   Rotimi Fani-Kayode, 'Traces of Ecstasy', in *Fault Lines*, p. 181.

21   Ibid., p. 180.

22   Mark Sealy, 'A Note From Outside on Rotimi Fani-Kayode', in *Fault Lines*, p. 185.

23   Lisa Fischman, 'Untitled (A Way In)', in *Fault Lines*, pp. 98–103.

24   Ibid., p. 99.

25   Prince Mbusi Dube, 'At least one person was killed' in *Fault Lines*, pp. 167–76.

26   Yasmeen Siddiqui, 'Emergent Forms: Sabah Naim Reconceptualises Movement',
     in *Fault Lines*, p. 235.

27   Sabah Naim, unpublished text, 2002.

28   Kader Attia and Jerome Sans, 'The Right Position', in *Fault Lines*, p. 106.

29   Ibid., p. 109.

30   Wael Shawky writes: 'An essential part of the *mulid* is *zekr* … it is a Sufi
     religious ritual to reach a higher spiritual level or it is a state of transition.'

31   Niru Ratnam, 'So You Wanna Be …?' in *Fault Lines*, p. 255.

32 Wael Shawky, unpublished text, 2002.

33 Achille Mbembe, 'Provisional Notes on the Postcolony', in *Fault Lines*, pp. 53–63.

34 Peterson, p. 154.

35 Langa, unpublished correspondence, 2003.

36 Kateb Yacine, 'The Poet as Boxer', in *Fault Lines*, pp. 125–9.

New Media, Art and Science: Explorations beyond the Official Discourse

GEERT LOVINK

Disclaimer: In this essay I want to raise the topic of why new media art is perceived as such a closed and self-referential scene. Why can't artists who experiment with the latest technologies be part of pop culture and the arts market? What's the after-effect of the 'exhuberant' dotcom era? And why is there such a subordinate attitude towards academic science within new media arts? Is the educational sector the only way out? In what follows, I am reluctant to list specific examples of artworks for fear of diluting the general argument. Each and every argument can be falsified with reference to specific projects that prove the opposite of what I am trying to prove. What I am interested in is the broader context in which new media arts currently exists—a situation I will argue is unnecessarily constraining at a time of rapid commercial development and social uptake of new media forms. The immediate call for 'positive examples' and 'alternatives' is not a constructive attitude but part of the problem, because it avoids making an actual institutional power analysis.

BEGINNINGS

I feel compelled to start with a definition. New media arts can best be described as a transitional, hybrid art form, a multidisciplinary 'cloud' of micro-practices.[1] Historically, 'new media' arose when the boundaries between clearly separated art forms such as film, theatre and photography began to blur, due to the rise of digital technologies.[2] The beginnings of new media arts are currently being investigated by scholars such as Dieter Daniels (Leipzig), Charlie Gere (London), Stephen Jones (Sydney), Paul Brown (Goldcoast) and Oliver Grau (Berlin).[3] The emerging field of 'media archaeology' as exercised by Zielinski, Huhtamo and others will contribute to this effort, as will studies by sociologists and art historians. Before we can start speculating what it is becoming, the stagnant new media arts must be analysed with the tools of institutional criticism.

The birth of new media is closely tied to the democratisation of computers. According to some it is an art form born out of the Geist of Fluxus with its video art and performance. Others stress the influence of 1970s electronic music and post-industrial art and activism of the 1980s. The term 'new media art' only arrived as a set of practices in the late 1980s, and is specifically tied to the rise of desktop publishing and the production of CD-ROMs. Internet involvement started relatively late, from 1994–95 onwards, after the World Wide Web had been introduced. New media art is first of all part of the larger 'visual cultural' context. While it has strong ties to written discourses, computer code, sound, as well as abstract and conceptual art and performance, we can nonetheless say that the visual arts element forms the dominant thread. The problem with these accounts of the 'beginnings' of new media art, however, is their over-emphasis on individual artists and their works. Such accounts lack institutional awareness. Whereas technology developed fast, institutional understanding in this sector has been equally slow. In this respect, new media art is a misnomer, since it reproduced time and again the modernist dilemma between aesthetic autonomy and social engagement. Add the word 'art' and you create a problem. In the case of new media arts there was—and still is—no market, no galleries, few curators and critics, and no audience. And most of all: there is no 'suprematist' feeling of acting as an avant-garde. What is lacking here is historical confidence. Instead, there is a strong sense of conducting 'minor' practices in the shadow of established practices such as film, visual arts, television, computer animation, games and graphic design.

New media art, as defined by the Australia Council for the Arts, for instance, 'is a process where new technologies are used by artists to create works that explore new modes of artistic expression. These new technologies include computers, information and communications technology, virtual or immersive environments, or sound engineering. They are the brushes and pens of a new generation of artists.'[4] The emphasis here is on exploration. New media art is searching for new standards and art forms. Its prime aim is not necessarily to create everlasting universal artworks. Instead, it paves the way for a next generation to make full use of the newly discovered language—outside of the new media arts context. The emphasis on the creation of a language, an infrastructure, could explain why there is so much hidden, voluntary work done on this scene and why self-exploitation is so common. Only pioneers understand that one first needs to create a language in order to write a poem. However, the 'laws of new media' are not simply there to be uncovered. What some see as an advantage, not having a complex set of rules and references, others such as I judge to be an inherently immature situation.

We have to be specific, that's true. Political climates in Western countries vary wildly. Whereas e-culture funding in The Netherlands has gone up over the past years, the situation in Berlin, Paris and London, for instance, remains bleak. Academia remains a safe haven in the USA, with little cultural funding available elsewhere. Yet, the overall tendency of stagnation is clear and needs to be analysed. This critique is not meant to disdainfully look down on the 'yawning vacancy of the technological sublime'.[5] New media arts is not a single entity. It is 'searching' and does not primarily focus on grand narratives or finished works that can be purchased in a gallery. They are forms in search of a form. As testbeds they obviously lack content. Many of the works are neither 'cool' nor ironic, as so many pieces of contemporary art are. Instead, they often have a playful, naïve feel. Electronic arts, a somewhat older term that is sometimes used as a synonym for new media arts, is an experimental setup rather than an established discipline that is highly dependent on the cultural parameters set by engineers. Many of the key players in the field position their practice in the fragile zone between 'art' and 'technology', which is asking for trouble. What does it mean to have to please both computer scientists and art curators? Neither the art world nor information and communications technology professionals are fans of electronic arts. *Wunderkammer* artworks are not in high demand. From the 'geek' perspective, they are made by users, not developers. New media artworks 'apply' new technologies and do not contribute to its further development. For the art professionals, on the other hand, new media art belongs in educational science museums and amusement parks, rather than in contemporary arts exhibitions. If we read the mainstream critics, art should transmit Truth and Emotion. In today's society of the spectacle there is no place for halfway art, regardless of how many policy documents praise new media arts for its experimental attitude and Will to Innovate.

MYTH OF THE BLANK PAGE

There is a widespread belief that new media art works have the potential to be works of 'genius'. Supposedly, there are not yet 'traces' or 'fingerprints' of the human on recently developed technologies, and the artist therefore has the full range of all possible forms of expression in front of him/her. Dirty society, with its evil economic 'pop' interests, has not yet spoiled the channel. The apparent absence of a digital aesthetics for personal directory assistants (PDAs), radio frequency identification (RFID) tags, mobile phones etc. is seen as exactly its potential. According to this 'myth of the blank page', new media artists are not limited by existing cultural connotations because there are no media-specific references, yet. It is the heroic task of the new media artist to define those cultural codes. In this argument the situation of new media art is too good to be true. The problem of this theory of the unspoiled perception is the uncritical belief in universal talent. So-called creative, contemporary artists, on the other hand, are focused on the market. They have to subject themselves to the laws of fame and celebrity and cannot waste their time in such 'uncool' environments as computer labs. For them, technology is merely a tool. But the search for the specificities of a new medium requires a long trial-and-error period in which neither funky images nor experiences are guaranteed. Pop and experiment do not go together very well. The geek as role model had its media moment during the Internet hype of the mid 1990s, but then quickly faded away. And the geek aesthetics remained as bad as it always has been. This is media reality, but the new media arts sector finds it hard to deal with. The uncool can only be pop once; after its demise it's just a failure.

THE DESIRE TO BE SCIENCE

There is an implicit holistic, New Age element in the desire to create a synthesis between arts and technology—and not go for confrontation. It's tempting to look away from the harsh reality of the arts markets. With the heroic Leonardo figure in mind, the 'artist-engineer' expects the world to embrace the desire to unite the humanities and hard science. Much to their surprise, the world is not yet ready for such good ideas. Often, the artist is not much more than a willing test user/early adaptor. In itself this wouldn't be such a problem. Who cares? But most new media art works are neither subversive nor overly conceptual or critical. To make things more complicated: they aren't 'pop' either. The new media art genre can't work out whether it's underground or urban subculture. But new media arts never really became part of the techno, dance or rave party scene either—let alone a subculture; certainly, it's never had anything to do with rap or other contemporary street cultures. VJ culture, for instance, is not part of the official new media arts canon. Like the self-insulated world of the ivory-tower modern academic, new media art situates itself in a media lab rather than a lounge club. The launch bed of works is the new media festival at which like-minded colleagues gather.

Instead of being loud and clear about the hybridity-in-flux, the somewhat odd and isolated situation of new media arts has turned into a taboo topic. A general discontent has been around for a while, in particular as a privileged inner-circle has focused on excessively expensive interactive 'baroque' installations that could be found at in places like ZKM (Karlsruhe, Germany) and ICC (Tokyo). But that excessive period of the late 1990s is over. We could almost become nostalgic about those roaring 90s. It was a good party for many and a goldmine for some. In contrast, this is a time of budget cuts, conceptual stagnation, artistic backlashes (with the 'return' of minimal painting) and political uncertainty—while simultaneously new media are penetrating society in an unprecedented fashion.

It is not considered 'good form' to openly raise 'crisis' issues in the new media area, for the simple reason that the gloomy mood may endanger future projects, a next job or an upcoming application. 'Negativism' sticks to people in this scene, which is silently dominated by 'new age' positivism, driven by the common belief that technology will ultimately save us all. There are only rare cases of individuals who speak out openly. The rest eventually shut up and move on to become complicit in traditional 'contemporary arts', or find a job in the industry. One source of the lack of negation could be the implicit influence of techno-libertarianism. Those who protest are quickly condemned as 'enemies of the future', but this is never done out in the open.

The collective discursive poverty within new media arts explains the virtual absence of lively debates about art works. There is little institutional criticism. With mainstream media uninterested, the new media arts scene is fearful of potentially devastating internal debates. Rival academic disciplines and policy makers could be on the lookout to kill budgets. Instead, a fuzzy tribal culture of consensus rules, based on goodwill and mutual trust. In order to develop a genuinely critical perspective on new media arts, one really has to either come from elsewhere, or move away from the scene to an entirely different field, such as the commercial art world, pop culture or dance parties. For all these reasons, the scene remains small and is stagnating, despite the phenomenal growth of new media worldwide. This is not exactly what young, creative tinkerers expect. A growing number of young artists who work with technology avoid the ailing sector and find their own path, either via the established art sector, 'tactical media' activism or small businesses. At the same time there are painters, sculptors and fashion designers who use computers as the primary tool of design, yet explicitly leave out 'new media' in their public presentations.

Instead of taking the heroic stand of the avant-garde, many new media practitioners have chosen to simply 'drift away' in clouds of images, texts and URLs. There is a certain cosiness in hanging out in the networks and not being confronted with the world. The importance of vagueness cannot be underestimated. The blurry, background aspect of many works needs to be acknowledged and taken seriously. In the present situation of immediate irrelevance, it is genuinely difficult to create a significant work that will have an impact. Digital aesthetics has developed a hypermodern, formalist approach and lacks the critical rigour of standard contemporary arts pieces. Serious international curators simply cannot afford to include halfway ready 'fairground' installations that lack critical content and decent aesthetics. Marketing and attempts at professionalisation cannot overcome this basic mistrust.

If new media arts has such an emphasis on experimentation, collaboration with engineers, bio-scientists, innovative interfaces, then why it is it not simply giving up this tragic alliance with the arts and ruthlessly seeking to integrate itself in the world of information technology business and computer science? Good question. Only outsiders can accuse the electronic arts of compliance with the 'capitalist system'. The sad reality is that artists aren't all that different from ordinary computer users, unless they are part of the celebrity high-end circuit. For the majority of artists, access to technology is limited to consumer electronics. Often, there is no money for more state-of-the-art machines and software.

Industries already have their own networks who do the demonstration design. This is the true tragedy of new media arts. Those who turn new media inside out and develop an aesthetic agenda have no place in today's production processes. Despite these institutional, disciplinary and economic realities, so many artists persist in their pursuit of a formalist nirvana. Is this symptomatic of a lack of imagination, or perhaps even an over-subscription to the exotica of the artist identity?

If digital formalism is not recognised by the museum, the market, or by the industry, and is such a dead end street, then why aren't artists walking over to the 'content side' and producing interesting narratives? Certainly, a lot of the new media artists try this move. But their stories are not connected to the mainstream distribution networks such as film, TV and the publishing industry. This is why numerous CD-ROMs and DVDs do not even reach their own core audiences. It is not seen as a priority to build up distribution networks through, for instance, museum bookshops. Another reason for the reluctance to 'comply' is the wish to alter interfaces, software and even operating systems. Rightly so (or not?), new media arts feels uncomfortable using mainstream products such as Windows XP. Critique in this context is focused on underlying structures, not the superficial level of mediated representation. It is the architecture of the Internet and open standards of the World Wide Web that shape your 'surfing' experience, not this or that 'cool' homepage.

New media arts operates well beyond the logic of the demo design. Marketing something that has not been conceived as a product in the first instance has proven to be next to impossible. Putting content online is a last resort, but funnily enough it's not very popular among new media artists. The Internet is looked down upon as a primitive device, left to an in-crowd of 'net artists' who prefer to do formalistic experiments, combined with a subversive political action every now and then, such as those instigated by groups such as <www.rtmark.com>. New media arts is (rightly so) not interested in traditional politics, but has yet to reach its own phase of political correctness. Even though the presence of female curators and administrators is substantial, this does not result in a more open field. Links to contemporary social movements are weak, and the awareness of post-colonial issues is absent. The 'white' scene is by and large an exchange between North–West–Central Europe, the USA, Canada, Australia and Japan.

Another reason for the alleged 'emptiness' of new media arts could be traced in the absence of regular critics and curators. Often, there are technicians or information technology managers around instead. There is no rich reference system or common language (even though, in theory, this could have been constructed by now). Instead, there is a romantic notion that artists are busy 'inventing' the language of new media. It's rare to see playful games of referencing each other's work. If classified, works appear under very general categories or are simply grouped under the rubric of the medium in which they were produced, or the genre to which they belongs.

Life for artists, in general, is an uphill struggle, and this particularly counts for those that deliberately position themselves in between disciplines. Instead of curiosity and support, what the pristine new media arts scene finds is a stiff competition between scientific disciplines, media and art forms. These are often fights over decreasing resources within a general climate of jealousy and ignorance. There is no convergence or harmony with the performing arts. Despite all the ideology, multi- and interdisciplinarity are at an all-time low. People simply can't afford to jump over to a competing form of expression. Theatre has to look down on TV. Video people are snobs when it comes to new media. There is nothing as trashy and second-rate as the Internet.

Much of what I write here is of a speculative nature and is formulated to open up a discussion, not to criticise specific persons or the pursuit of new media arts experiments. Allegations such as the existence of mafia networks, corruption and insider favours can be investigated but not published, because they will be met with defamation claims. People in power, even in this relatively progressive scene, have their lawyers close at hand to silence dissent. It is an old-boys' club in which only a handful of tough ladies can survive, presuming they are playing the game. As I have indicated, a lack of a rich and diverse discourse is one of the many problems. Sectarianism is another. The new media scene, even on a global scale, is simply too small. But what is more surprising: it is not even growing. For instance, theatre itself becomes digital (stage design, light, music etc.). It doesn't need the new media arts to do that; the same with film. The only observation one can make is that every civilised country needs to have its own festival or centre. But that doesn't say much. What stagnates is the 'penetration' into society.

New media images are not sacred, nor do they have an aura. Instead, we could describe these images as technical in the spirit of Vilem Flusser's definition of 'technical images'. According to Flusser:

[I]t is difficult to decipher technical images, because they are apparently in no need of being deciphered. Their meaning seems to impress itself automatically on their surfaces, as in fingerprints where the meaning (the finger) is the cause and the image (the print) is the effect ... It seems that what one is seeing while looking at technical images are not symbols in need of deciphering, but symptoms of the world they mean, and that we can see this meaning through them however indirectly. This apparent non-symbolic, 'objective' character of technical images has the observer looking at them as if they were not really images, but a kind of window on the world. He trusts them as he trusts his own eyes. If he criticizes them at all, he does so not as a critique of image, but as a critique of vision; his critique is not concerned with their production, but with the world 'as seen through' them. Such a lack of critical attitude towards technical images is dangerous in a situation where these images are about to displace texts. The uncritical attitude is dangerous because the 'objectivity' of the technical image is a delusion. They are in truth, images, and as such they are symbolical.[6]

I am quoting Flusser at length because he provides us with a clue to the 'faith' of new media arts: the technical nature of its images is profoundly uncool.

New media arts has a problematic relationship with the strategy of appropriation. Obviously, its image production is not claimed to be unique. Instead, they are probes into new laws of perception. The dominant appropriation point of view in art history can only deal with content, not with the medium itself. Data from other media are used as resources, as data trash, fuel that can fire up the exploration. There is no desire to further deconstruct the already weak modernist project. If there is anything that needs to be appropriated it is geek knowledge, not other art works.

The new media arts scene is no longer in need of further globalisation. It's international enough, despite the relative lack of work from non-Western countries. What new media arts cries out for is a quantum leap. The ghetto walls need to be taken down. As a revolt from inside is not likely to happen, we can rather expect a general implosion. A first step would be to raise civil courage and get out of closet. Right now people talk with two tongues. Questions are raised in small circles and private conversations, but in the end funding bodies and other officials have to be praised. There is a regime of fear that needs to broken down. Electronic art is in need of its own whistleblowers. People in positions of power are not questioned, and there is not even a basic awareness as to how a controversy could be ignited. We're in a situation much like that of the former socialist countries, with their two cultures and two languages—except that in this case dissidents are even too fearful (or cowardly?) to publicly declare that the existing dominant culture is one of corruption, misguidedness and irrelevance. The only legitimate option remains to walk away and change context, or not to enter the scene in the first place—which is what most young artists seem to do.

ELECTRONIC ARTS AND THE DOTCOMS

Let's focus now on the more specific topic of the absent relationship between new media arts and the 'dotcoms'. Superficially, the 'tech wreck' of 2000–01 and its following associated scandals did not affect new media arts. It always struck me how slow critical new media practices have been in their response to the rise and the fall of 'dotcom-mania'. It seemed as though they were parallel universes, with the arts dragging behind events. There was not even a 'spiritual anticipation' of the excess. The world of information technology firms and their volatile valuations on the world's stock market seemed light years away from the new media arts galaxy. The speculative heyday of new media culture was the early to mid 1990s, before the rise of the World Wide Web. Theorists and artists jumped eagerly at not-yet-existing and inaccessible technologies such as virtual reality. 'Cyberspace' generated a rich collection of mythologies. Issues of embodiment and identity were fiercely debated.

Only five years later, with Internet stocks going through the roof, not much was left of the initial excitement in intellectual and artistic circles. The artist-as-virtual-expert had lost their short-lived hype status of the early to mid 1990s, when artists could showcase their multimedia capabilities. Once concepts could be turned into money, there was no longer room for people with ideas. By the turn of the millennium artists and theorists had lost influence on the public perception of what new media was all about. What could have turned into a pop culture degenerated into a shrinking micro-cosmos.

Dotcom culture has been 'anti-art' in a rather open fashion. It was said that profit should be re-invested in the information technology sector and transferred into stocks, and ought not to be invested into art works, as the 'old money' was doing. Technology itself was art, and there was no need for artists to substantiate this assumed truth. Real artists were geeks. Applied art such as design was cool, but its role should not be over-estimated as it was the abstract and image-free 'code' that eventually ruled, not the world of images. Nineties cyber culture was fighting with this same paradox.

Eventually, experimental technoculture missed out on the 'funny money'. As a result, no commercial arts in this sector have been developed, nor have serious attempts been made to resolve the distribution and revenue/cash crisis. Most new media art is therefore produced with government support that tightly controls and guides production. It's stunning to see how, in detail, pseudo-independent bodies are overseeing the new media arts field, exercising their power over tiny individual applications. This, in turn, explains the relative importance of Northern European countries, Austria, Canada and Australia. Most work done in the USA originates from universities and/or is funded by a handful of foundations. Over the past few years there has been a growing stagnation of new media culture, both in terms of its concepts and state funding. With hundreds of millions of new users flocking onto the Internet and over a billion now using mobile phones, new media arts proved unable to keep up with the fast pace of change and had to withdraw into its own world of poorly attended festivals and workshops.

Whereas new media arts institutions, begging for goodwill, still portray their artists as working at the forefront of technological developments, collaborating with state-of-the art scientists, the reality is a different one. Multidisciplinary goodwill is at an all-time low. At best, the artist's new media products are 'demo designs', as described by Peter Lunenfeld in his book *Snap to Grid*. Often, the work does not even reach that level. New media art, as defined by institutions such as Ars Electronica, ISEA, Transmediale and the countless educational programs, rarely reaches audiences outside of its own subculture. What in positive terms could be described as the heroic fight for the establishment of a self-referential 'new media arts system' through a frantic differentiation of works, concepts and traditions, may as well be classified as a dead-end street. The acceptance of new media by leading museums and collectors will simply not happen. Why wait a few decades, anyway? The majority of the new media art works on display at ZKM in Karlsruhe, the Linz Ars Electronica Center, ICC in Tokyo or the Australian Centre for the Moving Image in Melbourne are hopeless in their innocence, being neither critical nor radically utopian in approach. It is for this reason that the new media arts sector, despite its steady growth, is becoming increasingly isolated, incapable of addressing the issues of today's globalised world. It is therefore understandable that the contemporary (visual) arts world is continuing the decades-old silent boycott of interactive new media works in galleries, art fairs, biennales and shows such as Documenta. The relative isolation of new media arts could, in part, also explain the rise of the 'creative industries' discourse, which presents itself explicitly as a way out of the miserable policies that surround the state-funded arts and education businesses. The irony, however, is that 'creative industries' themselves do not exist outside of the realm of state policies.

A critical reassessment of the role of arts and culture within today's network society seems necessary. Would artists be happier if they could work within the 'creative industries' and no longer be bothered with the question of whether or not they are producing 'art'? Certainly, there's a discursive legitimacy that awaits migrants to the Creative Industries, but whether it pays their rent has yet to be seen. The 'information economy' is still failing to extract value from content production, and if money is to be made, it profits whoever possesses the Internet provider rights—which typically isn't the creative producer, whose role is really one of service provision. So, what's the difference between the artist and the sales clerk in that scenario?

Let's go beyond the 'tactical' intentions of the players involved. The artist-engineer, tinkering away on alternative human–machine interfaces, social software, alternative browsers or digital aesthetics, has effectively been operating in a self-imposed vacuum. Over the past few decades both science and business have successfully ignored the creative community. Even worse, artists have actively been sidelined in the name of 'useability'. The backlash movement against web design, led by useability guru Jakob Nielsen, is a good example of this trend. Other contributing factors may have been fear of corporate dominance. Creative Commons lawyer Lawrence Lessig argues that innovation of the Internet itself is in danger.[7] In the meantime, the younger generation is turning its back on the specific new media arts-related issues and becoming anti-corporate activists, doing some web design for a living, teaching here and there, or turning to other professions altogether. Since the crash, the Internet has rapidly lost its imaginative attraction. File swapping and cell phones can only temporarily fill the vacuum. It would be foolish to ignore these trends. New media has lost its magic spell; the once-so-glamorous gadgets are becoming part of everyday life, similar to radio and the vacuum cleaner. This long-term tendency, now in a phase of acceleration, seriously undermines the future claim of new media altogether.

NEW MEDIA AS WAR OF THE GENERATIONS

Another 'taboo' issue in new media is generationalism. With video and expensive interactive installations being the domain of the baby boomers, the generation of 1989 has embraced the free Internet. But the Internet turned out to be a trap for the young ones. Whereas real assets, positions and power remains in the hands of the ageing baby boomers, the gamble of their successors on the rise of new media did not materialise. After venture capital has melted away, there is still no sustainable revenue system in place for the Internet. There is no life after demo design. The slow-working education bureaucracies have not yet grasped the new media malaise. Universities are still in the process of establishing new media departments. But that will come to a halt at some point. The fifty-something tenured chairs and vice-chancellors must feel good about their persistent sabotage. The 'positive generation' (Wanadoo) is unemployed and frustrated.

'What's so new about new media anyway?' the baby boomers ask. Computers are not generating narrative content and what the world needs now is meaning, not empty, ironic net art. Technology was hype after all, promoted by the criminals of Enron and WorldCom. It's enough for students to do a bit of e-mail and web surfing, safeguarded within a filtered and controlled intranet … If there is to be a counter to this cynical reasoning, then we urgently need to analyse the ideology of the greedy 1990s and its techno-libertarianism. If we don't disassociate new media quickly from that decade, and if we continue with the same rhetoric, the isolation of the new media sector will sooner or later result in its death. Let's transform the new media buzz into something more interesting altogether—before others do it for us. The Will to Subordinate to Science is nothing more than a helpless adolescent gesture.

One way out of this subordinate position may be to point to the social aspect of the production of science, as Bruno Latour and others do. According to their theory, the work of science consists of the enrolment and juxtaposition of heterogeneous elements—rats, test tubes, colleagues, journal articles, funders, grants, papers at scientific conferences and so on—which need continuing management. They conclude that scientists' work is 'the simultaneous reconstruction of social contexts of which they form a part—labs simultaneously rebuild and link the social and natural contexts upon which they act'.[8]

US performance artist Coco Fusco wrote a critique of biotech art on the Nettime mailing list (26 January 2003). 'Biotech artists have claimed that they are redefining art practice and therefore the old rules don't apply to them.' For Fusco, 'bio-art's heroic stance and imperviousness to criticism sounds a bit hollow and self-serving after a while, especially when the demand for inclusion in mainstream art institutions, art departments in universities, art curricula, art world money and art press is so strong.' From this marginal position, its bio-arts, post-human dreams of transcending the body could better be read as desires to transcend its own marginality, being neither recognised as 'visual arts' nor as 'science'. Coco Fusco: 'I find the attempts by many biotech art endorsers to celebrate their endeavor as if it were just about a scientific or aesthetic pursuit to be disingenuous. Its very rhetoric of transcendence of the human is itself a violent act of erasure, a master discourse that entails the creation of "slaves" as others that must be dominated.' Okay, but what if all this remains but a dream, prototypes of human–machine interfaces that, like demo-design, are going nowhere? The isolated social position of the new media arts in this type of criticism is not taken into consideration. Biotech art has to be almighty in order for the Fusco rhetoric to function.

Coco Fusco rightly points to artists who 'attend meetings with "real" scientists, but in that context they become advisors on how to popularize science, which is hardly what I would call a critical intervention in scientific institutions'. Artists are not 'better scientists' and the scientific process is not a better way of making art than any other, Fusco writes. She concludes:

> Losing respect for human life is certainly the underbelly of any militaristic adventure, and lies at the root of the racist and classist ideas that have justified the violent use of science for centuries. I don't think there is any reason to believe that suddenly, that kind of science will disappear because some artists find beauty in biotech.[9]

It remains an open question as to where radical criticism of (life) science has gone and why the new media (arts) canon is still in such a primitive, regressive stage. Coco Fusco's remarks were written before the US Federal Bureau of Investigation cracked down on Critical Arts Ensemble (mid 2004) because of their alleged biotech terror experiments.[10] This, however, does not affect her overall argument.

BECOMINGS

Western 'new media arts' lacks a sense of superiority, sovereignty, determination and direction. One can witness a tendency towards 'digital inferiority' at virtually every cyber event. The politically naïve pose of the techno-art tinkerers has not paid off. Neither the science nor the art world is paying any attention to its goodwill projects. Artists, critics and curators have made themselves subservient to technology and 'life science' in particular, unsuccessfully begging for the attention of the 'real' bio-scientists. This ideological stand has grown out of an ignorance that cannot be explained easily. We're talking here about a subtle mentality. The cult practice between dominant science and its slaves in the new media artists is taking place in backrooms of universities and art institutions, warmly supported by genu-inely interested corporate bourgeois elements, board members, professors, science writers and journalists who set the technocultural agenda. Here, we are not talking about some form of 'techno celebration'. The corporate world is not interested in the new media art works because in the end they are too abstract and seriously lack sex appeal. Do not make this mistake. New media art is not merely a servant to corporate interests. There has not been a sell out, for the simple reason that there has not been basic interest to start with. If only it was that simple. The accusation of new media arts 'celebrating' technology is a banality, only stated by ill-informed outsiders; and the interest in life sciences can easily be sold as a (hidden) longing to take part in science's supra-human 'triumph of logos', but I won't do that here. Scientists, for their part, are disdainfully looking down at the vaudeville interfaces and well-intentioned weirdness of amateur tech art. Not that they will say anything. But the weak smiles on their faces bespokes a cultural gap of light years. An exquisite non-communication is at hand here. Ever-growing markets for Internet, mobile devices and digital electronic consumer goods make it hard to sense the true despair. Instead of, again, calling for a more positive attitude towards the future, a more seductive strategy could be the 'becoming'; disconnecting the computer from labels such as 'new' and 'digital' and starting to build up networks with an even more brutal intensity.

NOTES

1   Earlier fragment of this essay <http://www.media-culture.org.au/0308/10-fragments.html>. Thanks to Ned Rossiter, Trebor Scholz and Scott McQuire for critical comments.

2   For an extensive debate on the merits of the new media term, see Lev Manovich, *The Language of New Media*, MIT Press, Cambridge (Mass.), 2001, pp. 27–61.

3   See <www.mediaarthistory.org>. Books of individual authors include, among others, Dieter Daniels, *Kunst als Sendung: Von der Telegrafie zum Internet*, Beck Verlag München, 2002; Charles Gere, *Digital Culture*, Reaktion Books, London, 2002; Oliver Grau, *From Illusion to Immersion*, MIT Press, Cambridge (Mass.), 2003; Siegfried Zielinski, *Audiovisions Cinema and Television as Entr'actes in History*, Amsterdam University Press, Amsterdam, 1999.

4   <http://www.cultureandrecreation.gov.au/articles/newmedia/>

5   Charlie Finch (Artnet) on Chris Kraus' book on the Los Angeles art scene, *Video Green*, Semiotexte, Cambridge (Mass.), 2004.

6   Vilém Flusser, *Für eine Philosophie der Fotografie*, Göttinger, West Germany, European Photography, c1984, trans. by the author; see Vilém Flusser, *Towards a Philosophy of Photography*, trans. by Anthony Mathews, London, Reaktion, 2000, pp. 14–15.

7   See <www.creativecommons.org and www.lessig.com/blog>.

8   Quoted from the website 'What is Actor-Network Theory', written by Nancy Van House, <http://carbon.cudenver.edu/~mryder/itc_data/ant_dff.html>.

9   Posted on nettime < http://www.nettime.org/>, 25 January 2003, <http://amsterdam.nettime.org/Lists-Archives/nettime-l-0301/msg00122.html>.

10   See <http://www.caedefensefund.org/>.

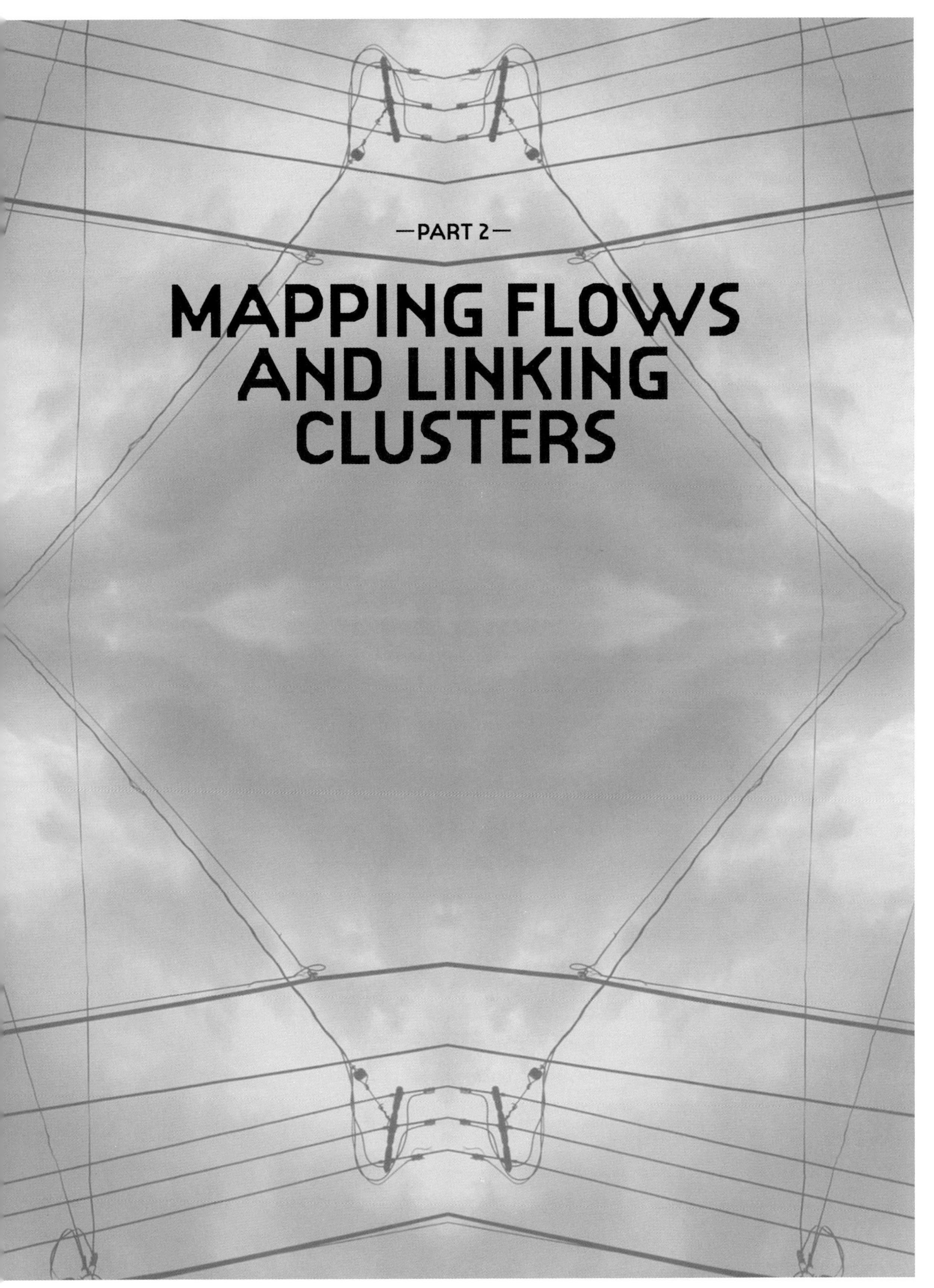

—PART 2—
MAPPING FLOWS
AND LINKING
CLUSTERS

Introduction: The Flightless South

KEVIN MURRAY

In the context of Empire, particularly for today's Anglo alliance, the south is a region that is often taken for granted. The recent film *Master and Commander: On the Far Side of the World* is a telling example of this complacency.

Master and Commander combines the strengths of the Anglo alliance. It is a skilfully made, ballet-like film, set on the seas around the South American coast in the Napoleonic era. Though a Hollywood production, the film benefits from the work of three seasoned Australian film masters—director Peter Weir, cinematographer Russell Boyd and actor Russell Crowe. In both content and realisation, the film celebrates the global adventure pursued by the British Empire.

The story begins with a surprise attack on the captain's ship by a French vessel, the *Acheron*. It's an Al Qaeda-like hit that signals the arrival of a deadly new enemy to threaten the survival of the British nation.

Incensed by *Acheron*'s terroristic strategy, Captain Jack Aubrey strays from his mission in dogged pursuit of the enemy ship. But not everyone agrees with the captain's obsession. Supporting him is Dr Stephen Maturin, the ship's surgeon, whose theatre of heroism is the wounded body rather than the high seas. The doctor is a man of science, eager to gather new knowledge from the world they pass by, particularly the Galapagos Islands and the flightless cormorant he spies from a distance.

United in their patriotism, the captain and doctor have a relationship that parallels that of US President Bush and British Prime Minister Blair. One argues for resolute action, the other attempts to moderate passion with reason. Despite their differences, they maintain the same course.

Eventually, their ship does catch up with the *Acheron*. Through a clever adaptation of the doctor's botanical knowledge, they capture the French vessel in bloody battle.

In gratitude for the doctor's support, the captain promises Maturin time on the islands to study the new world and to catch the elusive flightless cormorant. But a last-minute threat forces him to withdraw the offer and they sail off to pursue the enemy.

In consoling the doctor for this missed opportunity, the captain reminds him that the bird that so fascinates him is flightless, and therefore 'not likely to be going anywhere'. The two men share a knowing smile at this good fortune and head off into another thrilling adventure, happy that their world remains secure for the future exploration.

Master and Commander maintains a steady plot that is superbly realised on screen. But a question remains: to what extent was its colonial adventure based on the assumption that the south was a passive realm, unable to either resist or evade the claims of the industrious race from the north?

Such a possibility invites a challenge. Is there a way to understand the flightless bird as an active creature in its own right? Should it always be consigned to the margins of nature, as a curious joke like the dodo, moa or penguin? In finding dignity in the flightless bird, there may be a way to counterbalance the more restless interests that cruise the southern hemisphere.

Today, the south is dismissed in popular media as a region beyond the rule of reason. The news stories that appear about South Africa usually concern AIDS and violence. From South America, we hear only of drug cartels and political corruption. And the Pacific is reported upon in the press only when there is civil unrest. The news filter acts as a set of blinkers, leaving us undistracted in our absorption in the north. The north sets the pace, in fashion, technology and ideas. The south, like Dr Maturin's cormorant, is stranded.

Like Aubrey and Maturin, we are largely focused on the main stage, on which the clash of civilisations engages the devout east against the technological west. Whatever happens in the other half of the world seems nowhere as urgent as the battle between the empire and its ruins, between the Anglo alliance and Muslim warriors. In a playful manner, *Master and Commander* confirms the dominance of the main game in our world.

Thankfully, this scenario does not fit comfortably on the emerging global reality. There is a fresh energy in the south. The oppressive governments that isolated southern countries from each other have crumbled. Apartheid and military dictatorships that reinforced dominant economic powers have been replaced with democracies that are eager for dialogue with each other. President Lula in Brazil is reconstituting an axis of non-aligned nations, with South Africa and India as key players. Countries such as Argentina have learned how to survive the International Monetary Fund. Previously rogue nations such as Libya, Venezuela and Bolivia are now fostering bilateral relations. We can no longer take the south for granted.

This movement is given voice by the region's artists. Creative agents such as Kendell Geers, Lisa Reihana and Carlos Capelán are flexing their wings. Geers holds tenaciously to the raw reality that cannot be assimilated into the media simulacra. Reihana finds the traditional Maori structures that readily infiltrate modern technology. And Capelán eulogises the fluidity of the south, as it emerges in all four corners of the world.

One essential feature that distinguishes the south is the inevitable co-existence of traditional and modern worlds. Whereas in the north, traditional worlds are experienced purely on the cultural stage, in the south these worlds are an intrinsic part of the political reality. The rooted world of tradition lives alongside the mobile world of modernity. They are destined never to fit, only to intersect. It is in this southern dialectic that artists have a critical role to play. Like tricksters, their challenge is to bring the two worlds together in strange magical forms, involving both ancestral spirits and Coca-Cola.

Put together, the three artistic perspectives from Africa, the Pacific and Latin America do not cohere into a singular vision. At this stage in our thinking, it seems more important to take apart our preconceptions of the south as a region that can be largely taken for granted. It is from this unpicking that a new conversation can begin.

And who knows what might happen. Cormorants might fly.

In the so-called Age of Globalisation, countries like New Zealand, Mozambique, South Africa and Australia are still blurred zones on the map, as seen from the South American horizon. This chapter is about finding the way to use a broken map; the feeling of belonging to places that are not interrelated in the general discourse of culture, but shared in the growing sphere of personal experiences and desires. Groups connecting beyond national and geographical identities where sameness and differences work equally as tools for communication are central experiences of the contemporary global.

The south–south dialogue is still an unusual and difficult conversation. Could it be possible to make such a dialogue work beyond the mere notions of victimisation and marginal positions?

Broken Walks

CARLOS CAPELÁN—ENGLISH TRANSLATION BY A. PERNIN

While still a child, I had a friend in New Zealand whom I had never met. My father got to know him during a train journey in Uruguay before I was born. He was called Stuart Marshall and he lived at 8 Ranfurly Road in Auckland, where he had a farm on which he raised sheep. Stuart Marshall had been taking a trip of studies through South America. He did not speak any Spanish whatsoever. My father, as many others of his generation, was an autodidact in several areas. As well as Galician, his father's language, he had studied the very difficult Basque (his mother's family language), French, Italian and even Russian, to be able to read some classics in the original, as he used to say. Even though he read English, often and fluidly, he slaughtered the speech because of his complete lack of training. By the end of the 1930s, it was difficult to find opportunities to speak anything other than Spanish or Portuguese in the wide regions of South America. My father alleviated the problem by going down to the harbour to practise English with the sailors. He and Stuart Marshall became friends and exchanged letters for almost forty years.

I knew that I had been born in the southern-most capital in the world. This consciousness of the south was maintained in Montevideo by the presence of the Southern Cross and by the hurt penguins arriving on the winter beach. We used to take them home, where they regained strength with fish and poultices. When we took them back to the coast, they crossed the beach with comical urgency and swam straight towards the horizon, never looking back. I also knew that Cape Town and Santiago de Chile, which I envisaged as equally distant and imaginary places, shared a parallel with my neighbourhood. Lying on my bed, I tried to imagine Cape Town and Table Mountain, Santiago and the Mapocho, and imagined the children of these places looking at my stars at confused hours.

La Facción Popular Alter Ego (FPAE, también llamada La Disidencia) del Post Colonial Liberation Army (rematerialización) advierte de los peligros del aislamiento cultural y convoca a un simposio interregional en el cual se discutan e incentiven los eventuales peligros de un simposio como ese.

Como método para la convocatoria propone excluir de la misma a todas aquellas comunidades que compartan un mismo espacio geográfico continental, una misma etnia dominante o una misma lengua mayoritaria.

Entre las comunidades resultantes se dará prioridad a la participación de aquellas que sumen la mayor diversidad posible de factores comunes y/o diferentes.

El PCLA (r) declara que probablemente sea una buena idea orientar el simposio hacia la celebración pragmática.

The Alter Ego Popular Faction (AEPF, also known as The Dissidence) of the Post Colonial Liberation Army (rematerialización) warns of the dangers of cultural isolation and calls together to an interregional symposium where the eventual dangers of such a symposium should be discussed and incentivated.

As convocation methodology it proposes the exclusion from the symposium of all those communities sharing the same continental space, the same dominant ethnic group or the same majority language.

Among the resulting communities, those conflating the greater possible diversity of common and/or different factors will be given priority.

The AEPF declares that it would probably be a good idea to steer the symposium towards pragmatic celebration.

Each Christmas, and until I reached age eleven or twelve, Stuart Marshall would send me books of Rupert the Bear, which I listened to with devotion in strange paternal translations. And each Christmas my father translated my greetings into a letter of exotic and incomprehensible combinations that I copied letter by letter.

I know that on Stuart Marshall's farm there was a tree that was a curiosity in the region as it belonged to an unknown species. With my father's help the conclusion was reached that it was a South American variety (I cannot remember which). Probably, they agreed, it had grown from a seed carried in the wool of a sheep that had made the trip from the pampas to New Zealand. Ever since, I can evoke in New Zealand's landscape, hills and a lonely tree's profile I have never seen, but which I would recognise if I happened upon it.

I spent a good part of my childhood perched on a tree that grew in front of a house my parents had on the coast of the River Plate. There, I read books, took my afternoon meals, listened and told stories with my friends. I learned something about bird and insect life. There, among the branches and leaves of that casuarina, I have felt at home. I have always known that the sound of the wind among the foliage's threads was the sound of the south.

Por ello, el PCLA (r) propone un simposio bajo la forma de torneo de fútbol que trascienda cualquier antagonismo lineal y proponga una sana praxis de la justicia deportiva, o un concierto de música pop que no incluya el uso de micrófonos, guitarras eléctricas o blue jeans.

Therefore, the AEPF proposes a symposium in the form of a football tournament transcending any linear antagonism and proposing a healthy praxis of sporting justice, or pop concert excluding the use of microphones, electric guitars or blue jeans.

The horizons of the southern Atlantic regions of South America are level reaches, sometimes undulating. High skies and flat light, sparse vegetation, lonely prairies, processions of posts, lines of barbed wire and cattle. Sheep or cows graze with muzzles to the ground. Sometimes they look at us and then go back to their methodical and quiet routines. We know (and how could we not!) that those cows, those sheep, those horses between horizons stroll their shadows among rocks and lichens that had aboriginal names. Mixed with the cattle, the fences, the brush and the silent trails the landscape is spotted with small tree groves. They are planted there so that the relentless and energetic summer's sun would not burn the cattle's heads. In order to reach one of these groves one must walk through brush and pastures, as though shipwrecked. Actually, they are called 'islands' and are populated by bird's nests and echoes. Most of the birds are small parrots, green and boisterous, roused by just about anything and whose ongoing riot contrasts with the silence of the fields. Inside these islands, grass is particularly high and as one walks one brushes aside dead branches and dry cow pats. The islands are, mostly, eucalyptus woodlets that have substituted the indigenous flora.

Consecuentemente y en caso de que el simposio se decantara por la celebración de un torneo de fútbol, el PCLA (r) pone a consideración un conjunto de reglas generales para la redefinición táctico-estratégica del deporte rey:

a) que en los partidos participen tres equipos, dos de los cuales tratarán de ganar al otro mientras que el tercero tendrá por función estorbar el juego de los primeros;

b)   en caso de que uno de los dos equipos rivales fuera ganando al otro, la función del tercer equipo será la de ayudar al equipo perdedor hasta igualar el resultado;

c)   los equipos rivales se compondrán de tantos jugadores como de minutos se componga cada período del juego;

In consequence, and in case the symposium would be decanted by the celebration of a football tournament, the AEPF forwards for consideration a collection of general rules for the tactical-strategical redefinition of the king of sports:

a)   *that three teams should participate in the matches, two of which will try to win against each other while the third will have the function of hindering their play;*

Courtesy of the artist.

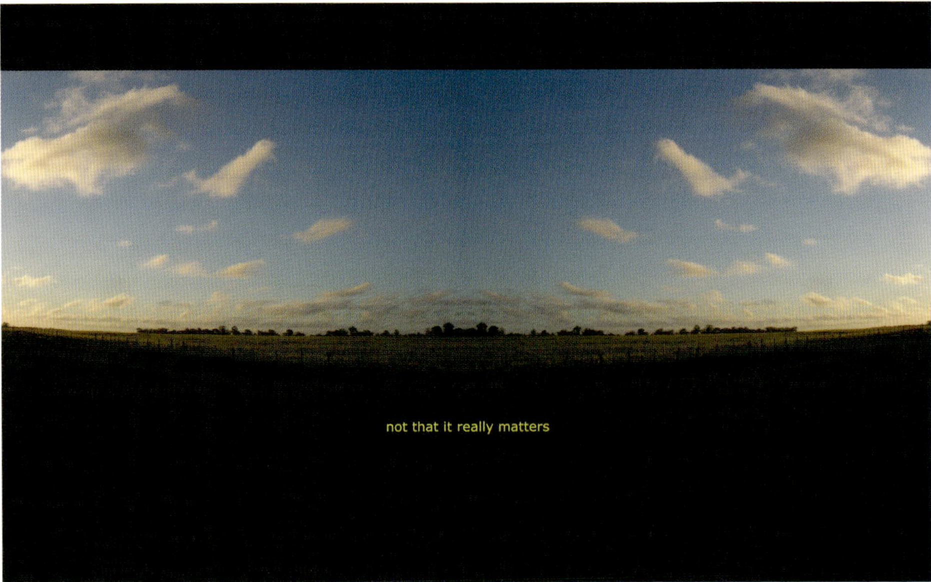

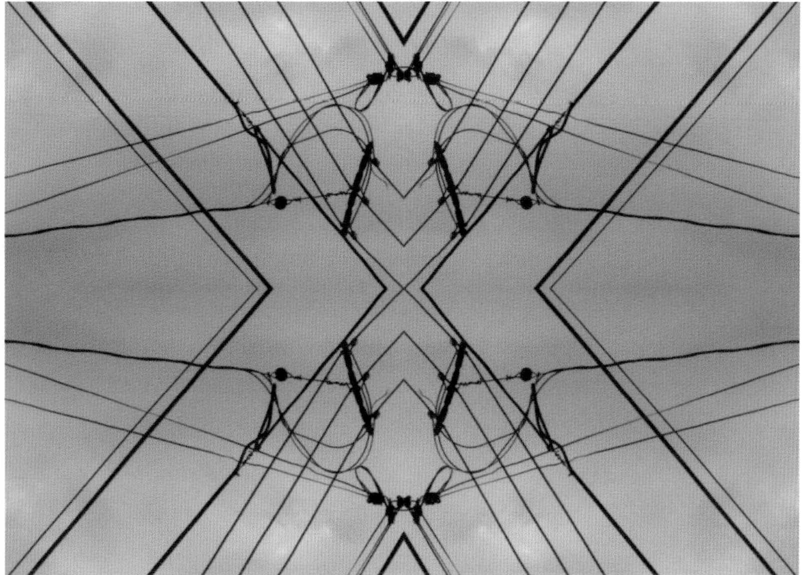

Courtesy of the artist.

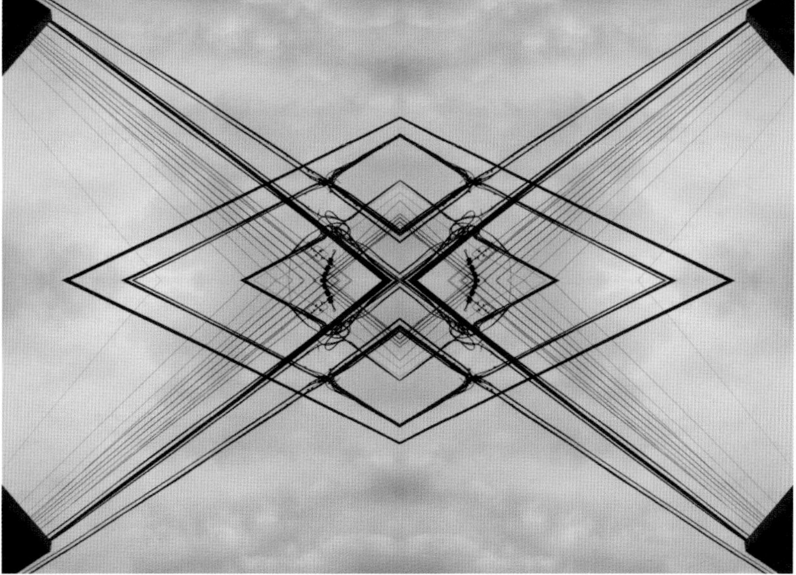

Courtesy of the artist.

b)   if one of the two rival teams should be winning against the other, the function of the third one will be to support the losing team until equalizing the result;

c)   that the rival teams will field as many players as there are minutes in each playing period;

We may or may not know it. We may be tired of being from places usurped forever. We may be used to the presence of Other among Us. Maybe not. We may have accepted incoherence as much as we accept logic's nervous gesture. Maybe daily life always has embodied in ourselves, breaks and failures, suspended tales. It may be that we do not care much about that. Maybe we do not care about anything.

Eucalyptuses are found all over the American landscape, from Patagonia to the northern coast of California. Annika, my wife, who was born in southern Sweden, cannot avoid associating the aroma of eucalyptuses with the woods she got to know in her first visit to Uruguay. Even in Spain, in the vast sea of eucalyptuses that replaces in Galicia the old oaks, chestnuts, walnuts, birches, pines and firs, she perceives the smell of South America.

d)   los equipos retiraran un jugador cada dos minutos desde el comienzo de cada tiempo y en un orden fijado provisoriamente por decisión de uno de los espectadores elegido al azar;

e)   los partidos se jugarán en una cancha regular de las usadas en este deporte y en la mayor penumbra posible;

f)   los jugadores dispondrán cada uno de dos linternas de mano que encenderán o apagarán a discreción y antojo;

g)   serán usadas dos pelotas de colores diferentes;

h)   todos los equipos jugaran egualmente et indiscriminadamente con cualquiera de estas pelotas;

d)   *the teams will withdraw a player every two minutes of each period and in an order provisionally stipulated by decision of one of the spectators chosen at random;*

e)   *the matches will be played on a standard field for this sport and in the deepest semi-darkness possible;*

f)   *the players will avail themselves of two flashlights each which they will switch on or off at their discretion and whim;*

g)   *two balls of different colours will be used;*

h)   *all the teams will play equally and indiscriminately with any of these balls;*

Rodnay Rosas Walker, with whom we shared a study in Montevideo barely after adolescence, took me once on a trip to the Blue Mountains. From the Three Sisters we saw the air coloured by these infinite woods. Numb with cold, we had to abandon this landscape and its disorder of feathers and screeches from the variegated parrots in the middle of a sleet storm.

In order to keep warm, I had bought a red, handmade pullover in a mountain village. Sheltering from the storm, we had a coffee in a small place, served by a Uruguayan woman who had lived in Mozambique. She became animated by the presence of two fellow countrymen, and gave away pieces of her life story in a brief conversation. She told us she loved Mozambique; that she had shared a house with a Swiss woman and two Spaniards until she separated from her husband, a Chilean engineer; that life in Australia was hard for the immigrants because of the racism; but that, in contrast to Montevideo, here there was really a democracy, civic culture and respect for the individual. I do not know what Rodnay was thinking then, but I know I thought that in that 'here' of the woman there were many and unnameable Blue Mountains.

i)   el arbitraje correrá por cuenta del jugador del tercer equipo más próximo a la jugada, el cual ejercerá justicia con el mayor rigor y criterio;

j)   el tiempo de duración de los partidos será: un primer tiempo de 15 minutos, un segundo de 45, un tercer tiempo amistoso de diez minutos (cuyos tantos no se tendrán en cuenta) y un cuarto tiempo de media hora flexible;

i)   *refereeing will be the task of the third-team player closest to the play, who will administer justice with the greatest cogency and criterion;*

j)   *the duration of the matches will be: a first period of 15 minutes, a second one of 42 minutes, a third friendly period of ten minutes (in*

Courtesy of the artist.

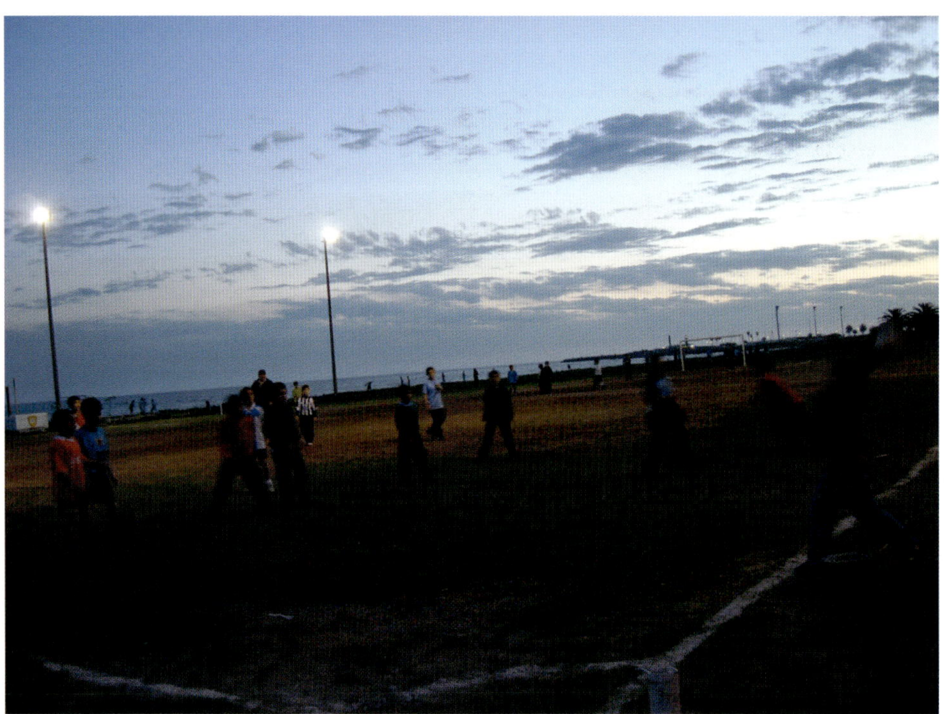

which goals will not be counted) and a fourth period of a flexible half-hour;

k)   the intervals will be resting periods of the duration of a light afternoon meal determined by consensus among the minors among the spectators;

We left at last the skyscrapers and suburbs of Johannesburg. We had just seen, in Northern Transvaal, the huge African geological fault, generated in the times of old Gondwana, together with Alfredo Pernin, who bored on with studies and curiosity for Geology. From the advantage of majestic, red bluffs, we had admired the huge gorges, the deep rifts and the plain extending all

Courtesy of the artist.

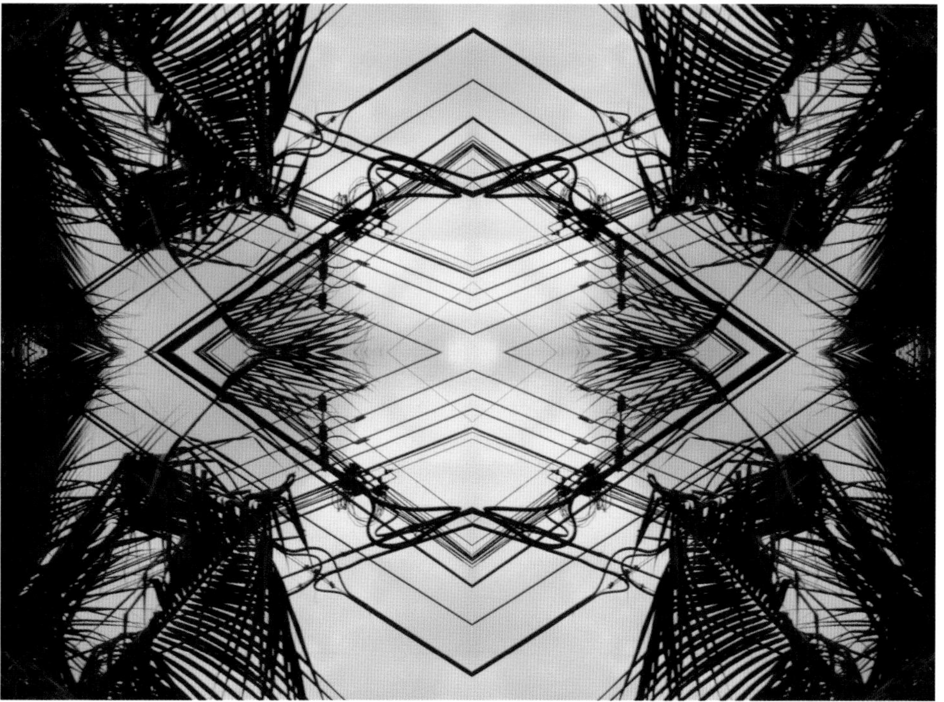

the way to the Indian Ocean. A baboon and I managed to scare each other when we suddenly met among the brushes. We ran away from each other, each howling in his own way, invoking the calm of each one's species.

That night, we rested in a hotel of small cabins with African names and paintings of wild animals on the walls. I recall that my bathroom had a painted hippo with its mouth open that ineffably parodied the WC with its open lid by its side. Alfredo and I registered, and the Boer owner of the place openly expressed his suspicion of two bearers of Swedish passports who were not blonde with blue eyes. We melancholically stared at him and avoided his rancorous hospitality by changing the subject and paying attention to the English songs with which his sister, sitting at a badly tuned piano, contaminated our dinner.

In Johannesburg we had met Pepe, son of Black and Hindu Africans. He was born in Durban and was tired of being looked at with racial distrust by Blacks, Whites and Hindus. He told us, in a moment of sincerity and anger, that he sometimes passed for Italian, which is why he called himself Pepe, that his innermost wish was to make it to Italy and disappear there, adapted for ever more ('another one among many', he said), and that he wanted to leave that land of others: Africa. He was lean, well proportioned, with fine features, easy smile and gestures between urgent and indifferent. According to him, his racial type and learned manners corresponded to a symmetry likely to be found in Rome. His second choice was Mexico.

1)   el resultado final del encuentro se determinará por votación entre todos aquellos que hayan participado o presenciado el encuentro (espectadores, jugadores, personal técnico y de todos los servicios incluidos);

m) este resultado se hará público por todos los medios disponibles no antes de un mes y no luego de 45 días de haber tenido lugar el encuentro;

n) etcétera

l)   *the final result of the match will be determined by vote among all those participating or spectating the event (spectators, players, technical and all service staff included);*

m)   *this result will be made public by all means at hand within 45 days but not before one month of the event;*

n)   *etcetera*

There are easy cheats when travelling that sometimes it is amusing to allow oneself. We had just had a speedy lunch on the outskirts of Sydney, while looking at a surfing school for children and small waves coated with white quick foam. We had a photo taken in front of the horizon and I knew, physically, that I was seeing again that line of water and sky that I had so many times seen from Chile's coasts. Seen from the other side, the horizon looked the same but it was not. Until that moment, there had always been something else beyond the horizon, but that morning in Sydney, it was me, beyond the horizon, looking towards this side.

'I, TerroRealist'

KENDELL GEERS

PART I

In the beginning was the Word, and the Word was with God, and the Word was God. He was with God in the beginning. Through him all things were made; without him nothing was made that has been made.

—John 1:1-3

We must find out what words are and how they function. They become images when written down, but images of words repeated in the mind and not of the image of the thing itself.

—W. S. Burroughs

'Did you pack your bags yourself? Were your bags with you at all times since you packed them? Could anybody have tampered with your bags? Are you carrying any electronic or battery operated devices? May I see them please? What is your occupation? Where do you live? How long have you lived there? Who paid for your ticket? How did you receive it? Are you carrying anything that could be used as a weapon? Please remove your laptop computer!! Please remove your shoes and belt!! Thank you and enjoy your flight … '

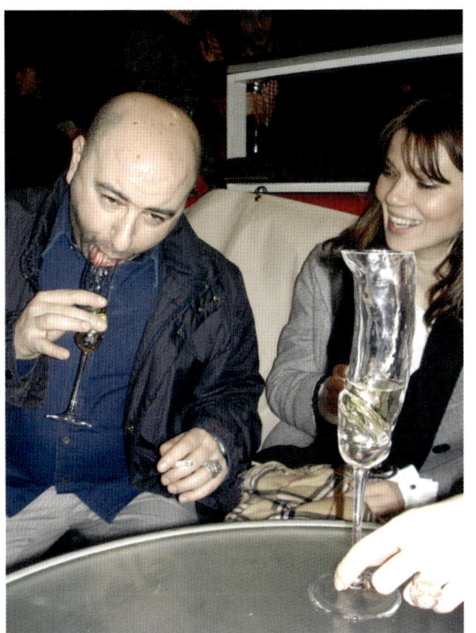

Kendell Geers, *cocktail* (2005), performance
and crystal glasses; courtesy of the artist.

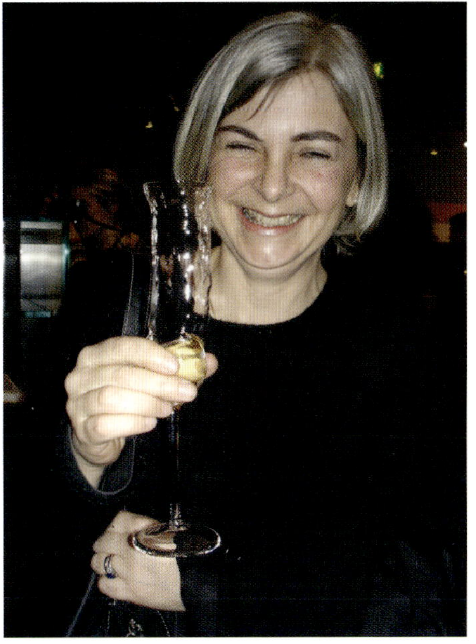

Kendell Geers, *cocktail* (2005), performance
and crystal glasses; courtesy of the artist.

Every time I fly to the USA I am amazed and shocked by the naïve stupidity of the security procedures at the airport. As if you would say that you did not pack the explosive bags yourself or that you intend to set your shoes on fire mid flight. Then, once you arrive in the USA, the visa forms require you to state whether you are a Nazi, terrorist, drug addict, alcoholic, or have a history of insanity in your family. The assumption is, of course, that if your intentions are to engage in any form of terrorist or subversive activity, that when asked you will readily reveal your intentions. Why would you go through all the trouble of acquiring sophisticated and undetectable explosive devices, spend months, if not years, planning your attack, engage in a secretive life hidden inside a sleeper cell and then at the eleventh hour admit that you are a terrorist and that you are packing a bomb? Why do we so readily assume that such a person would not lie and would not be carrying false passports hidden beneath the veneer of a fake lifestyle and grey suit?

God gave me language and my profit of it is that I can lie, and lie I shall for I am an artist. George W. Bush gives us two options: that we are either with HIM or we are on the side of terrorism. Following his logic, you would immediately become a terrorist should you lie about that vibrator in your bag that you would simply prefer not to show to the macho monkey in the uniform. Indeed, the truth is even stranger than fiction, for on 11 September 2001 the hijackers did not have the need for luggage, packed by themselves or not, nor were they carrying dangerous weapons, for they brought the capitalist world to its knees using credit cards, masking tape, box cutters and a great deal of faith, vision and courage. Perhaps our greatest shock was to discover that faith, vision and courage are still all you need to change the world.

In reality, if you really want to disrupt an international flight with an act of terror it's so much easier to simply open the doors mid flight, for the pressure alone will suck out at least two dozen people; a dozen more will die in the panic, ten will die from exposure to the extreme temperatures up there, and you can be certain of at least two more dying from heart attacks. If your accomplice forgot his nail file or toenail clippers, or if they were confiscated at the airport, he can break the neck off the bottle of in-flight champagne or red wine, and use it to cut the throats of a dozen more passengers. Alternatively, he can simply strangle his neighbour or drop sleeping tablets into the captain's coffee. Let's face it, it's about as easy to hijack or cause terror in an aeroplane as it is to lie about your intentions.

Terrorists are not born any more than their actions can be considered illegitimate. Irrespective of their political position, their actions and strategies are always forced upon them through a lack of alternatives. Denied a country, they have no voice or seat at the United Nations. Their plight is made illegitimate only by virtue of their being born disenfranchised and alienated from the seats of global power and capital. Outnumbered, out-gunned, undernourished and impoverished, they are supposed to disappear into the folds of history and silently assimilate into the culture of their oppressors and masters.

The concept of a 'terrorist', as opposed to that of a 'freedom fighter', is built upon the premise of an homogeneous society in which we all have the very same value system and subscribe to the same sociopolitical and ethical codes. The terrorist is the outsider; the other to whom our codes do not apply and who is, as a result, now our enemy. We classify them as terrorist only because they do not play by our rules, respect our currency or worship our gods, and they certainly do not respect our crusades and declarations of war. We expect them not to lie because we have been taught that only the truth shall set us free, and why should they be any different, especially if they aspire to our measure of civilisation with its so-called universal laws of democracy and justice?

Arriving in the USA today, everyone who requires a visa is then also digitally photographed and their fingerprints scanned. Of course, visas are not required for persons from the European Union, Japan, Australia or any other wealthy partner of global capital. The visa is, in effect, the very same method of controlling the movements and access of people deemed undesirable, as used by both the apartheid regime and the Nazis in Germany. The USA has, however, gone one step further than even Hitler could have imagined, with its introduction of the Patriot Act and the fingerprinting of visitors. Standing there as my body is scanned, I am reminded that I am alien to that culture; that I am unwelcome and shall be tolerated only for as long as I behave appropriately. My differences, my otherness, is in the process coded as criminal, captured and archived. My crime was to be born into a country classified as suspicious.

PART II

Indeed, terror is in all cases whatsoever, either more openly or latently, the ruling principle of the sublime.

—*Edmund Burke*

Terror is nothing other than justice, prompt, severe, inflexible; it is therefore an emanation of virtue.

—*Robespierre*

I gave birth to myself in May 1968, in a moment of terror, a riot of global proportions as Paris, Prague, Mexico City and San Francisco were burning

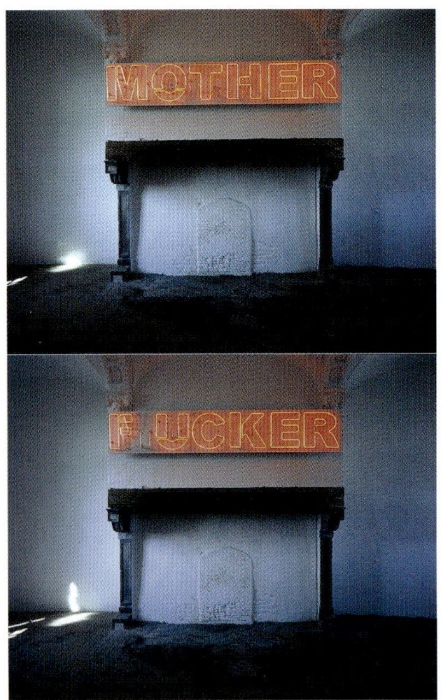

Kendell Geers, *bruce nauman, failed to bind* (2003), neon; courtesy of the artist.

and Carl Andre's bricks were being hurled into the faces of capitalist authority. The Molotov cocktail and dustbin lid transformed forever our understanding of the quotidian object and in the explosion the innocent milk bottle lost its virginity. It would take another three decades and another generation before the importance of that shift would be fully understood as Seattle, Genoa and of course the World Trade Centre finally caught fire, and this time it was on a scale hitherto unimaginable.

I did not grow up in Soho, nor was I ever invited to dine with the Queen or hide my emotions in a suburban haze while resting in a Matisse armchair. I do not speak the Queen's English because I grew up on the streets of Africa, a place where you can die for what you believe in, or for the small

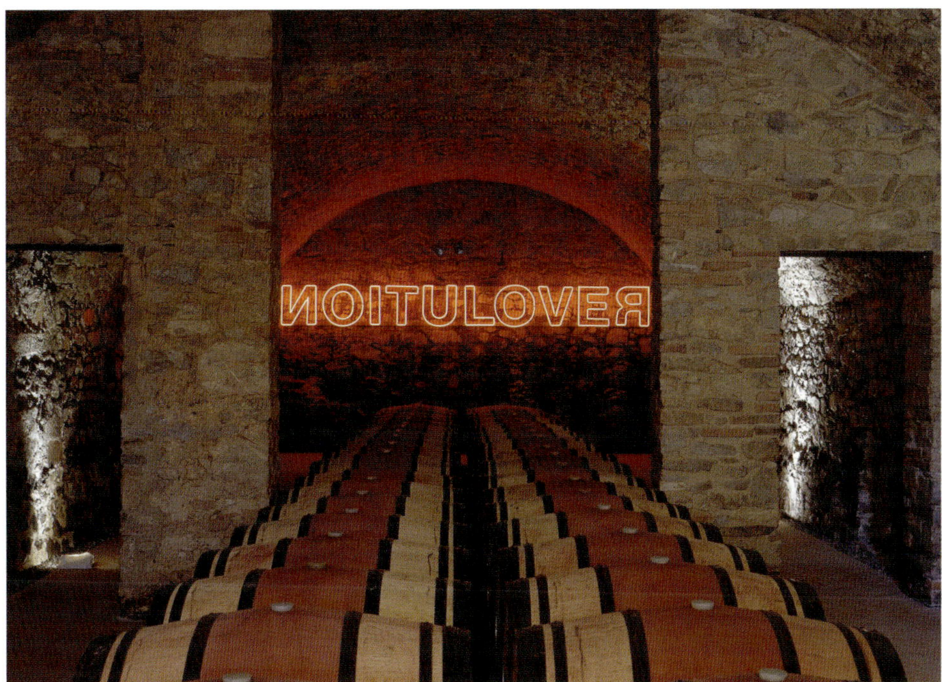

Kendell Geers, *noitu(love)r* (2005), neon;
courtesy of the artist.

change in your pocket. My accent is my resistance, for it reflects my lived experience; the realities of my being born twice. My accent separates me from the centre, by choice.

Language is oppressive, as it only acknowledges that which can be named. It is not the result of any particular individual's design as much as the external manifestation of a culture. The structures and codes that enable or disavow what may be articulated and expressed in any particular language are predetermined by the dominant class and culture to which it gives voice. In English, it is the Queen's accent and Oxford University that set the standard and norm, the structure of authenticity. It is therefore hardly surprising that English should be predisposed towards the prejudices, values and experiences of that social class. For example, the Royal habit of understatement, especially when it comes to the world of emotions, means that we have only one word, LOVE, to express what you feel for your Corgi, your mother, your lover, your wife, your favourite ice-cream flavour, a book, colour or chair.

A vastly different lifestyle and experience than the Queen's translates into an entirely different language, and while it is certainly true, for example, that French allows a far greater emotional vocabulary, the prejudices of its own ruling classes are embedded in the very same manner. Your only resistance is in terms of your accent, which is by no means neutral or impotent. The accent is an authentic voice that, while limited in terms of vocabulary, is empowered in terms of points of reference, allusion and intonation. It prioritises the spoken word over the written, transforming the tongue into a very sharp weapon. The accent is built upon the foundation of a lived experience that places the street, the parochial and colloquial at its semantic core, defining itself in terms of the shared experiences that bind that specific community and no other. Whether it's the Irish accent or the argot of prisoners, the accent embodies the conflict between the centre and periphery, a dialogue and negotiation between points of contact and points of resistance.

In creating their colonies, the modus operandi of the European superpowers were to duplicate the centre in every imaginable aspect, from the language to the names of the streets, the urban design, architecture and even the history lessons. I was, for instance, taught more at school about European history than about the continent on which my family had been living for 400 years. Teaching the natives how to read and write was a quick and efficient method for inserting the 'master's voice', and hence his values and beliefs, into the soul of the good students. With the Bible as textbook, the transformation quickly meant that there were more churches being built in the colonies than in Europe. According to the logic of the church and colonial master plan, the natives were divided between that of the 'good' natives who read their Bible diligently and who spoke, dressed, walked and thought like their master and in every way aspired to become that master, and on the other hand the 'bad' natives, who functioned according to an entirely different concept of good and evil and who were thus cast in the role of cannibal.

In 1928, Oswald de Andrade's Anthropophagic Manifesto recalled this same cannibal as the most appropriate voice for the native who sought a way out of the binary duplicity of the Christian European model. He explained that:

> ... the struggle between what one would call the Uncreated and the Creature illustrated by the permanent contradiction between man and his Taboo. The quotidian love and the capitalist modus vivendi. Anthropophagy. Absorption of the sacred enemy. To transform him into totem. The human adventure. The mundane finality. However, only the pure elites managed to realize carnal anthropophagy, which brings the highest sense of life, and avoids all the evils identified by Freud, catechist evils. What happens is not a sublimation of the sexual instinct. It is the thermometric scale of the anthropophagic instinct. From carnal, it becomes elective and creates friendship. Affectionate, love. Speculative, science. It deviates and transfers itself. We reach vilification. Low anthropophagy agglomerated in the sins of catechism-envy, usury, calumny, assassination. Plague of the so-called cultured and christianized peoples, it is against it that we are acting. Anthropophagi.[1]

I grew up watching *Dallas*, *Dynasty*, the *Smurfs* and *Rocky* 1, 2, 3, 4 and 5. I never saw the *Muppets* or *Coronation Street*, because the producers had the good sense to boycott apartheid South Africa. I did, however, read *Face* magazine, ate Kentucky Fried Chicken and drank Coca-Cola (even though the latter pretended to boycott South Africa by changing the name in the very small print on the side of the can, but the drink looked and tasted exactly the same as any can of Coke anywhere else in the world). To all intents and purposes, I was weaned on the same cultural crap as a kid of my age in London, New York, Melbourne, Nairobi or Sao Paulo.

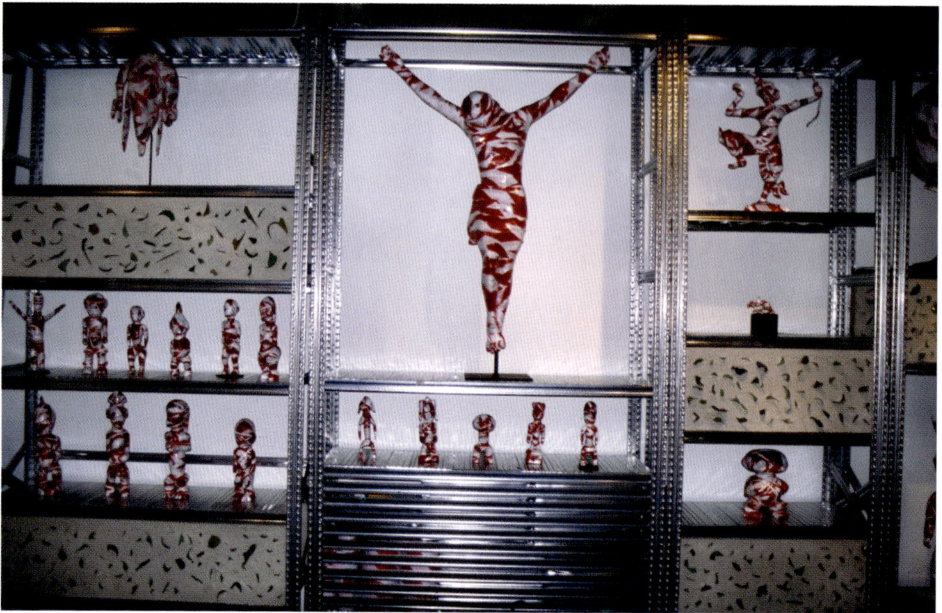

Kendell Geers, *mondo kane* (2002), installation;
courtesy of the artist.

On the other hand, the violence of my childhood colours my memory of
the *Smurfs* and nails one foot very firmly into African soil, giving my *Smurfs*
a slightly different shade of blue. I think I shall carry a coffin of Germiston
earth around with me like a vampire for the rest of my life. That's not necessarily a bad thing, for at least I will never forget where I came from and will
always be reminded that I am in fact the Frankenstein of a failed experiment
in social engineering.

It's been two years since the opening of what was meant to be 'our' Documenta, and I would argue that little has changed as a direct result. Those of
us born into the third world—the margins, the disenfranchised, the colonised, the disempowered—naïvely trusted that the tables would turn, that
we would finally be granted a seat at the table rather than waiting on it. I
believed in the hope of a global expression that would adjust the colonial

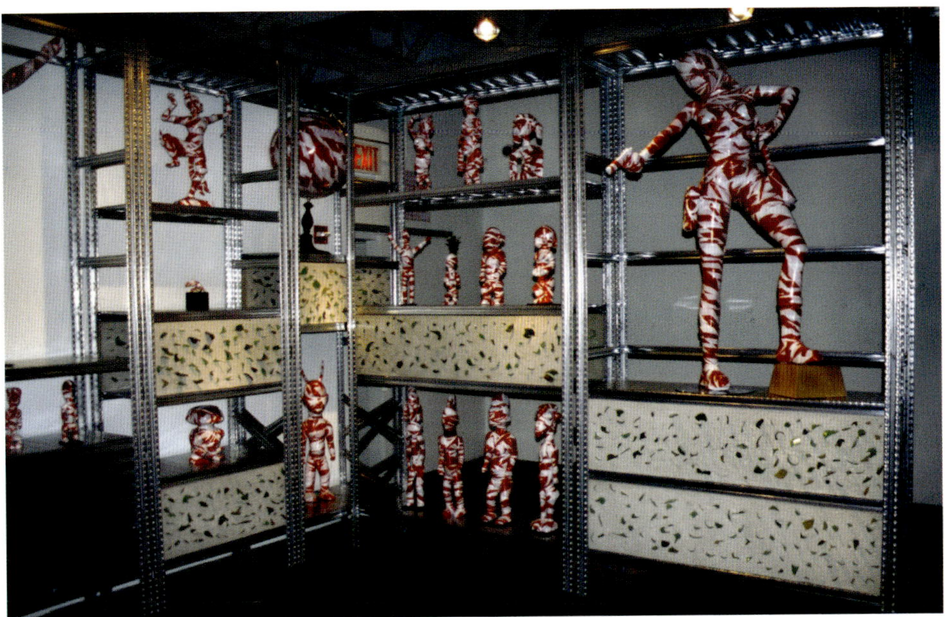

Kendell Geers, *kode-x* (2002), installation;
courtesy of the artist.

structure whereby I have always been judged by a model that prejudices quality in terms of proximity to the centre; how well I spoke the Queen's English. I listened aghast during the 'Empires, Ruins + Networks' conference in Melbourne in 2004 as the former pope of art explained to a naïve, isolated audience that no single person had the power to change the system. His words stood in stark contrast with my memory of the same man literally having to run through art fairs as the most powerful galleries, dealers, vendors and artists in the world chased after him with complete devotion and would jump to any height or sink to any depth to win his favour.

No sooner had Enwezor's appointment been made public than the punters began placing their bets. Everyone who had previously supported him, or had even been seen in his company, was scooped up into the net lest they become part of a new turn in the art market. We all benefited from that, and it certainly made a world of difference that otherwise would have taken a decade longer. It's very ironic, to say the least, that the punters took more risks and were infinitely more courageous than the show they were trying to pre-empt, and in the end it was they who changed the way we now understand art from the margins.

Dokumenta XI ushered into the mainstream the politically correct, multi-cultural (PCMC) artist from both the margins and the racially unequal centre. On the other hand, this ushering played into the hands of the neo-conservatives and left us with an art that is desexed, desensitised, devoid of content, apolitical (except for the predictable partisan accusations and propaganda), innocuous, calculated, decorative, bland, sentimental, saccharine and inoffensive. The PCMC artist is unlikely to change or even challenge anyone, except his/her own political nemeses. The direct expression and literal articulation of one political position is really as valid as any other, and with time the pendulum of fashion will swing in the opposite direction and disavow its predecessor. The 'holier than thou' PCMC artist starts off on the wrong foot with the assumption that he/she has the moral high ground and that the rest of us mere mortals should follow. The problem with such a position, irrespective of political bias, is that such work leaves us with a very predictable binary choice by which we are able to only agree or disagree; a small stone's throw away from George W. Bush's special version of reduced political logic. The partisan nature of such work neither challenges nor subverts any value system, and probably reinforces difference with its reductionism. Ultimately, it embodies precisely the same logic of power as that which it seeks to disavow, and it is thus as guilty as the mirror through which it sees everything in reverse.

Since the work of art is always an invested social relation and always the physical embodiment of a culture located at a specific point in time, the work of art will always be politically inscribed. It's not necessary to announce whom the artist voted for, since that should already be clear in terms of their choice of scale, medium, symbolism, imagery, strategy and so forth. To be truly subversive or revolutionary, the artist creates a context or situation through which the composition of power is disavowed and the viewer cast into a complex semantic labyrinth through which they must find their way back to safety alone. In reversing the polarity from passive consumer to active participant, the work of art functions more as a catalyst that starts a chain reaction whereby the sociopolitical and moral prejudices of the viewer become the checkerboard on which the delicate game of ideological chess is played out.

This dislocation process is really possible only when the field lies beyond the safety of the known. The work of art needs to move outside the logic of language into the dangerous world of terror. The codes of language and history are threatened only by terror and that which is unimaginable, unpredictable, unexpressible, untranslatable, unmentionable, unsayable, inappropriate and articulated through humour, contradiction, danger and extremism. Of course, having been articulated once, the code resets itself and assimilates and denies the threat by transforming it into fashion. It is here that the colloquial becomes so powerful, for the lived experience of life in the margins, be it geographical, emotional or moral, lies so far outside the conception of the centre, that complete assimilation is very problematic. In order to function it is necessary that the expression be articulated through the common ground of a mutually understood code. The point of contact here is language and history that, since we assume to be set in stone, plays straight into the hands of the cannibal with a different eye on what's permissible. The point of resistance is the emphasis on the accent and the cannibalisation of language and history by inverting its logic of power through an entirely different lived experience and relocating the centre to the outside.

When the slave finally gets to dine with his/her master, he/she can either decide to imitate the master and even fuck the other slaves, entirely forgetting where he/she comes from, or he/she can quietly poison the master's food and seize control of the entire farm and liberate all the other slaves.

PART III

The white cube gallery is the high temple of capitalism and its dealers are the priests who make daily sacrifices of integrity in order to keep the gods of profit happy. The entire institution of art, from the critics to the collectors, the trustees to the punters, makes the timely visits to these temples to renew their faith and maintain their shrines at home. Art has always been there and will always be. It differs from what we understand as culture, in that it is culture at its most rarified and pure.

Culture is an open-ended expression of heterogeneous individuals who have created particular forms that give material form to their social needs. These groups are united and divided by their individual relationships with these expressions. On the other hand, Art is the purest expression a homogeneous culture can give to its most holy beliefs, investing objects and images with symbolic power and ideological charge. At its service are the artists who are commissioned either formally or via the pressures of market demand to make manifest this value system. Only that which is able to perfectly express the unspoken will of the elite will survive, for only it will be taken care of and preserved for posterity by the commanding powers; for only they can afford, and only they have the vested interest in, protecting that legacy. The white cube gallery system is the manifest form of high capitalism and the physical form of its purest ideological expression.

Capitalism responds to every potential threat by assimilating the threat in the form of fashion. Since the 1960s, every subcultural challenge, from the underground threat to the mainstream from the Punk movement to the commune, from the drunken wail of Bukowski to the cut-up technique of Burroughs, from the bullet of Valery Solanis to the body fluids of COUM Transmissions, or the call to arms by Malcolm X, has been assimilated and translated into the safe cathartic rituals of fashion. No longer dangerous, the implicit violence and transgression has been recorded as mere history and the fabric cut into Prada's anti-fashion, no less fashionable, fashion. Che Guevara is now only a slogan on a T-shirt and his diaries a Hollywood script. The last Dokumenta shifted the multicultural and politically correct into the mainstream only because it was already dead.

PART IV

> *Hoaxes are warnings that contain incorrect information about malware or system events. These warnings often describe fantastical or impossible malware program characteristics that often fool the user into performing unwanted actions on their system or suggests that users should forward the warning to other users. A hoax can be considered a nuisance by the mere fact that by forwarding it causes a waste of time and bandwidth.*
>
> *—<http://www.trendmicro.com/en/security/general/glossary/overview.htm>*

I would like to return to my starting point, to the question of language, of truth and the ability to lie. Given that the semantic composition of the art structure embodies and represents the values and needs of the ruling class, and that their brokerage predetermines the outcome, the artists themselves are impotent. What I make, say and do has no value beyond how it can be used, traded and exchanged.

Enter the TerroRealist. I have previously attempted a somewhat crude analysis of a certain kind of marginal artist, an artist who speaks both within a language of vested power and simultaneously articulates the

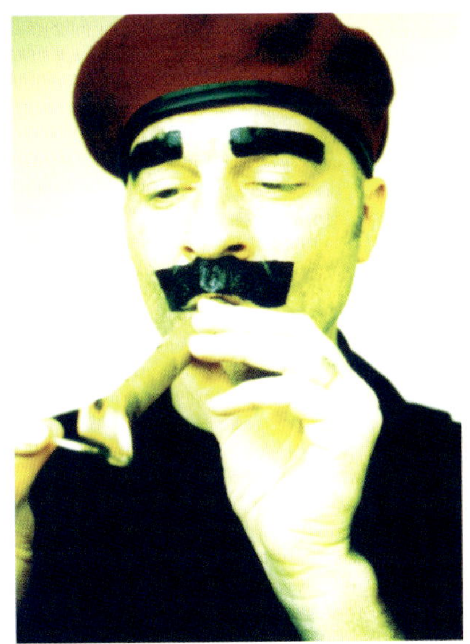

Kendell Geers, *auto-da-fé* (2003), performance; courtesy of the artist.

realities of an entirely different experience. I observed that artists who had grown up in countries that had been torn apart by war, revolution, conflict, crime and genocide created work according to an entirely different set of aesthetic principles. In place of the cool, detached, passive showroom aesthetics of the white cube shrine, their work was invested with a reality principle that sought to disrupt the viewer's pleasure more than satisfy it. While most of these artists may be known to the institutional powers, their practice seems to preclude full assimilation.

On the one hand, the artists typically grew up or lived significant parts of their lives in countries that had experienced extreme ideological switches, such as the former Soviet Union, Yugoslavia, Serbia, Croatia, South Africa, East Germany and so forth. Having witnessed such extreme ideological reversals and dramatic shifts in their social realities and moral codes, these artists would naturally be more critical of any social codes and ideological promises. I was thinking here of artists such as Milica Tomic, Ilya Kabakov, Aleksandra Mir, Christian Jankowski, Sisley Xhafa, Oleg Kulig, Alexander Brenner, Marina Abramovic, Irwin, Fernado Alvim and so forth. There exists, also, an entirely similar group of artists who grew up or lived in countries in which capitalism has failed to take root, countries that embody the empty promise of profit and the criminal inequality of a system designed around the needs of the G8. The *favelas*, streets and ghettos of São Paulo, Mexico City, Rio, Havana and Bogota have witnessed a very similar strategy coming from artists based, once again, on a loss of faith in a political system that disqualifies and disenfranchises them even before they begin, and this experience has created artists such as Cildo Meireles, Felix Gonzales Torres, Helio Oiticico, Victor Grippo, Lygia Clark and Carlos Capelán, to mention a few.

The USA was naturally shocked and deeply traumatised to see the twin towers burning in 2001, but in countries like Iraq, Angola, Russia and in cities like Johannesburg or Bogota, such terror attacks are daily events. Every day families are traumatised by rape, kidnapping, murder, bombs, assassinations and incarceration, for no other reason than being in the wrong place at the wrong time.

Almost immediately as I had articulated the theory of the TerroRealist that—albeit somewhat forced—still made sense, I was uncomfortable with it, for a great many artists from the centre demonstrated the very same characteristics; for example, David Hammons, Jimmie Durham, Maurizzio Cattelan, Carl-Michael von Hausswolff, Jens Hanning, Giani Motti, Gino de Dominicis, and so forth. In the case of Spanish artist Santiago Sierra, I would say that his is a simple case of the colonial structure of raping and enslaving the natives for profit, but for the rest I needed to expand the logic somewhat.

The terrorist must infiltrate in order to survive, slowly integrating him/herself into the culture he/she is seeking to destroy. The more successful they are in being able to lie about their intentions and disappear into the social fabric, the greater their chances will be to later rip it all apart. While the ensuing attack will certainly be articulated in terms of terror, it can be as effective with a well-placed rumour as with a benign but suspicious-looking package, or a spectacular car-bomb explosion made from fertiliser. The terrorists' weapons are all recycled from everyday life so as to, on the one hand, avoid suspicion, and on the other because they have no access to other means. Their greatest weapon is their precise analysis of the social fabric, its strengths and weaknesses, and where a well-placed object or telephone call would be the most disruptive. Since it can sometimes take years for a plan to be set in motion, it is very important that they keep focused on their goal, with a very strong sense of faith and courage, hiding behind subterfuge and equivocation. As a role model there can be no better for the contemporary artist, for the terrorist needs to, by definition, study and perfectly understand the structure of power and the logic of the social, political and economic classes of the society of its enemy.

The artists I have attempted to define as TerroRealist would refute such a definition, for they would be suspicious of the power and control that follows the process of naming. Their work is difficult to define because it concerns

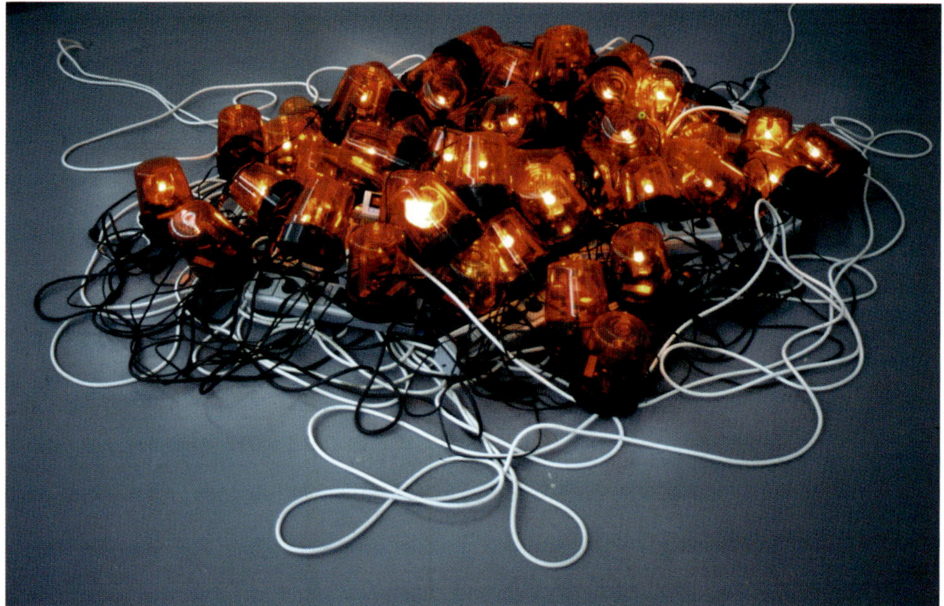

Kendell Geers, *Cry wolf* (1999), installation;
courtesy of the artist.

itself more with the social fabric than the objects or images that are the external expression of that fabric. Their work is performative and disruptive, anti-social; and yet at the same time they can sometimes use fashion as a vehicle. Most importantly, the TerroRealist distrusts power, whether it is in the form of language or history, the logic of the institution or an individual. Power is defused with humour, contradiction, disavowal and history is thrown back into the dustbin from whence it came.

Perhaps the most important aspect of such artists is that they begin every project from the perspective of the self. Unlike the PCMC artist, the TerroRealist does not speak on behalf of others or create victims by imprisoning either the viewer or their subject. Instead, the self is located at the centre, as the subject from which the world may be analysed and decoded. The self is fixed in another time, language, history, place and culture and, as such, it is

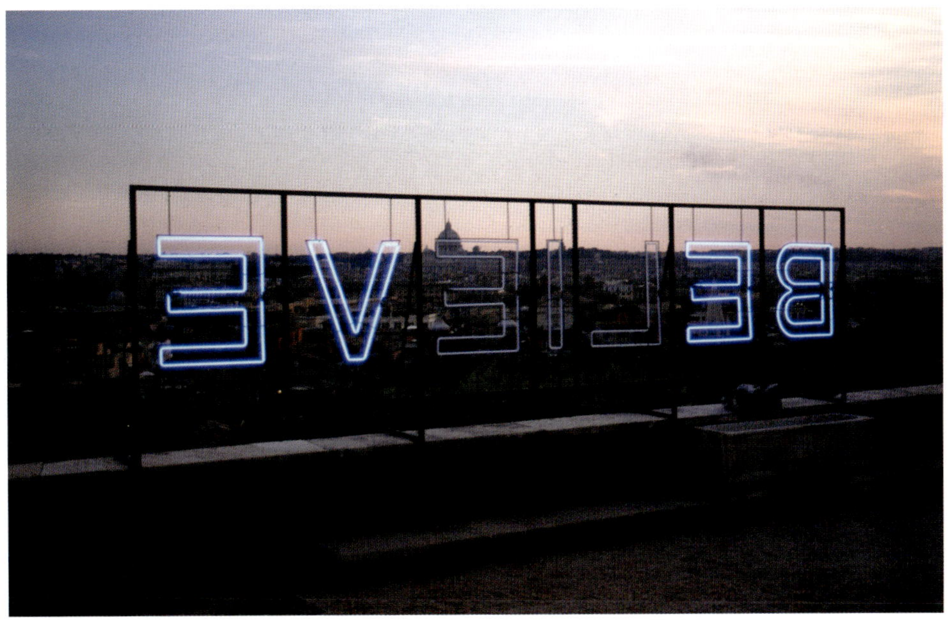

Kendell Geers, *be:lie:ve* (2002), neon; courtesy of the artist.

the most subversive place to begin for it holds all the keys to the dislocation of the centre. The lived experiences, the colloquial subjectivity of this space provides all the clues necessary to create the bumps and potholes on the gallery floor of an homogeneous culture.

PART V

According to the Hindu tradition of cosmology, we are now entering into the age of Kali Yuga, a dark spiritual age of chaos, rampant sexuality, greed, violence, debauchery and lies. The gods that were once feared have since been reduced to one-dimensional clichés like Bush's Episcopalian America or Muslim fanaticism, or even entirely forgotten as profit replaced the prophets. Most contemporary art practice reflects this condition in its vapid banality and decorative emptiness. The gestures become more slight and the expressions more flat. The veneer disease of 'Empty V' television is spiralling out of control and artists have absolutely nothing to say about nothing and are happy to simply go on photo-shopping. There is no spiritual dimension to contemporary art beyond celebrating the sale and exchange value of the objects. I would argue that this absence of faith is directly related to the emptiness and boredom of living. The excess of profit has created lifestyles in which death, disease, pain, trauma and the fragility of the body are removed from experience. According to the ancient Shamanistic ways, it is necessary that you confront and deal with the realisation and experience of your own death before you can express life. Throughout the history of art, the proximity and experience of death and disease, revolution and war, translated into entirely different strategies and expressions than during periods of luxury. In our own lifetime, the AIDS epidemic in New York brought death, suffering and empathy into the lives of a generation of artists who as a result produced work that was far more engaged with life and its fragilities than the decade either before or after. The same may be argued for the work created in the time of the Vietnam War, although we have yet to see what the attack on the twin towers and the unjustifiable war in Iraq will translate into.

Memory is a scar that holds onto the body in pain, ecstasy, anger, orgasm, hysteria and excess, constantly reminding itself about that moment when every word, every vowel or syllable it had been programmed with was un-able to save or protect it. This loss of control threw the body into a space beyond language that was closer to God than any other experience before or since. The memory of it remains a scar because time has no way to cover the wounds with words or cultural expressions, and only the experience itself can describe the experience. God is the ultimate terrorist, constantly creating and destroying our world with violence and beauty, simultaneously express-ing infinite terror and infinite joy.

I have ripped out the tongue of my master and with it firmly in my cheek

I would now like to speak about the spirit and the soul. This is not the sentimental quoting of yet another faith I have read in a book, but a baptism of fire into the secret life of objects as ideological receptors. It's about returning the body to a space for desire, sex, blood, sweat, pain, love, death, the awakening of the Beast within, the cannibal in Dionysus devouring Apollo in order to assimilate him …

NOTE

1   Oswald de Andrade, '*Manifesto Antropofágico*' (Anthropophagic Manifesto), *Revista de Antropofagia* magazine, São Paulo, Year 1, May 1928.

Virtual Marae 2020 AD

LISA REIHANA

In recognition of the *tangata whenua,* or indigenous people of Australia, I begin this talk with an image of the Aboriginal flag, and examples of different Maori tribal flags. These alternatives to the colonial red/white/blue designs flown by New Zealand and Australia are reminders of a long struggle to assert self-determination. I am an urban woman of *Ngaa Puhi*, Welsh and English ancestry.

For 'Empires, Ruins + Networks', I hope to impart a sense of the vibrancy of our culture, and what it feels like to be connected by *whakapapa,* or genealogy. The *Marae* is a fundamental structure that supports Maori to connect with each other. One could argue that a contributing factor to the evolution of the *Marae* was as a resistance to colonial desire for land. This sound you hear is the *karanga* [keening welcome] performed by women. It is the first thing you hear as you are welcomed onto the *Marae*. Physical structures such as *Wharenui* [sleeping houses], *Wharekai* [eating houses] and *Niu* poles were used to mark tribal ownership. The highly decorated interior space signals an evolved spiritual life. Generally, the *Marae* is on tribal land, but now it is not unusual to see them at schools or universities—in these cases they function as pan-tribal spaces.

The video playing beside me plunders work I've made over the past fifteen years and intersperses it with images of customary practice. The work of Pine Taiapa and Tene Waitere, to name just two of many *Tohunga Whakairo*

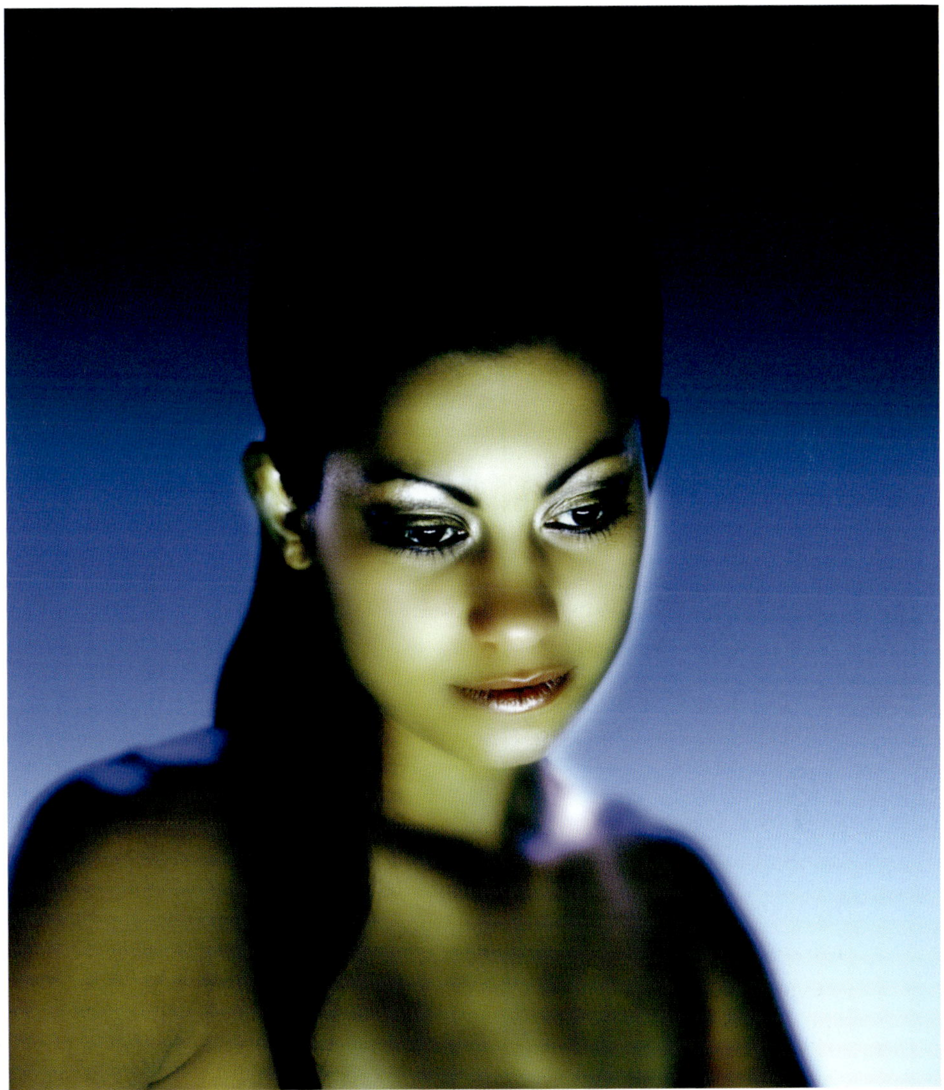

Lisa Reihana, *Hinewai* from *Digital Marae* (2001),
colour cibachrome photograph mounted on
aluminium, ed. 2/5, 120 × 140 × 0.35cm.
Collection: Queensland Art Gallery;
courtesy of the artist.

[esteemed carvers], provides me with a foundational and aesthetic context for my films, photographs and sculptures. The images of *Wharenui* [meeting house] are embodiments of mythological and tribal ancestral figures—so when you enter a meeting house you are, in effect, walking back into the body of an ancestor. The entrance has a head and outstretched arms; inside you can see the *heke/kowhaiwhai* or ribs. It is in here that Maori *whaikorero* [speak], debate, share food, cry, sleep and are rejuvenated.

My love of Maori architecture is manifold. Each *Wharenui* has its own unique personality, and their solid presence affirms 'We Are Maori'. They have an incredible amount of visual material—we didn't have a written language. Our language is embedded in carving, *tukutuku* [weaving, painting], encoded in each physical component. It is through this visual material that I connect to Nga Puhi and other Maori. I do not speak *Te Reo Maori* [Maori language] but I am visual.

Here is an excerpt from *Tangi* written by Witi Ihimaera. He is important because he showed a way that contemporary writers could straddle the gap between traditional visual models and contemporary and culturally based written language. You may be familiar with his novel *Whalerider*, recently made into a feature film. This story of the emotional struggle a young man faces when his father dies is selected because the book begins with the Maori Creation Story. This myth is quoted time and again in traditional and contemporary art forms.

My mother was the Earth
My father was the Sky
  They were Rangitane and Papatuanuku, the first parents, who clasped each
other so tightly that there was no day. Their children were born into darkness.
They lived among the shadows of their mother's breasts and thighs and groped
in blindness among the long black strands of her hair.
Until the time of separation and the dawning of the first day.

DIGITAL MARAE

Because certain knowledge is reserved for *Tohunga Whakairo* [esteemed carvers], it can be tricky—even dangerous—to work within this cultural domain. I want to go beyond romantic constructions of Maori mythological figures, so I include cityscapes rather than natural bush settings and empty landscapes. My dilemma is that I irrevocably change the course of Maori art practice. For the exhibition *Purangiaho,* held at Auckland Art Gallery, I unveiled my installation *Digital Marae.* This work includes five ancestral figures, presented like carvings, in large photographs of a video and children's shoes. A *Tuhoe* descendant told me I had breached tribal protocol by presenting *Hinepukohurangi,* and ascribing her with humanistic attributes. As the signature image for the exhibition, she had already entered the public arena. Luckily this selection was made by the *Tuhoe* curator, Ngahiraka Mason, who reassured me that I had made a beautiful image in good faith and with integrity.

In conclusion I'd like to quote Geraldine Barlow, who says that:

Cultural knowledge is a powerful and fragile expression of identity, owned by communities—by necessity, in the custody of individuals. We may struggle to keep even a part of it intact, and yet to remain dynamic and alive it must also be subject to change, revision and creative adaption. Information must be balanced with intuition as the next generation finds its way, drawing upon the old to create the new.[1]

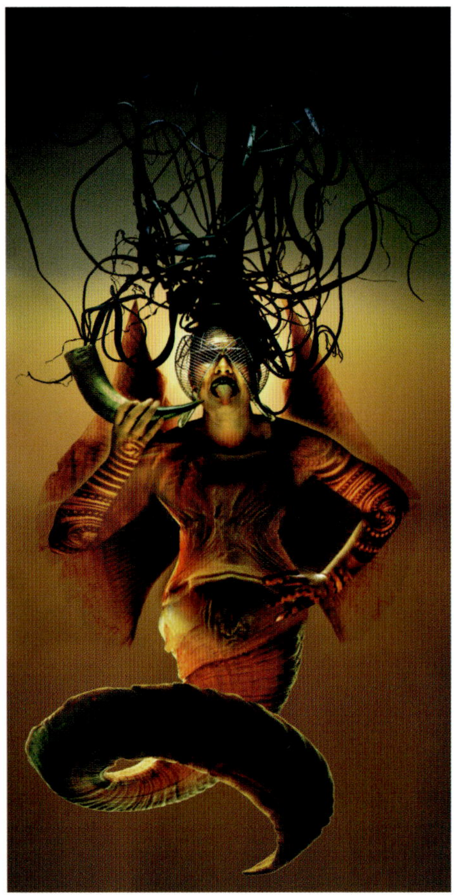

Lisa Reihana, *Marakihau* from *Digital Marae* (2001),
colour cibachrome photograph mounted on
aluminium, ed. 2/5, 200 × 100 × 0.35cm.
Collection: Queensland Art Gallery;
courtesy of the artist.

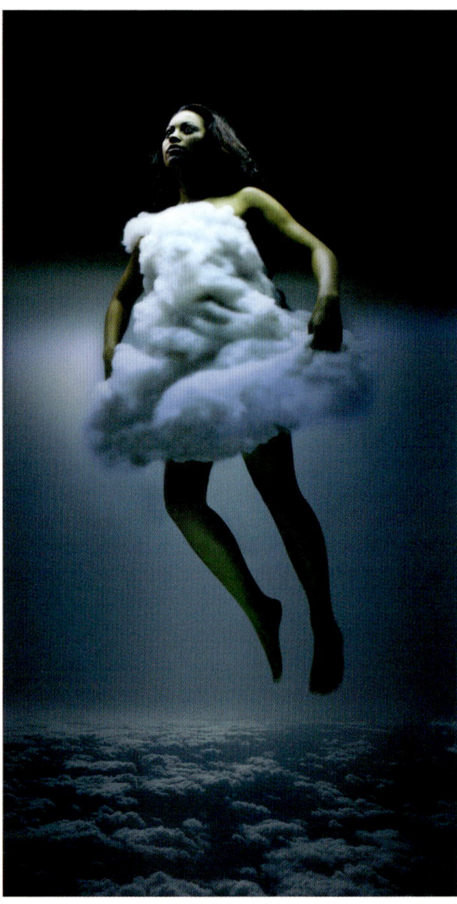

Lisa Reihana, *Hinepukohurangi* from *Digital Marae*
(2001), colour cibachrome photograph mounted
on aluminium ed. 2/5, 200 × 100 × 0.35cm.
Collection: Queensland Art Gallery;
courtesy of the artist.

NOTE

1   Geraldine Barlow, 'New 04: Parekohai Whakamoe: How to tell of those who
have gone before?', *NEW 04* exhibition catalogue, Australian Centre for
Contemporary Art, Melbourne, March 2004, p. 11.

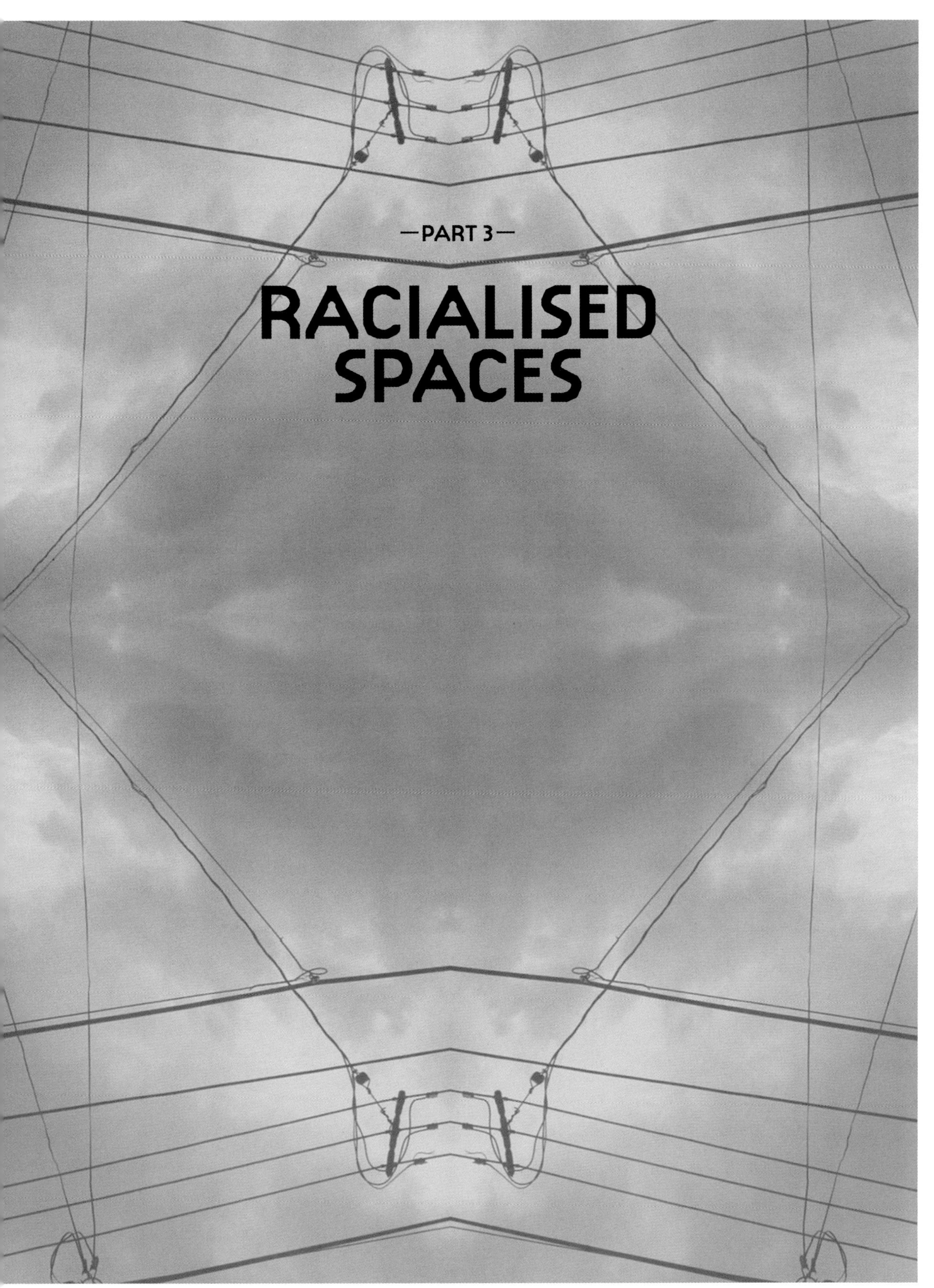
—PART 3—
RACIALISED
SPACES

Introduction: The Paradox of Space in Contemporary Art

NICK TSOUTAS

It seems anachronistic that we invest in and build new architectural museums to house the archive of art (the history and traditions of culture), but consider it more appropriate to house the new contemporary art (the art of the now and the future) in 'renovated', 'revitalised', 'restored' historic buildings. The art of the present, the new direction of art that defines and invents our future, is housed in buildings of the past—buildings that were never intended to function as venues for contemporary art, but as sites of industry, offices, warehouses, and colonial administration palaces—while the art of yesterday is given the privilege of being housed in architectural structures that represent the vision of the present and the future.

This inversion of the relationship between contemporary art and new architecture signifies an attempt to consign contemporary art to a subservient and subordinate relationship to history, while privileging the primary function of the historical archive. To me this suggests a contradiction in systems of cultural valuing. The expedient practice of fitting new contemporary art forms into conserved, redundant buildings is a policy that reflects very little trust in or knowledge of the function of contemporary art. It gives priority to the fiction of history and its preservation. I know that it has been suggested that all buildings are subject to change during their life cycle and that a changed context produces new meanings, but politically I am not convinced that abandoned buildings adequately provide for the demands, functions and new directions of contemporary art.

Art is not fixed and is constantly and radically reinventing itself, renewing its parameters as it invests in creating new spaces. The challenge, then, for communities, government and contemporary arts organisations, along with our architectural thinkers and sociologists, is how to develop the spaces of the contemporary. Recycling abandoned spaces is not the answer, as abandoned spaces are not free spaces. They come burdened with residual political meanings from their previous functions. Art needs the freedom to create and rethink its potential. When the government gives you an abandoned site, is this an intervention into the historical meaning of the site or a sanctioned, authorised intervention that co-opts the contemporary and empties its capacity for any form of opposition?

Today one may well ask: What is a gallery? What is a museum? For, as Uta Meta Bauer suggests, this institution conceals enormous potential. It has at its disposal authoritative financial and symbolic capital, and the perception that it has the responsibility for the construction of history—albeit a history that is linear and predominantly focused on the West and modernity. While the museum/gallery is a space of consumption, the platforms of contemporary art are multifaceted. Indeed, an exhibition itself is a site of displacement; a temporary space of both transition and translation, that functions as a space of refuge for the radical and an opportunity for experimental and critical investigations that transport us beyond the institutional codes. The contemporary space is a space with the potential for many centres and many edges, with a capacity for the yet unknown; a space that is not self-contained but discursive, open and constantly fluid. It is a speculative space without boundaries: a cultural laboratory.

What do we mean by the term 'laboratory'? The term itself is strangely Victorian—perhaps modernist—as it implies a site for experimentation, a site for testing, a place where you begin with a hypothesis or formulate an assumption, and then set out to prove it by gathering data and realising certain tests/demonstrations which, after considered analysis, eventually prove beyond a shadow of doubt that the hypothesis is true—empirically and scientifically true. The laboratory functions as a space for cognitive investigation that not only sets up conditions to challenge the system of certainties, but is itself in the business of establishing certainties, of maintaining the idea of knowledge as pure, incontestable, stable and reliable. It presents itself as a theatre of proof, as an economy of fixed constants, an end game of modernity which desires a scientific, inalienably accurate understanding of everything—life, the planet and the universe.

The laboratory is symbolically an isolated construct, a restricted and secret space that sits outside the real world. However, while it is apparently disconnected—outside nature and society—it mediates and authorises itself unconditionally and, as a corollary, is the perfect arbiter for the authorisation of the real world. Yet, despite our ability to manipulate life, we are still largely ignorant of the natural world and how to live within its limits. Today, despite the enormous achievements generated by and through the laboratory, our understanding of nature and its intricate diversity is underdeveloped, immature, and leaves us in the most precarious position of our entire history. In this context, how do we now consider the laboratory as a purveyor of definition and truth? Can we still rely on such systems and structures to realise the truth? What are the ethics involved in realising such truths when truth itself has been so manipulated and commodified? Herein lies our dilemma: the more we desire the logic of the laboratory, the more we seem to misunderstand the very nature of so-called truth in relation to the idea of the future. For whoever seems to own and control the laboratory also lays claim to ownership of the truth that it produces.

The artist's studio has long been equated with the idea of the laboratory, and at times it has been argued that the function of the artist's studio is parallel to the methodology of the scientific laboratory: the assumption is that artists methodically undertake research into the limits and possibilities of cultural knowledge. For me, this assumption is somewhat problematic and perverse, for it obscures the fact we cannot readily understand the forces that are effective in the production of art and culture. It implies that the artist can produce fixed meanings and objects for consumption. It very neatly fits into a contemporary art economy of signs that serve the market demand for fixed empirical evidence and objects that satisfy and acquiesce to the ideas of commodity and exchange.

Okwui Enwezor goes even further by stating: 'My question is simple. Don't you think that Andy Warhol's identification of his studio as an industrial factory or laboratory perverted the nature of the art object, by locating art in an industrial factory environment?' It implied fixed objects of consumption rather than mutable or unfixed territory. Such assumptions not only provide certainties for the marketplace, but more significantly are the constructs that empower the notion of the archive, the museum, and the idea of cultural history itself. For it is here that the archive both understands itself and, indeed, authorises itself not only as a repository of art production and the history of art, but as the signifier of social value. It articulates a policy for the collection of objects that becomes a standard for both taste and exchange. In general, the archive or museum has great difficulty in dealing with the mutable or unfixed territories of art—with the ephemeral and the temporal—other than, perhaps, in the form of documentation. Even the idea of an installation, which today is a commodified standard of international practice (particularly in the context of Biennales), remains a difficult proposition for the archive or the museum. Open systems of art practice continue to perplex the museum, as they operate against the conditions of collectability and offer a challenge that demands that the museum shift both its ideology and its function.

By way of example, I shall refer to several art projects that defy their institutionalisation while also presenting new artistic strategies, models for collaboration in the making of art, and notions of community. These projects reflect a performative and ephemeral way of thinking, which problematises the production of objects as collectable evidence, and privileges a radical social interaction—not only between the participating artists themselves but also within the communities in which they operate.

Lu Jie's extraordinary *Long March* project, a walking visual display in which a group of artists and thinkers undertook to follow the route of Mao Tse Tung, took place in China a couple of years ago. It was a monumental and heavily debated project that remains (or was declared to be) unfinished. Its logistics were as enormous as its objectives, yet its objectives, in the words of Lu Jie, were developed by the 'road that led us along'. Ultimately, it had twelve sites and twelve communities to engage. It confronted the problem of power in a complex social system, as twenty-eight artists of varying degrees of idealism and commitment dealt with the issues of collectivity; with the very idea of what constitutes art; and with the economy of scale and its relationship to the people as well as to the hierarchy of international cultural systems, in which 'Western' culture is automatically privileged. It was a utopian project that was as much about the critical dialogues en route as it was about the opening of new spaces for ideas—spaces that were not subject to the constraints of the academy, nor to the signifying processes of museum culture. It was as much a confrontation with the relentless power of globalisation as it was an effort to define or understand what we mean by Chinese art—particularly when that art is considered in relation to China's position in relation to the West. Fundamentally, the *Long March* explored the revolutionary history of China and its legacies in everyday life.

Similarly, the *B-fact* projects, initiated by Turkish artist Hüseyin Alptekin, are ongoing and interconnected networks of transnational activities that seem to defy any form of cultural categorisation. The projects question the place of art, and more fundamentally, the role of the contemporary artist working in what appears to be an almost permanent state of borderless global mobility. Often nomadic, and always geopolitically collaborative, *B-fact* explores the mutual realities that exist within the processes of trans-border artistic exchange between and across cultures, as a means of expressing interregional solidarity. These cross-cultural collaborations precipitate complex interrelational interventions, which in turn produce a contemporary remapping of an 'other' geography, and generate alternative networks for mediating the fragments of community discussions, performances and culturally artistic events. Their deterritorialising investigations are transformative and disruptive as they interrogate the divisive implications of borders, nationalism and global economies.

The critical inspiration for Hüseyin Alptekin's *B-fact* projects came from Jules Verne's novel *Keraban le Tetu* (*Keraban the Stubborn*), which tells the story of Keraban, a Turkish tobacco merchant living in Istanbul. When Van Mitten, one of his agents from Rotterdam, arrives for a visit, Keraban invites him to dinner in Uskunder, a district on the Asiatic coast (the other side) of the Bosphorus. When they arrive on the shore they find out that the fee for crossing over the Bosphorus by boat has increased. Although it is a small amount, Keraban considers the charge unfair, and decides to take his guest to dinner by travelling all the way around the Black Sea coastline until they reach Uskunder. The rest of the novel is the story of the two friends' journey from Istanbul to Istanbul via the Black Sea coast, meeting many people and having many adventures.

Jules Verne wrote the novel at a time when life in the Ottoman Empire was overlaid by a cosmopolitan texture of cultures and languages. Today, the Black Sea region contains, or is contained within, a completely different set of cultural conditions. The West is perceived as a closer destination than the neighbouring countries. Communication within the Black Sea region seems to be more difficult than communication with the West. However, people from the Black Sea region and the Balkans are in constant motion. They buy, sell, trade, smuggle, marry and construct their own routes. Thus the map of the Black Sea is in constant flux, altered by big and small movements, individual and community decisions whereby, one by one, men and women take their destiny into their own hands and move, until *heimat* becomes where they are.

Current economic and global theories cannot fully explain these movements, yet it is evident that strong social forces are at work. What these movements signal is the necessity of rethinking the geographical construction of the Black Sea. Following the spirit of Keraban, a re-routing is required—one that refuses the established national boundaries set by political fault lines and entrenched by Western hegemony.

A major *B-fact* project, the *Bunker Research Group* (BRG) was Hüseyin Alptekin's contribution to the 2003 Tirana Biennale, a collaboration that included international artists from Sweden, Finland and Turkey. BRG entered the paranoid schizophrenic world of cold war Europe by working in the now defunct military defence installations on Albania's costal border. 600 000 concrete bunkers were constructed by the Enver Hoxha regime as a protection from the politically exaggerated threat to Albania from the west. Now obsolete, these minimalist architectural domelike structures were surveyed, documented and subjected to a rigorous social reinterpretation. Previously, in 2002, Hüseyin Alptekin had removed a bunker from the coastal town of Durres and installed it at the National Gallery of Tirana, but failure to meet bureaucratic requirements meant that the bunker was subsequently demolished. Undeterred, Hüseyin Alptekin persisted. The bunker was relocated to the courtyard of the National Gallery. It was subsequently covered by collaborating artist Kaija Kiuru with lace tablecloths produced by the artist or procured from Albanian and Finnish communities. Recoded and decontextualised, these obsolete bunkers of destruction were feminised and returned to the community irrevocably transformed. The BRG project is ongoing, with new displacements presented in Istanbul, Havana and Kassel.

Further *B-fact* projects include *A Paddle Trip Through the Baltic Sea, Danube and the Black Sea*, in which two Swedish artists, Love Enqvist and Martin Berling, undertook a journey using a kayak, with the intention of reaching Turkey by following the canal river systems and networks that intersect throughout Europe. Without ever setting foot in Europe, they engaged with the communities they met through their shared experiences of displacement. At the end of the three-month journey, the project concluded in Istanbul. This was a deterritorialising project that deliberately disrupted the notion of borders and represented the underside of globalisation. The dream of a completely fluid and passable world-space was perhaps the last utopia of the twentieth century. Nevertheless, borders of various kinds—conceptual, material, territorial—remain operative all around us. In contrast to some interpretations of globalisation, which consider the heightened volatility of cultural flows largely from a position of privilege in which those with wealth and power are able to move seamlessly across different territories, the experience of border crossing needs to be considered in terms of both fluidity and friction. The artistic projects to which I have referred reclaim the initiative of constructing art outside the institutional power structures of museums, government funding policies and objectives, white cube galleries, and dealer networks. They have located their practice outside the available spaces and extended the meaning of spatiality and temporality in contemporary art.

These projects have established new territories for artists. They are bound by difference, and rely on different relationships to the cultural industry. They enter uncharted territory and their laboratory is not understood in terms of scientific convention, but rather in terms of their transformative potential for change in the socioeconomic and political structures of globalism. These projects not only challenge the ability of the museum to consume and archive them, but more significantly, challenge the role and function of art spaces. They reveal the depths of the paradox in the cultural industry: We have yet to build institutions and art spaces for and of our present.

Standing Still

SIMRYN GILL

On various trips back to South-East Asia after the Asian economic collapse of 1997, I was struck by the growing number of rather ambitious development projects which were simply being abandoned before completion, and were slowly starting to crumble back into the damp and humid landscape. These remains were often just shells of what would have become large shopping centres or apartment blocks or private mansions or even mini-towns. They never reached a state of arrival or finish. The economic crash changed these fantasies of ultra-modernity into lonely ruins. From the future to the past without a present.

I started looking at these strange decaying giants in relation to the older abandoned buildings which seem to punctuate the towns and the countryside in Malaysia, where these photographs were all taken. These are empty and derelict buildings—houses, shops, hotels—which are mainly pre-independence (Malaysia became independent in 1950), though some are more recent. It's hard to know why they have been left to rot. Sometimes it's because they have a bad history, such as having been used during the war by the Japanese for the kinds of activities that can make places inconsolably haunted; sometimes it's because of family disputes about inheritance and such matters, but often they are left and allowed to fall apart simply because they are old.

I explored some of these places a few months ago while thinking about some new ideas. I had been approached by the Petronas Gallery in Kuala Lumpur to make a new work. This invitation was enticing because the gallery is located on the third floor of the Petronas Twin Towers, the structure that sits at the very heart of Malaysia's need to be-in-the-world; a building which had mushroomed out of exactly the same economic boom that created these derelict sites. The gallery staff were cautiously interested in the abandoned projects idea: they were not keen for me to wash dirty Malaysian linen in public, and it was clear that they did not want the work to travel out of the country.

To me this restriction is a very interesting proposition, but for another reason. We often hear calls from bureaucrats and patriots to show our countries abroad in a 'good light'. Unpacking this mild exhortation could offer some interesting challenges with respect to 'site specificity' and the nature of the portability of an experience of place. The abandoned buildings in the Malaysian countryside, because they are so tied into recent local history, offer powerful material through which to think about the complex contextualising layers of local knowledge, and what the nature of the translation might be when we try to export experience.

In my initial nosing around with my camera and tripod, I found the sites almost unphotographable. They are already so enclosed, so complete in their stories of unfulfilled fantasy and power, that the act of 'taking a picture' didn't seem to have anything to add to the presence of the sites. Yet I did make records of these crumbling places, maybe because I remember seeing some fragments from Smithson's *Planque Hotel* series of photographs in a book: a series of images of the entropy that so mesmerised Smithson—a hotel in Mexico in a perpetual state of construction and decay.

The question remains: whether, and how, I should do anything in these derelict sites? If I attempt to contain their presence in an art work, what sort of references will I filter this work through? What light will I show them in?

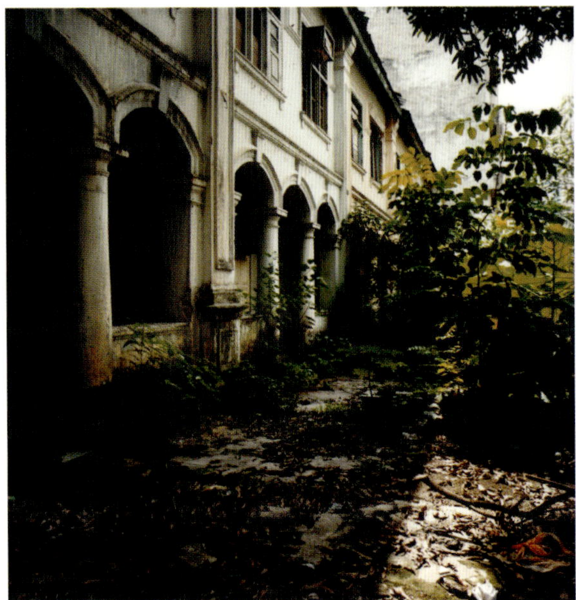

Simryn Gill, *Standing Still* (2000–2003), series of 117 photographs, type-c photographs 31.5cm × 31.5cm; courtesy of the artist.

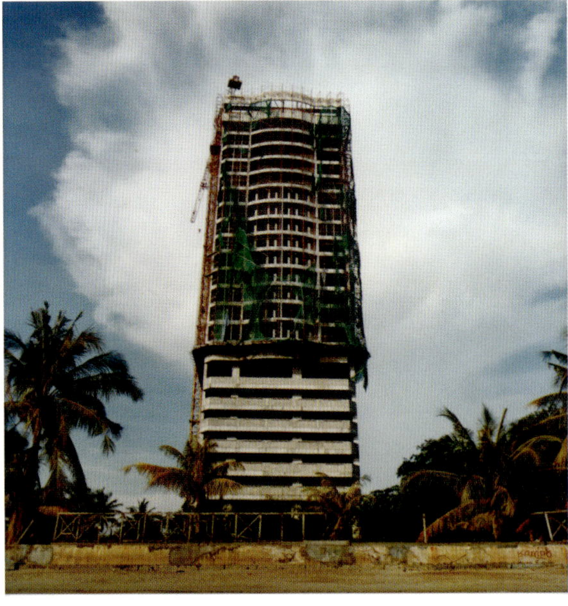

Simryn Gill, *Standing Still* (2000–2003), series of 117 photographs, type-c photographs 31.5cm × 31.5cm; courtesy of the artist.

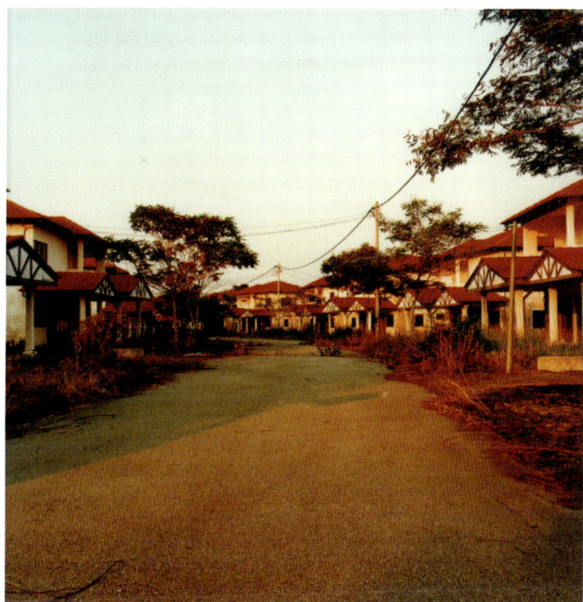

Simryn Gill, *Standing Still* (2000–2003), series of 117 photographs, type-c photographs 31.5cm × 31.5cm; courtesy of the artist.

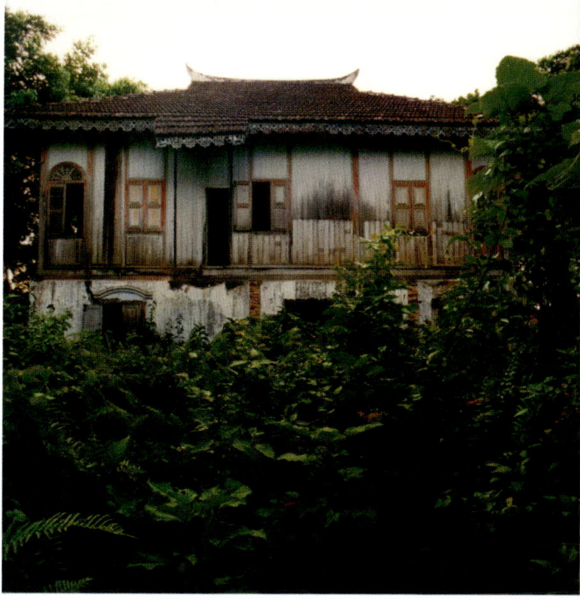

Simryn Gill, *Standing Still* (2000–2003), series of 117 photographs, type-c photographs 31.5cm × 31.5cm; courtesy of the artist.

Should I, perhaps, set the ruins against the eighteenth-century British fashion for classical and neoclassical ruins, which they built as follies for their monumental landscape gardens? And in that act should I suggest that these instances of the modern-in-ruins are the underpinnings of the culture of the global in the same way that the classical-in-ruins underpins the culture of Europe? Or could I approach them as places of the triumph of nature in levelling the residue of human activity, a play on the Ballardian fable that all things will go back to the bosom of the earth? Or perhaps these derelict places are most interesting as fuel for the rhetoric about the thinness and the superficiality of enactments of modernity in newly industrialised countries. In this version, modernity in these sites becomes unintentional parody, desolate mimicry of real or imagined arrival into the grace of capitalistic success—into postmodernity.

I could turn a cold documentary lens on these ruins, and make a moody film in an enigmatically suggestive science fiction style. Why did the inhabitants of this planet leave unexpectedly? What calamity prevented them from completing the construction of these towns and dwellings? Or I could photograph them in the all-knowing, cheery *National Geographic* manner—another place, another story, another aspect of the global village. Or perhaps I could make maquette likenesses of these never-finished structures out of tropical materials like bamboo and palm fronds, idealising their crumbling abandonment and the mismatch of the grandiosity of their intention with the geography of their placement. Monuments to natives who step beyond their place in the world.

Along the Passiac River banks were many minor monuments such as concrete abutments that supported the shoulders of a new highway in the process of being built. River Drive was in part bulldozed and in part intact. It was hard to tell the new highway from the old road; they were both confounded into a unitary chaos. Since it was Saturday, many machines were not working, and this caused them to resemble prehistoric creatures stuck in the mud, or, better, extinct machines—mechanical dinosaurs stripped of their skin. On the edge of this prehistoric Machine Age were pre- and post-World War Two suburban houses. The houses mirrored themselves into colorlessness. A group of children were throwing rocks at each other near a ditch. 'From now on you're not going to come to our hideout. And I mean it!' said a little blonde girl who had been hit with a rock.

…

Across the river in Rutherford one could hear the faint voice of a PA system and the weak cheers of a crowd at a football game. Actually the landscape was no landscape, but 'a particular kind of heliotype' (Nabokov), a kind of self-destroying postcard world of failed immortality and oppressive grandeur. I had been wandering in a moving picture that I couldn't quite picture, but just as I became perplexed, I saw a green sign that explained everything:

YOUR HIGHWAY TAXES AT WORK

Federal Highway Trust Funds 2,867,000	US Dept. of Commerce Bureau of Public Roads 2,867,000

New Jersey State Highway Dept.

The zero panorama seemed to contain ruins in reverse, that is—all the new construction that would eventually be built. This is the opposite of the 'romantic ruin' because the buildings don't fall into ruin after they are built but rather rise into ruin before they are built. This anti-romantic mise-en-scène suggests the discredited idea of time and many other 'out of date' things. But the suburbs exist without a rational past and without the 'big events' of history. Oh, maybe there are a few statues, a legend, a couple of curios, but no past—just what passes for a future.

—Robert Smithson

'A Tour of The Monuments of Passaic, New Jersey'

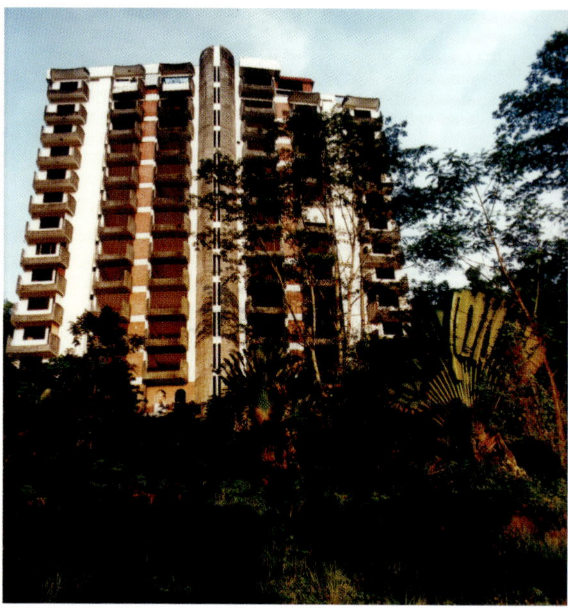

Simryn Gill, *Standing Still* (2000–2003), series of 117 photographs, type-c photographs 31.5cm × 31.5cm; courtesy of the artist.

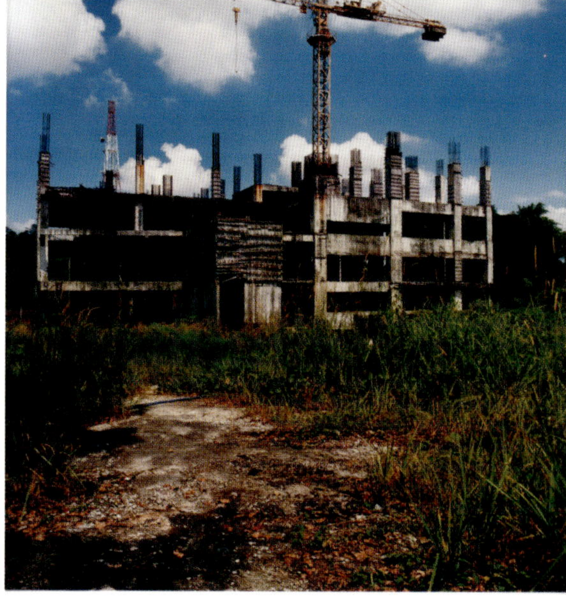

Simryn Gill, *Standing Still* (2000–2003), series of 117 photographs, type-c photographs 31.5cm × 31.5cm; courtesy of the artist.

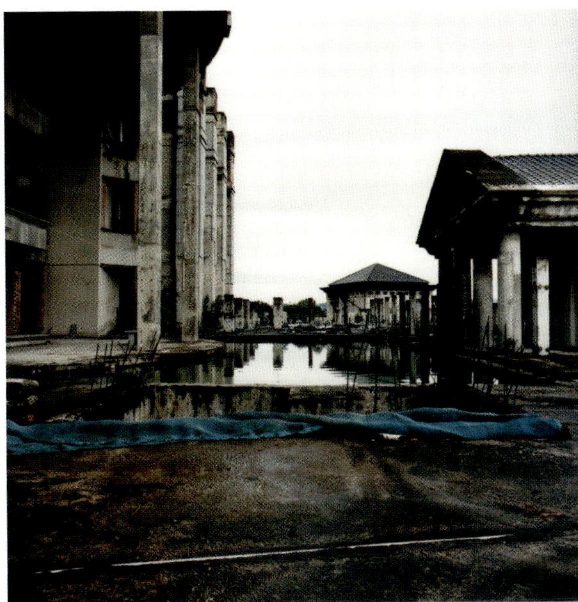

Simryn Gill, *Standing Still* (2000–2003), series of 117 photographs, type-c photographs 31.5cm × 31.5cm; courtesy of the artist.

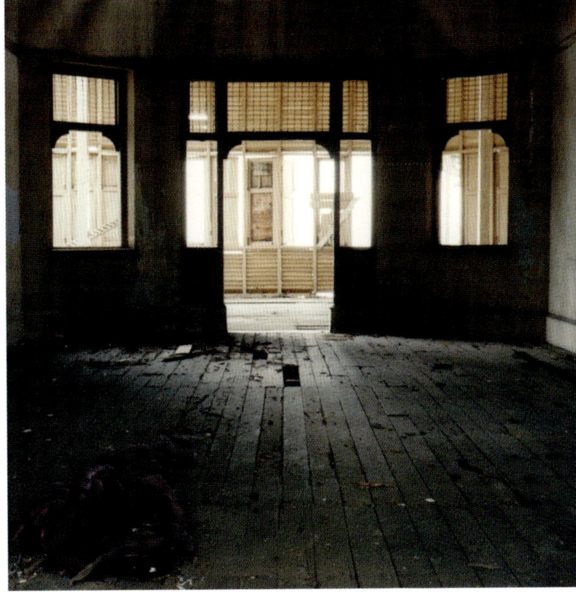

Simryn Gill, *Standing Still* (2000–2003), series of 117 photographs, type-c photographs 31.5cm × 31.5cm; courtesy of the artist.

He had commandeered the Ritz the day after their arrival, eager to exchange his cramped cabin among the laboratory benches at the testing station for the huge, high-ceilinged state-rooms of the deserted hotel. Already he accepted the lavish brocaded furniture and the bronze art nouveau statuary in the corridor niches as a natural background to his existence, savouring the subtle atmosphere of melancholy that surrounded these last vestiges of a level of civilisation now virtually vanished for ever. Too many of the other buildings around the lagoon had long since slipped and slid away below the silt, revealing their gimcrack origins, and the Ritz now stood in splendid isolation on the west shore, even the rich blue moulds sprouting from the carpet added to its 19th-century dignity.

The suite had originally been designed for a Milanese financier, and was lavishly furnished and engineered … Although it had been unoccupied for ten years little dust had collected over the mantelpieces and gilt end-tables, and the triptych of photographic portraits on the crocodile skin desk—financier, financier and sleek well-fed family, financier and even sleeker fifty-story office block— revealed scarcely a blemish …

A giant Anopheles mosquito, the size of a dragon-fly, spat through the air past his face, then dived down towards the floating jetty where Kerans' catamaran was moored. The sun was still hidden behind the vegetation on the eastern side of the lagoon, but the mounting heat was bringing huge predatory insects out of their lairs all over the moss-covered surface of the hotel. Kerans was reluctant to leave the balcony and retreat behind the wire mesh enclosure. In the early morning light a strange mournful beauty hung over the lagoon; the sombre green-black fronds of the gymnosperms, intruders from the Triassic past, and half-submerged white-faced buildings of the twentieth century reflected together in the dark mirror of the water, the two interlocking worlds apparently suspended at some junction in time, the illusion momentarily broken when a giant water-spider cleft the oily surface a hundred yards away.

—J. G. Ballard

The Drowned World

The solitude of the walk, the emptiness of that stretch of downs, enabled me to surrender to my way of looking, to indulge my linguistic or historical fantasies; and enabled me, at the same time, to shed the nerves of being a stranger in England. Accident—the shape of the field, perhaps, the alignment of paths and modern roads, the needs of the military—had isolated this little region; and I had this historical part of England to myself when I went walking.

Daily I walked in the wide grassy way between the flint slopes, past the chalk valleys rubbed white and looking sometimes like a Himalayan valley strewn in mid-summer with old gritted snow. Daily I saw the mounds that had been raised so many centuries before. The number of these mounds! They lay all around. From a certain height they were outlined against the sky and looked like pimples on the land. In the beginning I liked to tramp over the mounds that were more or less on my walk. The grass on these mounds was coarse; it was long-bladed, pale in colour and grew in ankle turning tufts or clumps. The trees where they existed were wind-beaten and stunted.

I picked my way up and down and around each mound; I wanted in those early days to leave no accessible mound unlooked at, feeling that If I looked hard enough and long enough I might arrive, not at an understanding of the religious mystery, but at an appreciation of the labour.

Daily I walked in the wide grassy way—perhaps in the old days a processional way. Daily I climbed up from the bottom of the valley to the crest of the way and the view: the stone circles directly ahead, down below, but still far away: grey against green and sometimes lit up by the sun. Going up the grassy way (and though willing to admit that the true path might have been elsewhere) I never ceased to imagine myself a man of those bygone times, climbing up to have this confirmation that all was well with the world.

...

And in spite of [the] crowd and the highway and the artillery ranges (with their fluorescent and semi-luminous targets), my sense of antiquity, my feeling for the age of the earth and the oldness of man's possession of it was always

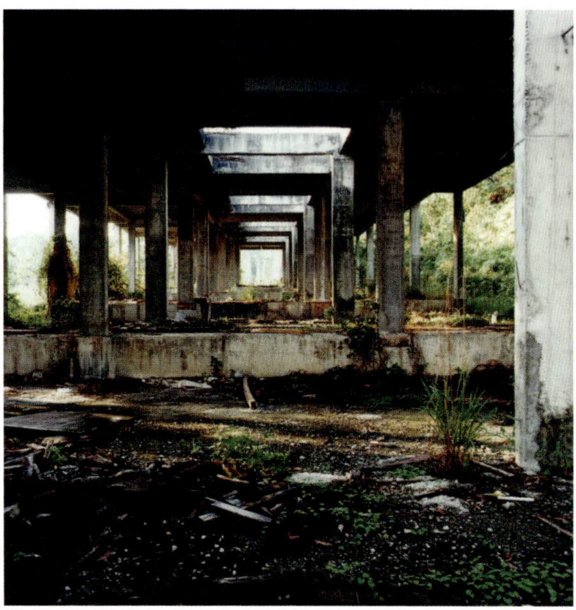

Simryn Gill, *Standing Still*
(2000–2003),
series of 117 photographs,
type-c photographs
31.5cm × 31.5cm;
courtesy of the artist.

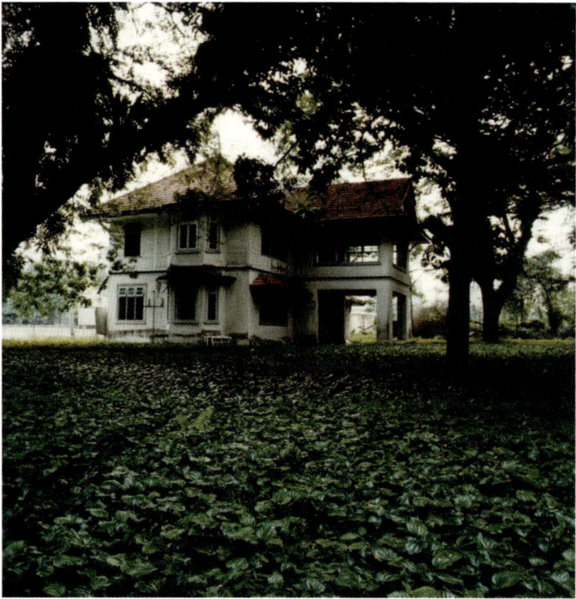

Simryn Gill, *Standing Still*
(2000–2003),
series of 117 photographs,
type-c photographs
31.5cm × 31.5cm;
courtesy of the artist.

with me. A vast scarred burial ground, bounded by the sky—of what activity these barrows and tumuli spoke, what numbers, what organisation, what busyness in these now virtually empty downs! The sense of antiquity gave another scale to the activities around one. But at the same time—from this height, and with that wide view—there was a feeling of continuity.

—V. S. Naipaul

   The Enigma of Arrival

He was known as the Ven. Luong Chun, he said, and he had lived on the premises of Angkor Wat most of his life. He had entered the monastery at Angkor Wat in his adolescence, and he remembered a time when the layout of the temple grounds was quite different. At the time a pagoda sat directly in front of the colonnaded galleries of the temple (it can be seen clearly in turn of the century photographs—an untidy, thatched-roofed structure, flanking the great flagstoned causeway). His grandfather, who had spent some time in the monastery too, had told him the story of how the pagoda came to be moved.

The French archaeologists who were restoring Angkor Wat had decided that the pagoda had to go: an actual, functioning shrine had no place in their pristine vision of the temple. They wanted it to be shunted off the premises altogether, but the monks had resisted. There had been a Buddhist monastery within Angkor for centuries and they could not conceive of abandoning the site altogether.

Eventually the seniormost monk had led a delegation to the then ruler of Cambodia, King Monivong ... At the King's intercession the monks were allowed to remain within Angkor Wat, but in purdah, as it were—on the condition that they moved the pagoda off its old site and rebuilt it at a suitable distance.

The Ven. Luong Chun had himself worked for the French archaeologists as a boy. Along with hundreds of others, he had been hired to crush stones from Angkor Wat and Angkor Thom, so the roads could be built to connect the monuments to Siem Reap.

The Ven. Luong Chun was living in Angkor Wat in April 1975 when the Khmer Rouge seized power. There were about four hundred monks in the monastery: several of them were killed, some right on the threshold of the pagoda. He, along with the others, was taken away to a work camp some distance away. He was stripped of his monk's robes which were cut up and made into trousers, and he spent the three years of the 'Pol Pot Time' working in the ricefields.

In January 1979, after the Khmer Rouge had been driven from power by the Vietnamese invasion, it was announced at his work camp that Angkor Wat was badly in need of cleaning and people who were familiar with it were welcome to go back. He set off for the temple soon afterwards, and for the next two years he and a few other monks tried to clear the monuments as best they could.

In tending the temple during that time the Ven. Luong Chun was doing what monks like him had done for centuries: there is evidence that monks continued to live in Angkor Wat even after the Angkorian period, when the complex fell into general decline. Thus the most powerful of the myths that surround Angkor—the legend of its accidental discovery by the nineteenth-century French explorer Henri Mouhot—is no more and no less true then any of the others inscribed upon the temple. For if it is true that Angkor was already well-known to the Buddhist Sangha and to the nobility of Cambodia and Thailand—not as a fetish, perhaps, but in the quotidian way in which medieval monuments are usually absorbed into living history—it is also true that Mouhot and the French did indeed make a discovery. They discovered a mirror for themselves: of the imperial state, l'État, in all its power and splendour.

—Amitav Ghosh
 'Stories in Stones'

Borders: The Other Side of Globalisation

MULTIPLICITY

The dream of a completely fluid and passable world-space may be the last utopia of the twentieth century. The smooth quality supposedly inherent to contemporary space, though, seems to fail upon a closer look at the territory. One of the immediate results of global interconnections and movements appears to be a proliferation of borders, security systems, checkpoints, physical and virtual frontiers. This phenomenon can be observed both at the micro-level of our surroundings and on the macro-scale of global flows. Borders are, in fact, all around us. They are both conventional and geographical, abstract and real, ordinary and controversial. An encompassing view of this combination of flows (of people, goods, ideas …) and restrictions on a given territory unfolds the complexity of both individual and collective identities that are, at the same time, constructed and diffracted by the experience of border-crossing.

BORDER DEVICES

Multiplicity, together with Domus Academy, Milan and Berlage Institute, Rotterdam, undertook a research project to detect this proliferation of border devices in the Euro-Mediterranean context.

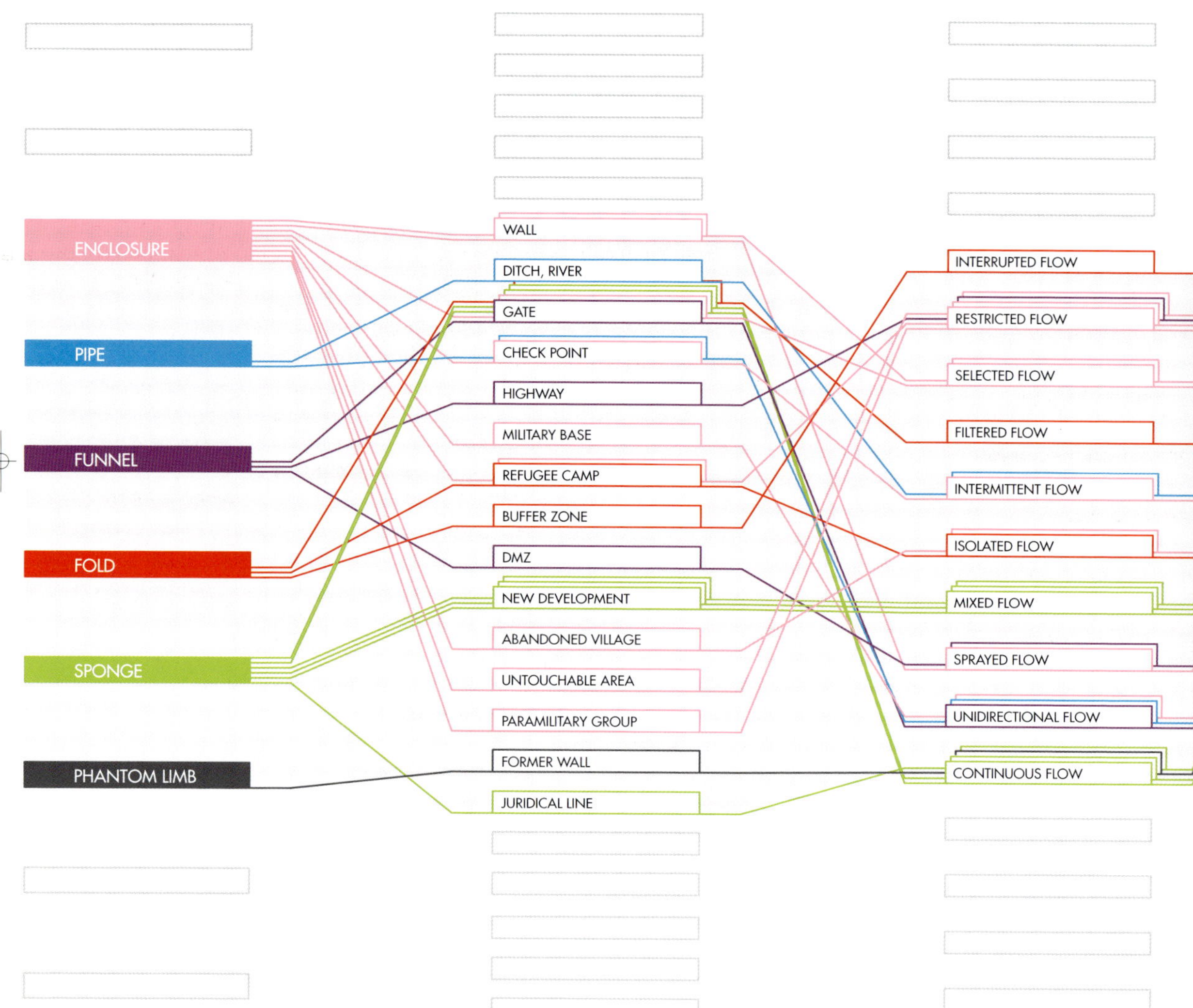

Multiplicity, *Border Device(s): the Matrix of Borders* (2003),
printed wall-paper; courtesy of Multiplicity.

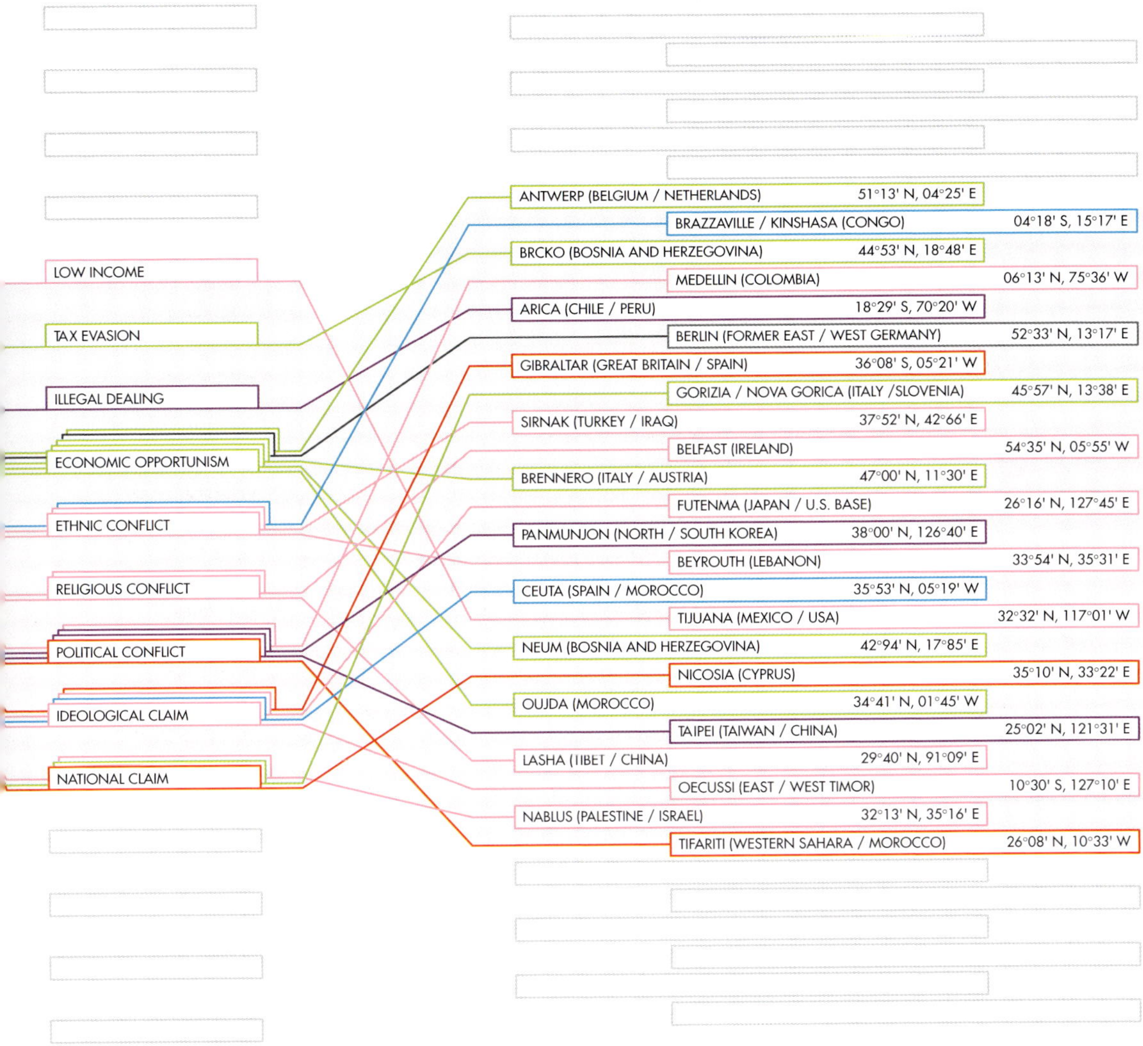

LOW INCOME

TAX EVASION

ILLEGAL DEALING

ECONOMIC OPPORTUNISM

ETHNIC CONFLICT

RELIGIOUS CONFLICT

POLITICAL CONFLICT

IDEOLOGICAL CLAIM

NATIONAL CLAIM

ANTWERP (BELGIUM / NETHERLANDS)   51°13' N, 04°25' E
BRAZZAVILLE / KINSHASA (CONGO)   04°18' S, 15°17' E
BRCKO (BOSNIA AND HERZEGOVINA)   44°53' N, 18°48' E
MEDELLIN (COLOMBIA)   06°13' N, 75°36' W
ARICA (CHILE / PERU)   18°29' S, 70°20' W
BERLIN (FORMER EAST / WEST GERMANY)   52°33' N, 13°17' E
GIBRALTAR (GREAT BRITAIN / SPAIN)   36°08' S, 05°21' W
GORIZIA / NOVA GORICA (ITALY /SLOVENIA)   45°57' N, 13°38' E
SIRNAK (TURKEY / IRAQ)   37°52' N, 42°66' E
BELFAST (IRELAND)   54°35' N, 05°55' W
BRENNERO (ITALY / AUSTRIA)   47°00' N, 11°30' E
FUTENMA (JAPAN / U.S. BASE)   26°16' N, 127°45' E
PANMUNJON (NORTH / SOUTH KOREA)   38°00' N, 126°40' E
BEYROUTH (LEBANON)   33°54' N, 35°31' E
CEUTA (SPAIN / MOROCCO)   35°53' N, 05°19' W
TIJUANA (MEXICO / USA)   32°32' N, 117°01' W
NEUM (BOSNIA AND HERZEGOVINA)   42°94' N, 17°85' E
NICOSIA (CYPRUS)   35°10' N, 33°22' E
OUJDA (MOROCCO)   34°41' N, 01°45' W
TAIPEI (TAIWAN / CHINA)   25°02' N, 121°31' E
LASHA (TIBET / CHINA)   29°40' N, 91°09' E
OECUSSI (EAST / WEST TIMOR)   10°30' S, 127°10' E
NABLUS (PALESTINE / ISRAEL)   32°13' N, 35°16' E
TIFARITI (WESTERN SAHARA / MOROCCO)   26°08' N, 10°33' W

The research is a part of the larger *Solid Sea* project (Kassel-Documenta XI 2002, Rotterdam Film Festival 2003, Vienna–Generali Foundation 2003) and was presented at the Venice Biennale (within the Utopia Station space, June–November 2003) and at the Musée d'Art Moderne de Paris (within the *Déplacements* exhibition, July 2003).

THE ROAD MAP

The territories of the West Bank are almost completely covered with enclosures and fences. They are war zone barriers, bypass roads, military zones for the Israeli army, Palestinian villages and cities, refugee camps, areas with no jurisdiction, networks of infrastructures. They are all arranged on top of each other like a giant web: a kaleidoscope of enclosures and borders impossible to reduce into two main areas. The West Bank represents the death knell to any dream of a symmetrical division and to any belief in a unique border.

1. BORDERS: THE OTHER SIDE OF GLOBALISATION

FLOW AND/OR BOUNDARIES

A widespread interpretation of the processes of globalisation tells us that the world is ever more interconnected, underpinned by the profit mechanisms of the multinationals and characterised by a cross-border flow of humanity, goods and information. It is a world where interpersonal relations and exchanges seem to permeate and redraw not only the subdivision of nation-states but even reach down to local levels. These subdivisions seem to transform themselves—especially in the richer countries—into large networks in which social and cultural divions are chipped away until they 'melt' into a mass of individuals, swallowing up minority and group identities.

Some recent social commentary has identified an apparent and pervasive 'fluidity' in social and cultural relations found in modern society—especially in Europe—and have presented the view of a 'smooth' geopolitical map. In this map the social substrata and the hierarchical superstructure are reduced and the individual takes its place over and above the whole social organisation. Many such views on the importance of population flows in the contemporary world are verified by studies in architecture, town planning and geography. These are disciplines that should keep their finger on the pulse of living conditions in the urban context, but often seem more interested in studying the flux and flow rather than the locally felt friction.

Although these different, but ultimately convergent, interpretations are symbolically persuasive in their message about 'flow' in the contemporary world, they tend to observe the movements that have been deemed media-worthy and are in the public eye. A careful study of our surroundings, however, shows a contrasting phenomenon. Wherever one looks, living spaces today offer a proliferation of borders, walls, fences, thresholds, signposted areas, security systems and checkpoints, virtual frontiers, specialised zones, protected areas and areas under control. The multiplication of fences and sub-system controls (which in the contemporary world take on many different and often changing appearances) is an inevitable if not surprising outcome of any study and mapping of territory.

As much as this proliferation of walls and borders can and should be seen as the result of pervasive population flow, their heterogeneous nature shows that the two processes—population flows and confinements—are not simply opposing or complementary. Flows and confinements are not two extremes of the same process of a territory's economic and social adaptation; they are not the opposites of an evolutionary phase in our society. From a study of the infinite restrictions that space places on an uncontrolled flow of population into a particular territory, and the social relations that follow it, a kaleidoscope of boundary devices can be called up that has nothing to do with the mirroring of geographical fluctuations in population or even with the traditional subdividing of the modern map into large political, social and cultural areas.

With *Border Devices,* we wish to develop a new hypothesis based on a careful study of geographical boundaries, one which gives a different representation of the world and of our societies. Our hypothesis is one that can read the proliferation of fences and signposted areas (the controversial as well as the ordinary ones) as a reflection of the many highly charged instances of identity and protection that explode every day between groups in our multifaceted societies. It is one that can reveal the densely differentiated and kaleidoscopic nature of our contemporary societies. On this hypothesis, our local territories can be interpreted as important metaphors for the whole of society. The research presents the numerous studies in the last few years that have observed the network of population influx, alongside a careful study of boundaries and their genealogical heritage, which can provide a clearer picture of what has been happening around us.

THE WORLD LABORATORY

The territories that make up the State of Israel and the area under the governing authority of the Palestinians are the most stirring examples of conflict over traditional and historical precepts. This is a conflict that the media and international onlookers tend to describe as if it were absolutely symmetrical. Without considering interpretations of imbalances and guilt, it is basically presented as a conflict that separates two people, two territories and two traditions; a conflict generated by the absence of agreements that could provide territorial symmetry.

The fact that this is perceived as an 'imperfect symmetry' (by the people who live in this part of the world as well as by international observers) is shown by the numerous proposals to end the conflict. These proposals seek to rationalise and harmonise the imperfect symmetry. One significant proposal came from Abraham Yehoshua, who called for the construction of a wall following the unilateral withdrawal of the Israeli forces from the Gaza Strip and the West Bank. From Yehoshua's proposal one can see the idea of a utopia in two phases: the construction of one shared borderline that serves to distinguish the two people as a necessary preliminary to eventual cohabitation,

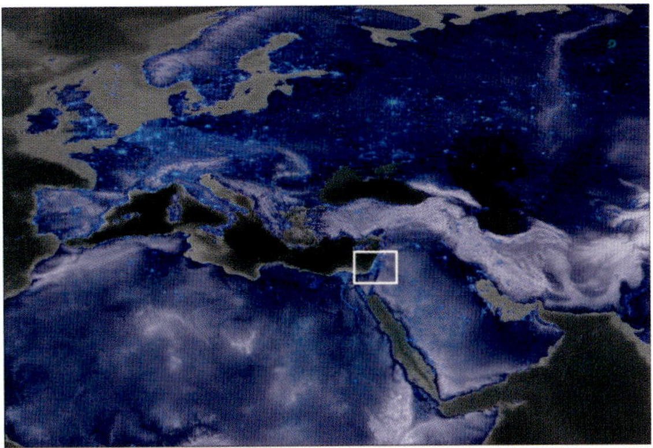

Multiplicity, *Solid Sea Case 03—the Road Map* (2003), printed wall-paper; courtesy of Multiplicity.

with the spatial separation a precondition to any political integration.

However, a close observation of these territories shows us something different. The maps produced by the Israeli architects Eyal Weizman and Rafi Segal in the West Bank show a territory where it is impossible to recognise, let alone to imagine, one demarcation line. It shows us an area almost completely covered with fences. Fences are falling over each other, apparently haphazardly. There are war zone barriers, bypass roads that join them, military zones for the Israeli army, Palestinian villages and cities, refugee camps, areas that have no jurisdiction. It is a network of infrastructures, all juxtaposed on top of each other like a giant web.

Rather than revealing the outcome of military control in the territories of the Gaza Strip and the West Bank, the kaleidoscope of fences and borders shown on the Weizman and Segal maps instead depicts a polyarchic territory, impossible to reduce into two areas—not least because of the bordered areas' resistance to being swallowed up into one or other of the two demarcated areas.

The West Bank represents the death knell to any dream of a symmetrical division and to any belief in a utopia based on one unique border. But it

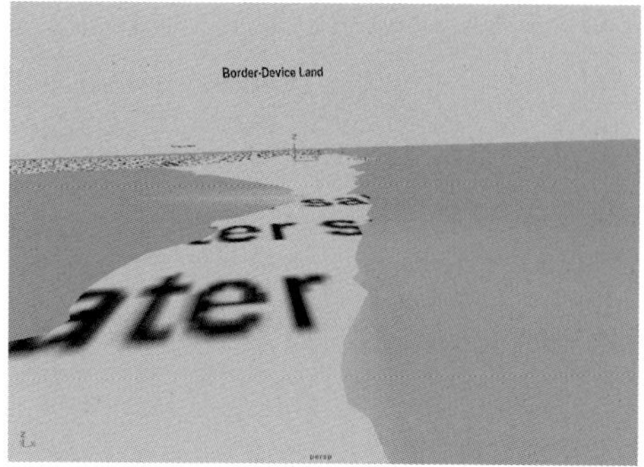

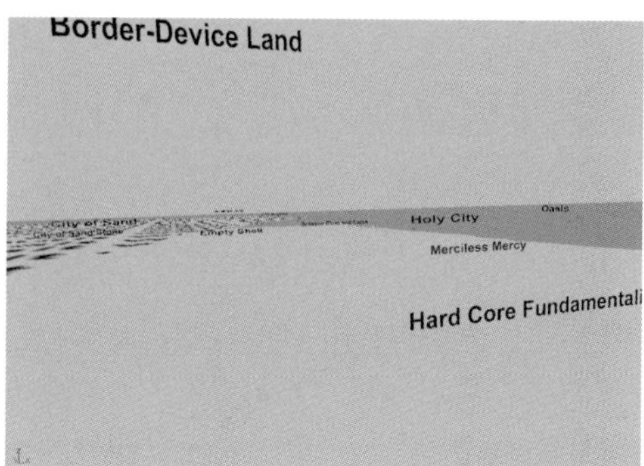

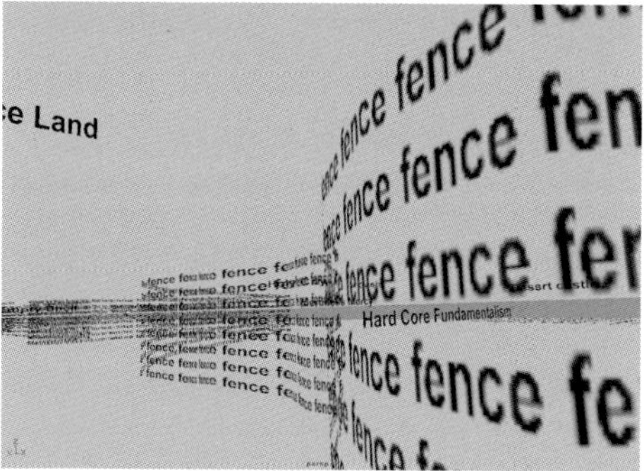

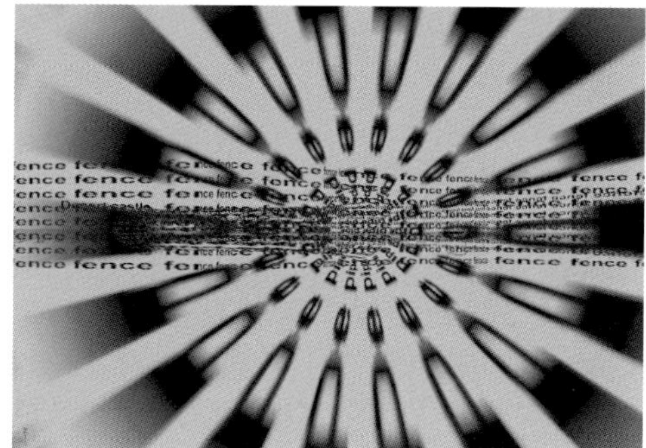

Above and opposite: Multiplicity, *Borderdevice(s): Border Device Land* (2003), animated video graphics; courtesy of Multiplicity.

does open the way to a second, concrete utopia. Edward Said, a Palestinian intellectual, has best expressed this idea in the last few years. He has never ceased to underline the necessity of cohabitation between the two peoples. Despite their innumerable ethnic, cultural and religious differences, there is the need for reciprocal co-operation within the same territory, including in the area of economic production. He insists that the idea of one state is inevitable, with no internal boundary line and no small and separate principalities, and argues that the territory is capable of containing at least eight different populations in a micro-experiment in new forms of cohabitation.

If Yehoshua's utopia calls for an integration and a reduction of the differences but within two symmetrical, territorially separate spheres, Said's utopia

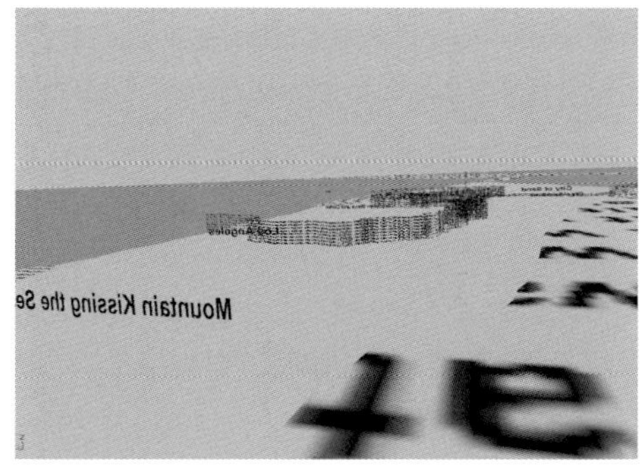

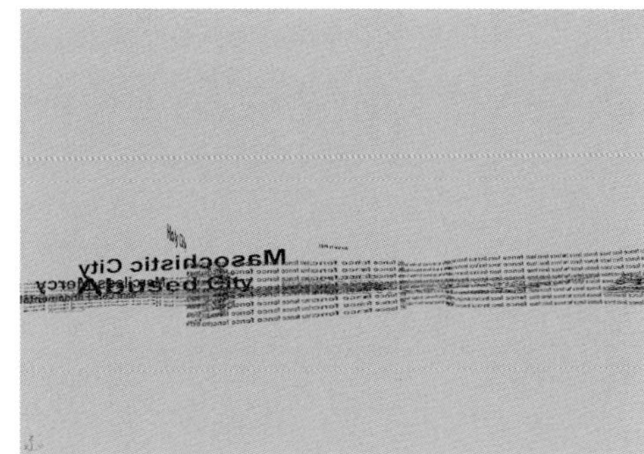

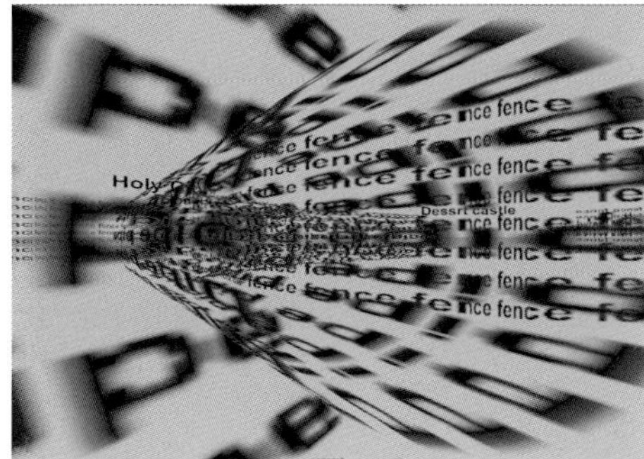

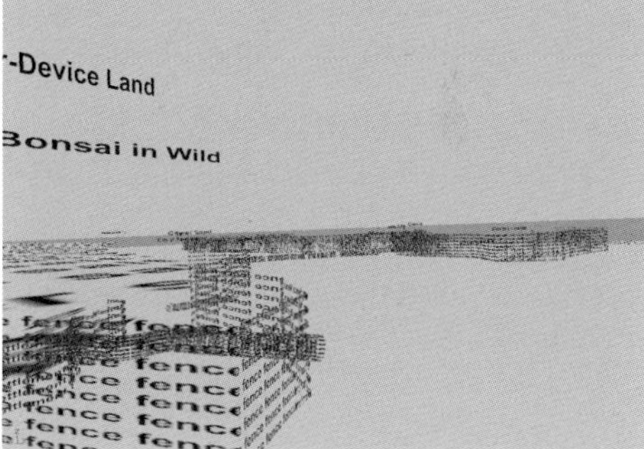

suggests, instead, that the kaleidoscopic character of the area should be accepted as a precondition, and that heterogeneity should be preserved. But the 'space' between these two utopias—in a certain way equally cynical and totalitarian in their pronouncements—is extreme, and today completely empty. It is the gap into which the political onlookers and negotiators have fallen in their incapacity to escape the rhetoric of symmetry; their inability to go beyond a solution that insists on stability based on equal division of territory between the two sides. It is an empty space literally, too, given that we do not have a geographical map showing the existing situation within the territory in question. It is this empty space that *Border Devices* examines—an empty space which, even though it is at the centre of world attention, is invisible and unknown.

THE MEDITERRANEAN

The tragedies continue, the conflicts, the prevarications, the difficult attempts at peace. All that is happening in the Palestinian territories and in the State of Israel can be linked to an inescapable geopolitical and historical root belonging to the people who inhabit the land. But it can be noted, too, that this conflict is also connected to the major events of this 'brief century' in Europe and the world: the wars, the persecution of the Jews, the eclipse of the bipolar balance of world power, the new international relations that are redefining the geopolitical world map. Less evident—and less observed—are the tensions and the analogies that link the recent evolution in the Middle East with the geopolitical processes taking place in the Mediterranean basin. Many events lead us to think that a major change is before us on both the geographical and political fronts of this large, fluid continent and its borders. The image of the Mediterranean as a 'cradle' of civilisation where different languages, religions and traditions meet in reciprocal respect and in a commonly acknowledged physical geography; the idea that it is a world where diversity has a certain ease thanks to solid, historical collective images (in the culture and the memory of coastal populations with a 'sea in common', and common flora and fauna), today seems to be fraught with tensions. The Mediterranean has become the scene of a growing number of networks of channels through which flow a steady stream of humanity and goods.

The growing importance of these channels suggest quite a different picture from that of old. The common sea, with its courses and trajectories, is becoming top-heavy and grinding to a halt, from both a geographical and a purely functional viewpoint. The coastal points of passage, which have become very real funnels of population and mercantile flow (for example, clandestine immigration, tourism linked to cruise ships, and military purposes), give these trajectories a rigid, 'sealed' character. The many varied and changing populations that exist on the borders or on the communal sea are forced to

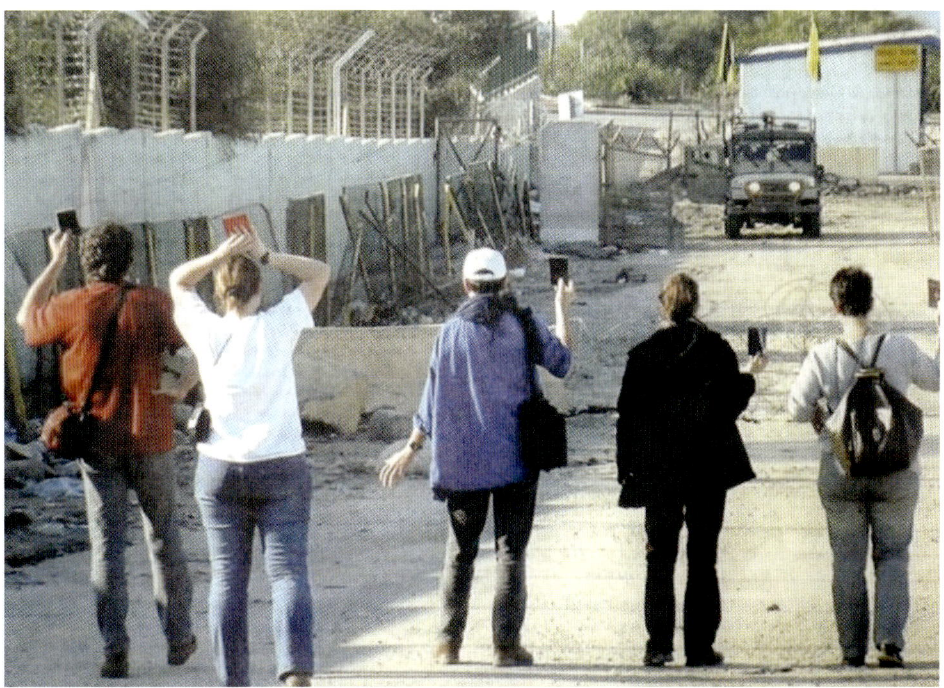

Multiplicity, *The Road Map—Palestinian Traveller*
Video: Checkpoint (2003), video; courtesy
of Multiplicity.

accept a type of 'mask', a schematic and pre-conditioned identity: the fisherman, the clandestine immigrant, the soldiers, the sailor, the tourist. The fact that each of these masks leads back to a rigid and non-interconnecting system of channels and courses, and the fact that these often use common sea-paths but at different levels or at different moments of the day, and are invisible to each other, lead us to conclude that the Mediterranean is undergoing a certain 'solidification'.

In its new 'solid' capacity it is interwoven with a series of networks, specialised and non-communicable pipes, and surrounded by a ring of funnels. It is a continent where differences do not have a chance to express or compare themselves but are rather shoved to the background and simplified. And it is a place where rigid border definitions prevail over the permeable internal flow. In southern Sicily or along the Pugliese coast, in Croatia, in Cyprus and along the Turkish and Lebanese coasts, in Alexandria and in Gibraltar, events confirm this transformation and suggest some important analogies with the Israeli–Palestinian conflict. They are analogies that this international seminar intends to examine and verify.

2. BORDER DEVICES: A DESCRIPTION

Borders, buffer zones, walls, control systems, protected areas: you only have to leave your house or watch the news to realise that the space around us ripples with boundaries. Our lives are marked by a succession of badges, passwords, entry and identification codes. These boundaries are another face of globalisation, framing the world's flow of individuals, goods and information. They proliferate to defend privileges and customs; they are used to control territories and to regulate cultural and language exchanges. For this reason, boundaries today are not merely lines or walls.

Some boundaries are like **FUNNELS**[1] that channel disorderly flows of individuals and objects to a place—along a coast or border—as in the case of the boats that carry the immigrants between the two sides of the Mediterranean. Others seem to be impenetrable **PIPES**[2], such as the highways that cross Israel and Palestine. There are boundaries that emerge between the **FOLDS**[3] of two territories in conflict, such as the strip of desert cutting through the middle of Nicosia; but also boundaries which, like **SPONGES**[4], attract populations and investment to create new communities. Like **PHANTOM LIMBS**[5], other boundaries continue to function even when they no longer exist.

But above all, everywhere in the world, there are **ENCLOSURES**[6], made of barbed wire or concrete, or mobile like those which, for different reasons, isolate from the rest of the world the inhabitants of the cruising ships *Odessa* and *The World Residensea*.

Boundaries are the sensors of contemporary world dynamics. They proliferate everywhere, but in some parts of our world, they become capable of governing our daily life.

Like dynamic 'devices,' borders vibrate with the energies and resistance that drive current history for the better and not just for the worse.

3. SOLID SEA 2003: THE ROAD MAP

The territories of Israel and Palestine are, in these days, a laboratory of the world. This is a region where, in a few acres, an incredible variety of borders, enclosures, fences, checkpoints and controlled corridors are concentrated.

On 13 and 14 January 2003 we tried to measure, with our EU passports, the density of border devices in the surrounding area of Jerusalem.

On 13 January we travelled along with a person with an Israeli passport from the colony of Kiriat Arba to the colony of Kudmin. The following day, we travelled along with a person with a Palestinian passport from the city of Hebron to the city of Nablus.

The two routes both start and end in the same latitude; at some points they overlap.

Their travelling times, though, are profoundly different.

To move between the two latitudes, the Israeli traveller took around one hour, while the Palestinian took five and half hours.

The West Bank territories are divided into three different zones:

ZONE A: under Palestinian Authority military and administrative control. It includes most Palestinian cities.

ZONE B: under Israeli military control, but under Palestinian Authority administrative control. It mostly includes Palestinian villages.

ZONE C: under Israeli military and administrative control. It includes most Israeli colonies.

This partition produced a leopard-skin-like territory, where the three zones

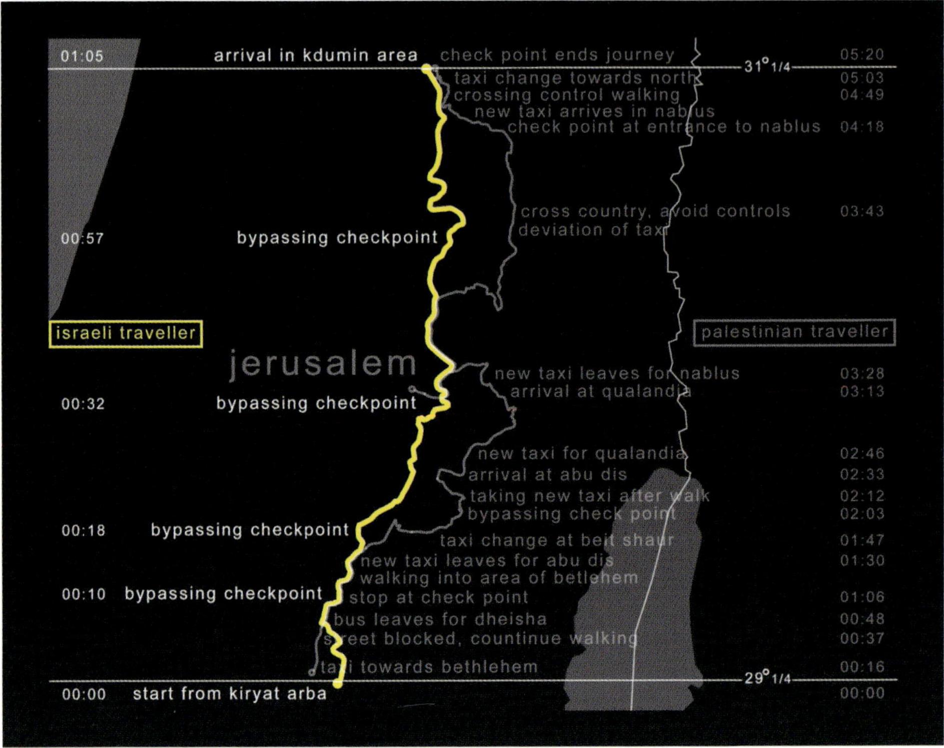

Multiplicity, *The Road Map—Israeli Traveller Route* (2003),
video graphics; courtesy of Multiplicity.

alternate without any apparent logic.

The different travelling times for the two routes are due to the fact that
to move from one settlement to another—from a Zone C to another Zone C—
Israeli travellers can use the so-called bypass roads, that is, highways, often
in tunnels or elevated, which link the colonies and bypass Palestinian villages.

On the other hand, Palestinian travellers who want to move from one city
in Zone A to another city in a different Zone A must pass through B or C Zones
which are under Israeli military control, crossing a number of permanent and
temporary checkpoints—or trying to avoid them. The checkpoints, which are

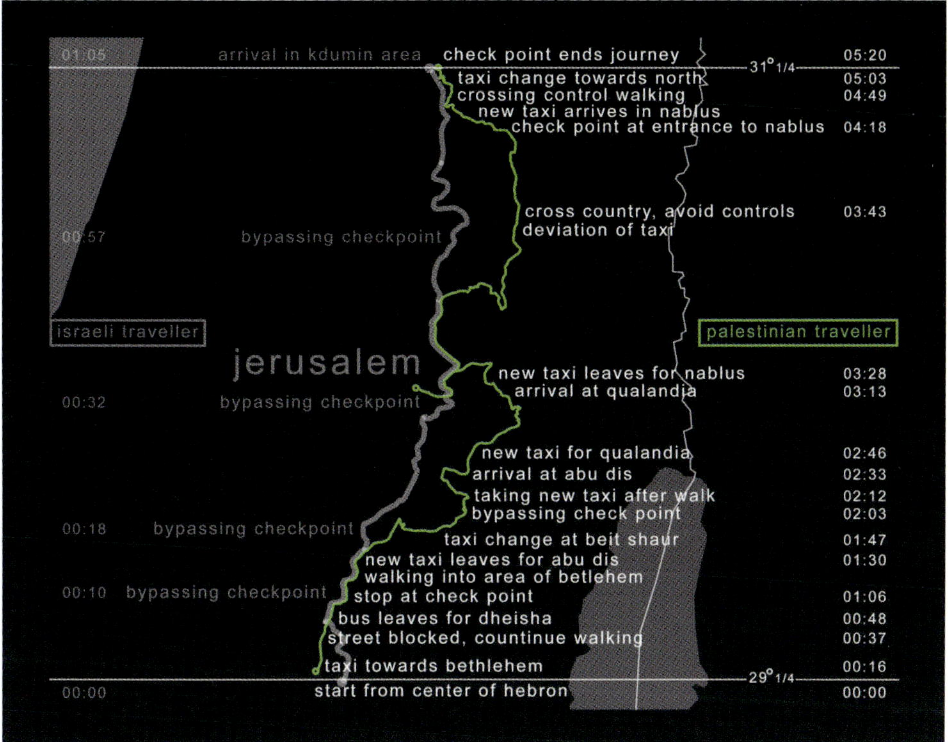

Multiplicity, *The Road Map—Palestinian Traveller Route* (2003),
video graphics; courtesy of Multiplicity.

situated along the 'Green Line' that runs between Israel and the West Bank,
as well as on the edges of East Jerusalem, cannot be crossed by those who
have a 'travel document' issued by the Palestinian Authority, unless they are
also provided with a special permission issued by the Israeli government.
Other checkpoints are activated and removed on a daily basis, according to
Israeli government security guidelines.

NOTES

1   **FUNNELS** are boundaries that gather and select different and dispersed flows within a circumscribed threshold. They normally channel a flow from one side of a fence to the other, selecting elements and giving direction. Often the diameter or control of the funnel defines its permeability. Control can be either unilateral or bilateral.

2   **PIPES** are cylindrical surfaces surrounding a flow (of people, goods, information …). Entry and exit are normally located at the extreme ends of the pipe. Control can be either unilateral or bilateral.

3   **FOLDS** (or sacks) are surfaces which pop up from the doubling up of a principal line and which take on a 'third' nature. They are, in a certain way, 'other' than the two spheres separated by the principal boundary line. They are no-man's-lands, interstitial or residual spaces, characterised by a void condition. The folds are controlled either by a neutral third party or by nobody.

4   **SPONGES** are border devices generated around a former border, attracting flows. People, goods, buildings and capitals gather along a borderline, often producing a linear environment. This is a pregnant, double borderline.

5   **PHANTOM LIMBS** are borders that continue to serve even after they physically disappear. The memory and enduring presence of a former situation often regenerates a border. None of the parties originally separated by the old border control the 'phantom limb'.

6   **ENCLOSURES** are encircled environments that host within them groups of individuals or systems of activity. They imply protection of what is inside the enclosure and exclusion of what is outside. The control of the perimeter-border is often unilateral.

Surveillance, Identity and Historical Memory in Ivan Sen's Beneath Clouds

TONY BIRCH

Ivan Sen's 2002 debut feature film *Beneath Clouds*[1] utilises the highway to interrogate the state of race relations between indigenous and non-indigenous Australia. The two central characters of the film, Lena (Danielle Hall) and Vaughan (Damian Pitt), walk the roads of rural New South Wales and head toward the metropolis of Sydney in search of 'home'. In the course of their journey Lena and Vaughan confront both the value and the burden of an indigenous identity in Australia. *Beneath Clouds* also interrogates colonial violence in Australia, contemporary and residual, the history and ramifications of which are located in physical and psychological landscapes. As *Beneath Clouds* illustrates, these sites remain contestable spaces within a nation-state that is more colonial than post-colonial.

Lena and Vaughan share a desire for relative autonomy and freedom, both as individuals and as members of a marginalised community that suffers the hypocritical sociopolitical juxtaposition of being 'out of sight, out of mind' within white Australia's social conscience while remaining under the claustrophobic scrutiny and surveillance of the ever-vigilant state. Within the genre of Australian road movies, the road trip often dissects stretches of empty blacktop in a search for meaning located somewhere within a Euro-centric construction of the 'outback'—a metaphysical and material location

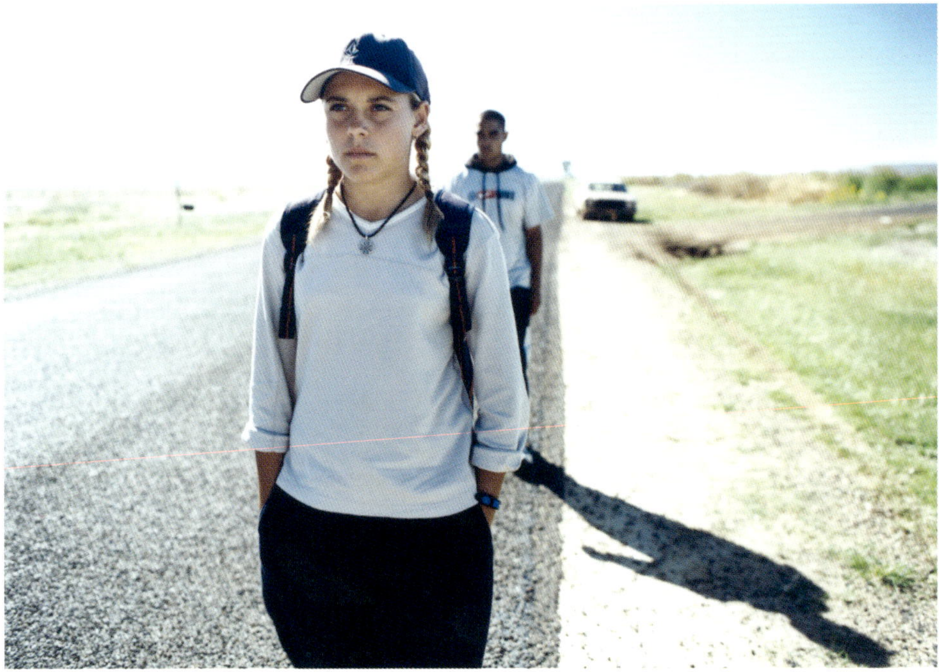

Ivan Sen, *Beneath Clouds* (2002). © SBS Independent.

constituted by wide flat horizons, rocky iconic outcrops and an absence of 'civilisation'. (Too much clutter may create an aural and visual din, interfering with an aesthetic concerned with an existentialist trip along the road to nowhere.[2])

Beneath Clouds subverts this search for spiritual realisation, in that Lena and Vaughan attempt to escape their particular predicaments (she from a damaged home life, he from prison), by heading toward a major Australian city rather than an untainted and essentialist indigenous heartland (or rather, more specifically, the 'dead heart' of white Australia's identity). *Beneath Clouds* refuses a simplistic resolution to loss and marginalisation. Lena and Vaughan do not discover their indigenous salvation in a space inscribed by clichéd sacredness, whereby indigenous characters and white audience alike discover their 'true' selves (as is the case, for instance, in the revelatory experience literally unearthed in the subterranean spiritual spaces found beneath the city of Sydney in Peter Weir's *The Last Wave* (1977)—a realisation that unfortunately comes too late, unable to prevent Armageddon raining down on the city).

Ivan Sen's film shares similarities with that historically vital Australian road movie, Philip Noyce's *Backroads* (1977). The cultural critic Stephen Muecke has commented that an informed engagement with the Noyce film is 'determined' by its display of provocation and unease, conveyed through the tense and occasionally violent interaction between characters in the film. *Backroads* exposes Australia's version of postwar apartheid, a dynamic that remained entrenched in some parts of Australia into the 1970s, more than a century after the first reserves and missions were established during the era of British colonial rule. *Backroads* refuses a comforting race relations quick fix or a digestible melancholic finale. The indigenous characters in the film are not patronised or demonised. The lead indigenous character in particular, Gary (Gary Foley), displays not the slightest sense of either noble savagery or of being the ubiquitous down-beaten fringe dweller. He is a genuinely self-determining political raconteur and frontier outlaw (hence the slightly comical 'western movie' shoot-out at the end of the film). With its honesty conveyed in part by its technological rawness, *Backroads* continues to resonate in Australia's regressive post-reconciliation environment.

Beneath Clouds, made a quarter of a century after *Backroads,* provides an insight into the extent to which some aspects of the lives of the indigenous communities of south-eastern Australia remain as they were prior to white Australia's brief moments of social 'enlightenment' during the past twenty-five years.

This has been the era of land rights struggles across Australia (supported by limited but foundational legislative reforms), including the historically significant 1992 Australian High Court *Mabo* decision, that, in an albeit limited judgement, recognised prior occupation and 'ownership' of Australian lands by indigenous nations. The mid 1990s also witnessed an energetic growth within the reconciliation movement, culminating in mass marches that involved hundreds of thousands of people in cities across Australia in 2000. But despite these political and social shifts, real change has been limited, with many young indigenous people damaged, not only by immediate family and community disadvantage (as *Beneath Clouds* does not shy from), but also by deeply ingrained forces of racism located in both the contemporary socio-political landscape in Australia and its historical landscapes of violence.

Critiques of *Beneath Clouds* have focused, not surprisingly, on the theme of dysfunctionalism within indigenous communities and a seeming confusion or secrecy in relation to indigenous identity, centred around Lena's search for her white father and her apparent denial of her Aboriginality. This is a simplistic reading of the film, although not an unexpected one, as it provides some comfort (and perhaps 'relaxation') for a non-indigenous audience ignorant of the residual impact of colonisation on young indigenous people, articulated time and time again in *Beneath Clouds* through both external and internalised forms of surveillance and self-inspection, and through the necessary but ultimately humiliating performance of deference by young indigenous people before the prying eyes of white authority.

'WHERE YOUR PEOPLE FROM GIRL?'

Several commentaries on *Beneath Clouds* have dealt (and dwelt) with the issue of identity, focusing on Lena, who is conceived too narrowly by many critics as a 'fair skinned, blue-eyed child of mixed race' attempting to escape both her impoverished indigenous family and herself.[3] While this description is not without some legitimacy, it is an essentially literal and singular representation of a more sophisticated and complex character. Lena uses the road to escape a marginalised rural indigenous community. But it is not only her indigenous identity that she questions and is perhaps running from.

It is also the inherent disadvantages and pervasive impositions of a post-twentieth century atmosphere of colonial rule that Lena finds oppressive.

Early in the film Lena expresses her hostility toward the rural town life that imprisons many indigenous youth, telling a friend (who has just confided in Lena, 'I think I might be pregnant'), 'you're never going to get out of this place … you know that, don't ya. You'll be stuck here forever like the rest of them.' Lena quickly decides that she will not remain 'stuck' in a town dominated by a towering wheat silo, menacing road trains and a trawling police patrol car. The forces of disadvantage and isolation have also pervaded her home life. Lena is disgusted by a stepfather who drinks straight from the bottle and a mother whose only comment on her young son being taken away in a police car is the reflection that it will 'give me a fuckin' break from him anyway'.

This confrontation with her parents is the immediate catalyst informing Lena's decision to hurriedly pack a bag and leave, clutching a photograph album containing images of her absent (white) father and the far-off idealised landscape of Ireland. With no clear intention, Lena catches the first bus out of town, heading for distant Sydney. To fully appreciate what Lena is escaping, we need to examine more closely the wider social and cultural landscapes confronting her. She must not only deal with the immediate breakdown of a family and a community debilitated by alcoholism and crime. Her frustration and anger, her reaction to the realisation that she also may not 'get out of this place', is directed also to those who have attempted to put indigenous communities in their (marginalised) place in the nation.

'Their place' and the ominous spectre of colonialism are both illustrated in the opening of *Beneath Clouds*. The frame is dominated by the image of the towering concrete wheat silo, casting its shadow across the landscape. Many rural towns in regional Australia were established primarily to service the economically tenuous wheat industry. Some of those towns are living; others are 'hanging in there' or suffering terminal economic and social decay. The

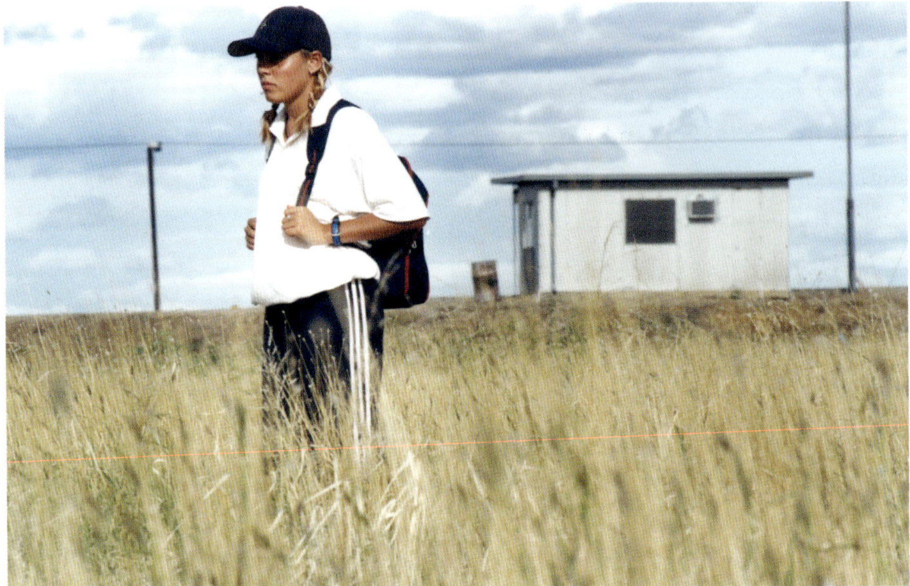

Ivan Sen, *Beneath Clouds* (2002). © SBS Independent.

wheat silo has become an iconic but ultimately deceptive temple of colonial prosperity and *ownership* of Australian landscapes. The impact of agricultural industries on indigenous communities has been profound, not only as a result of the extent of indigenous land taken and degraded to create 'fields of gold', but also as an outcome of the economic and social apartheid that tradition-ally accompanied colonial agricultural development and expansion (a point driven home in *Beneath Clouds,* in which indigenous workers are relegated to employment as itinerant and poorly paid cotton chippers).

In the same opening scenes introducing Lena, a police car slides across the frame, peering into the lives of young indigenous teenagers. This cameo is foreboding, with the finale of the film graphically illustrating the potential explosiveness of such surveillance and the escalating tension it creates. Lena's desire to escape is a desperate and eventually futile attempt to remove herself from this suffocating environment. The further that Lena physically removes herself from this situation, in a mythical quest for whiteness (or Irishness, to be specific), the more she must confront her individual and communal indigenous identity, through interactions with and a hesitant emotional connection to Vaughan.

A literal reading of Lena's expression of her identity is that she is 'passing', denying her Aboriginality. In fact, she does not do this. Certainly, some of those whom Lena and Vaughan meet along the road assume that she is a relatively harmless (and even vulnerable) white teenager, while Vaughan is portrayed as an unwanted and even menacing indigenous youth. I suspect that many non-indigenous viewers of *Beneath Clouds*

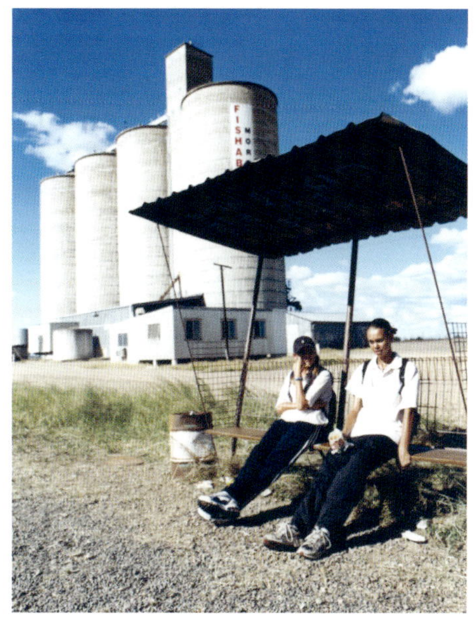

Ivan Sen, *Beneath Clouds* (2002). © SBS Independent.

extract comfort from a reading of Lena's grappling with her identity as a simple and betraying act of passing. Consciously or not, such attitudes are a social throwback, assuaging both an assimilationist ideology and the reinforcement of caste history in Australia. They privilege the 'voluntary' passing of so-called mixed-blood indigenous people over an affirmation of an indigenous identity through cultural and kinship relations. Even the most liberal-minded among non-indigenous Australians continue to look at 'fair-skinned' indigenous people with *natural* curiosity (and sometimes with disbelief, particularly when they may have paid for an indigenous scholar to 'perform' at a university conference).

In two key scenes from *Beneath Clouds*, Lena is directly confronted about her identity. The first scene is soon after Lena and Vaughan meet on the highway.

During a confrontation between them Vaughan angrily *accuses* Lena, 'Well, you're fuckin' white, aren't ya?' Her reply, 'Is that right?' challenges Vaughan's perception that she is white, rather than affirming it. Her response, directed with defiance, clearly implies that his accusation is wrong. (While it may appear that Vaughan possesses little insight into Lena's true identity, in a later scene, when the two of them seek shelter in an abandoned church and Vaughan's comment to Lena, 'You're not really from there, are ya?' (Ireland), reveals something more than is stated—that Lena is indigenous.)

The church scene is also the moment when Lena and Vaughan begin tentatively to convey some trust for each other. For much of the film their conversations are presented as a form of verbal shadow-boxing, whereby they each attempt to remain secured against either personal scrutiny or emotional engagement, a situation common to many indigenous youth when faced with the experience of being prodded by inquisitive outsiders. Many of the exchanges between Lena and Vaughan are all too brief and are cut off by deflection. For instance, when Vaughan enquires of Lena, 'So what's your story?', she looks away to a group of cotton chippers working in a field before returning to Vaughan with a question of her own, 'What are they doing?' Additionally, when Lena asks Vaughan 'What's your name?' he comes back with the defensive reply, 'What's yours?' Any notion that Lena is able to hide her identity from Vaughan fails to recognise this complex social dynamic that is constantly being negotiated between them and with others whom they meet. Much of what the characters (both black and white) in *Beneath Clouds* engage in is performative, as a mechanism of protection and negotiation.

In the second scene involving Lena's identity, it does come as a revelation to Vaughan. He appears shocked, but the shock comes in the form of a realisation of the deep knowledge about indigenous identity carried within indigenous culture. We witness this cathartic moment soon after Lena and Vaughan have hitched a ride with three of his mates. An indigenous elder rides silently in the back seat of the car while the young male occupants make small (bravado) talk. The old woman, remaining expressionless, looks across the back of the seat at Lena, who uncomfortably feels the eyes of the older woman on the back of her head. They share the knowledge of Lena's true identity, a situation that Lena realises before a word is spoken between them. When the elder asks Lena, 'Where your people from, girl?' she is not asking Lena *if* she is indigenous, but rather, who are you, Lena? Where are your 'people' (her land, her nation), where is Lena's country?

This is a powerful moment in the film. It indicates to Lena that she cannot easily escape herself. Her identity is not a self-determining process alone. It is embedded in indigenous culture and knowledge and is affirmed through the authority of an elder. The identity and status of young indigenous people is undermined in *Beneath Clouds*. But this is not due to Lena, who is doing nothing more than seeking some relief from a pervasive sense of adversity and surveillance. It is the wider social and cultural forces that threaten. And it is in dealing with such issues that *Beneath Clouds* is most persuasive.

'WHAT'S YOUR NAME, BOY?'

A second dominant theme of *Beneath Clouds* is the relationships of negotiation between young indigenous people and non-indigenous authority figures, including the police, prison guards and other representatives of colonial authority, such as the (benevolent) landed gentry, the pub owner and the (hostile) farmer. Through these characters an atmosphere of sometimes understated but ultimately claustrophobic surveillance pervades the film. From the moment that the police patrol car is viewed in the first frames of the film, an atmosphere of mutual antagonism between police and indigenous youth becomes apparent, although it is conveyed for much of the film through 'role play'—with each 'actor' performing the role of coloniser or colonised with a suitable display of bigotry and deference, respectively.

The police in particular 'perform' their role as the ultimate arbiters of contemporary frontier justice with a sense of lethargy and resignation, while the indigenous youth generally defer to the authority of police, accepting clichéd statements and gestures of racism, albeit with frustration and repressed anger. In Vaughan's first scenes in *Beneath Clouds* he is working at a tree plantation inside a prison farm. He receives a visit from his sister, who tells him their mother (who has never visited him in gaol) now wants to see Vaughan. He is told that his mother is dying.

On the way to the meeting with his sister Vaughan is under the escort of a prison guard. The interaction between Vaughan and the guard is minimal and their exchange is peripheral to the subsequent emotional interaction between Vaughan and his sister. But this brief encounter provides an insight into subsequent exchanges. The two avoid any social interaction beyond the necessity that their shared situation demands. The guard in particular conveys a sense of weariness or even boredom when he orders Vaughan to 'make it quick' (the visit). There appears to be no real need 'to make it quick', beyond reinforcing the roles of prison authority and the imprisoned (coloniser and colonised).

Similar performances occur following Vaughan's escape from prison, through a series of brief encounters between the two young runaways and various authority figures, with each party engaging in a variety of staged performances. The characters remain 'in character', performing their roles dutifully. This controlled atmosphere shifts dramatically in the defining scenes toward the end of the film when the constraints and tensions contained in these performances can no longer be contained or governed by gesture.

An indication of a growing shift in this emotional dynamic is provided early in the film. Soon after Lena and Vaughan begin hitchhiking toward Sydney they get a ride from an indigenous cotton chipper and his family. The partner of the driver is in the back seat of the car. She is nursing a young child. It is not long before the car is pulled over by the police. All the while the car radio wails an ironic black country and western lament, 'Oh, I wish that I

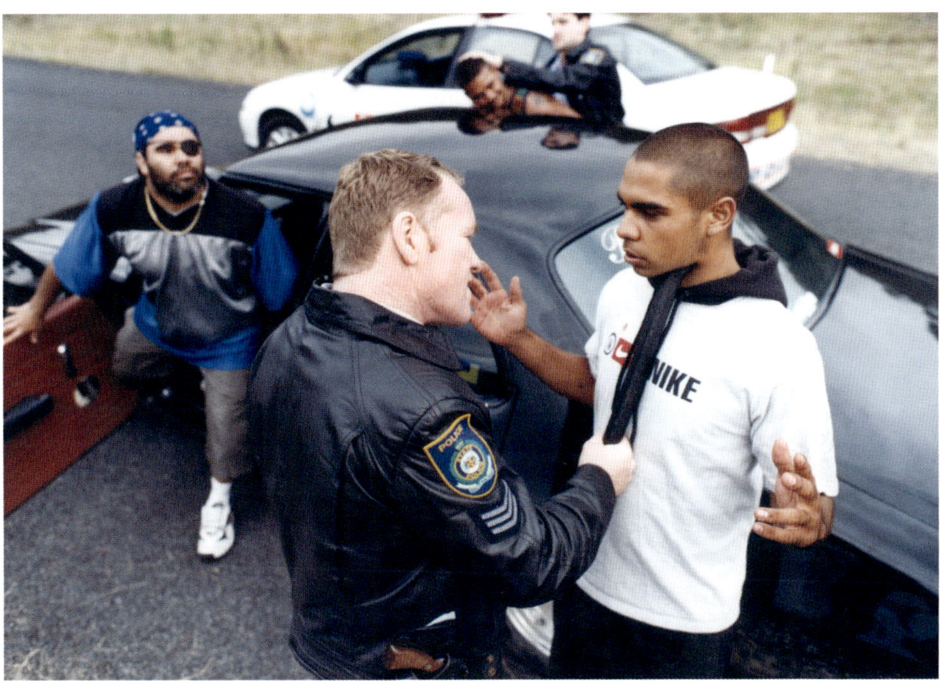

Ivan Sen, *Beneath Clouds* (2002). © SBS Independent.

was back in the Dreamtime.' The police officer lazily performs the role of the arbiter of state power, underpinned by appropriately bigoted language. He repeatedly refers to the driver as 'boy', informing him at one point (after the theatrical kick of a bald tyre), '[If I] see you driving this piece of shit again, I'll fine your arse.' During the conversation the policeman stares intently at the driver, silently reinforcing what they both know: 'See what I can do to you.' The stare of the police officer simultaneously attempts to provoke a reaction from the driver and leaves him in no doubt as to the consequences of his actions if he does retaliate. The driver defers to the authority of the police and the crude display of racism before he is eventually allowed to continue on his way to work.

This characterisation of the policeman seems to lack depth, being overtly two-dimensional and clichéd. It is also intentional. The non-indigenous characters in *Beneath Clouds* represent the psychology of colonial authority more generally within contemporary Australia, whereby power relationships are maintained through particular forms of etiquette and performance that are sometimes ambiguous, contradictory and conveyed with anxiety. By the end of *Beneath Clouds* it is realised that when the finely balanced relationships between indigenous and non-indigenous people are shaken, the façade of appropriate relationships collapses, resulting in catastrophic outcomes.

The young indigenous driver involved in this scene with the police is humiliated by the process, although it is only after he is told by the policeman to 'get going' that we realise the depth of his anger. The child in the back seat of the car begins to cry. The agitation on the face of the driver is apparent, as is the fear on the face of the child's mother. The driver screams at the woman, telling her to 'shut that kid up … I said shut that fuckin' kid up.' He then suddenly turns around to the back seat and hits the woman across the face.

As Lena screams at Vaughan after they have abandoned the hospitality of the driver (at her insistence, when she defiantly yells at the driver 'stop the fucking car'), it is no 'fucking excuse' for Vaughan or anyone else to conveniently lay the cause for this explosion of violence at the feet of the racist cop. But *Beneath Clouds* also informs us that causal relationships do exist between acts of racism and resulting humiliation and indigenous violence, whereby disempowered indigenous people transfer their humiliation into expressions of anger, self-harm and domestic violence.

In the penultimate scene of *Beneath Clouds* characters on both sides of the colonial divide break out of their respective roles, with disastrous consequences. This occurs during the same car ride in which the elder confronts Lena about her identity. The police pursue the car. They pull the vehicle onto the side of the highway. One of the officers quickly senses that Vaughan may be the prison runaway. In an increasingly tense scene one of the police asks Vaughan, 'What's your name, boy?' before attempting to get him to turn around so that he can be searched and, most likely, handcuffed.

It is at this moment, when he is most defenceless and about to lose his briefly savoured freedom, that Vaughan expresses his *true* character. He spits in the face of the policeman and smiles at him with a satisfying and childish grin, having realised that in a situation of impending and absolute powerlessness the only *real* act of defiance left to him is to spit in the face of colonial authority. And as much as it is an act of futility, it provides Vaughan with the briefest moment of clarity. There is no doubt that his action will have dire and immediate consequences. It is without question that he will suffer for what he has done. He knows beforehand, but decides on this costly but informed act of defiance.

What follows is an acceleration of violence between the police and the youths, an inevitable consequence of a barely repressed mutual hatred. The outraged policeman hits Vaughan across the face with a metal baton, establishing a chain of events that result in both officers being badly beaten by the youths, including Vaughan. (On each occasion that I have viewed the film I have been intrigued by the extent to which the predominantly non-indigenous audience 'barrack' for Vaughan and his friends as the officers are beaten.) It is only after this scene, with the car speeding away and the police officers left lying on the roadway, that we realise that in the circumstances, such a confrontation was inevitable and necessary to the logical outcome of the film. The film mirrors the rapid escalation of violence when indigenous people react to state violence, whether it is on the streets of Redfern or the tropics of Palm Island. Such reactions *are* inevitable and will continue to occur as long as indigenous communities are subject to the levels of surveillance and violence that serve as a form of colonial governance in Australia.

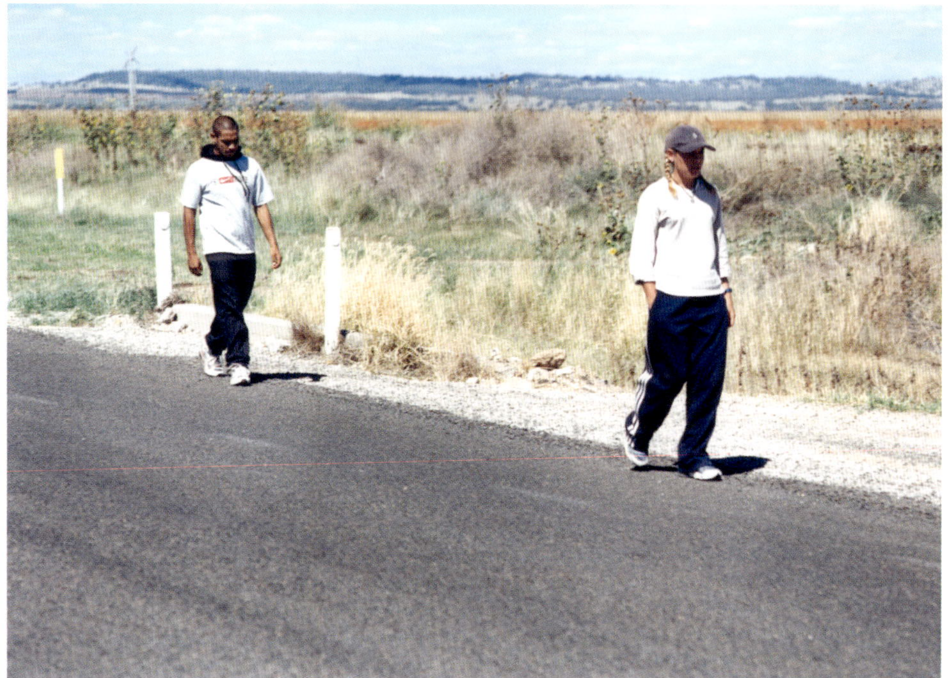

Ivan Sen, *Beneath Clouds* (2002). © SBS Independent.

'NOBODY GIVES A SHIT'

In order to understand the state of relationships between indigenous and non-indigenous Australia we must confront our colonial past rather than sanitise or forget it. *Beneath Clouds* interrogates incidents of colonial violence in Australia, providing an understanding of the depth of both this past and white Australia's *selective* preoccupation with history-making. While texts can be created that privilege particular representations of the past, in *Beneath Clouds,* as in indigenous culture, the land itself is the repository of historical memory. In a scene that begins with deceptive tranquillity, Vaughan and Lena walk along the highway during a more contemplative moment. They are beginning

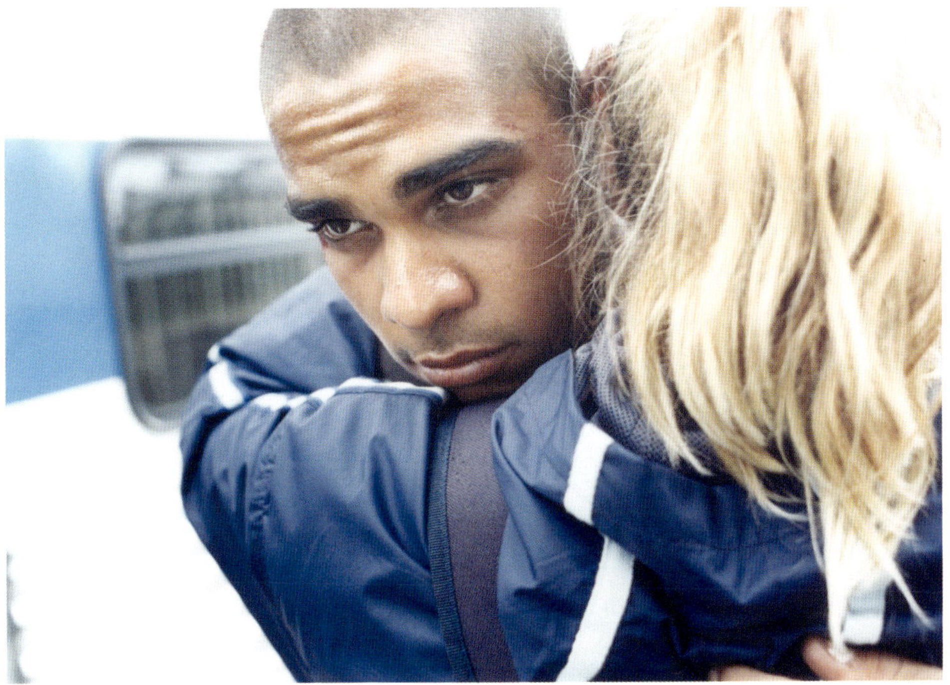

Ivan Sen, *Beneath Clouds* (2002). © SBS Independent.

to display some trust toward each other and their conversation is noticeably less guarded. Vaughan and Lena are dwarfed by the mountainous and heavily treed landscape surrounding them. It is an aesthetically comforting place. They simultaneously look across to a distant hilltop. Vaughan comments, 'It's pretty, hey?' He then tells Lena a story about this landscape, the hidden history of this place: 'My pop, he used to tell me about that place. The farmers chased all the blackfellas up there. They just shot them and pushed them off.'

Vaughan then looks across the highway to a family picnicking next to their car on the side of the road. He remarks to Lena, 'And now, nobody gives a shit'—clearly placing the responsibility for this 'Australian silence' at the feet of non-indigenous people. His next comment (along with Lena's reply) is a revealing reflection on the social and psychological damage that this irresponsible loss of colonial memory has inflicted on indigenous people. Vaughan says, 'No wonder she left me [his mother]; she didn't want a criminal for a son.' Lena's reply is equally revealing, absent of any of her earlier romantic fancies, which located a sense of belonging and love in the photographic image of absent white father. She tells Vaughan, 'My Dad left me; blames me for him and mum splitting up.'

This moment of emotional transparency between Lena and Vaughan conveys a sense of the depth of the legacy of colonial violence and its impact on indigenous people. Sadly, it manifests itself too often as an overwhelming sense of demoralisation and even self-hatred among young indigenous people who carry the burden, and who live with the knowledge that too many white Australians do not 'give a shit' about this violence, even when confronted with the reality of its existence.

In a later scene Lena and Vaughan are travelling in the car with the indigenous elder. The three of them look out of the window and across to the cliff face. Although no words are spoken, in this shared *silence* each conveys the depth of indigenous knowledge that passes between them, informing *us* (the viewers, and the Australian nation) that we know, we all know about this violent past—and we 'don't give a shit'.

In this one scene Ivan Sen has presented us with an opportunity to examine ourselves as a community. (I am reminded here also of the writer Ross Gibson, who, in his recent book, *Seven Versions of an Australian Badland,* asks white Australia to confront a history of violence embedded in landscape, in an effort 'to goad us into thinking more boldly about how that past produces the present. This remembering is something good we can do in response to the bad in our lands.'[4]) In its silence this scene indicates that, regardless of sustained attempts to forget colonial violence, neither selective amnesia, political expediency nor the production of a phony 'history war' can erase Australia's conscience.[5]

Beneath Clouds also reminds us that those who carry the burden of this memory on behalf of the nation are now young indigenous people, the custodians of the violence committed against their elders. This is an unfair responsibility. Young indigenous people are owed a debt of social responsibility by the nation. But too often Australian society pushes these people to the margins and then contains them in holding pens—made not of locks and wire, but a glance, a word, or simply a strategic refusal to recognise their value.

NOTES

1   *Beneath Clouds* (2002), directed by Ivan Sen, distributed by Ronin Films.
2   For a discussion of the Australian road movie genre see Stephen Muecke, 'Backroads: From Identity to Interval', and Meaghan Morris, 'Fate and the Family Sedan'. Both essays are located at <www.sensesofcinema.com>.
3   The list is inexhaustible. The above quote is from *inside film*'s online review. See <www.if.com.au>.
4   Ross Gibson, *Seven Versions of an Australian Badland*, University of Queensland Press, St Lucia, 2002, pp. 2–3.
5   For a summary of the 'history wars' debate, in all its sallow and tiresome but eventually destructive banality, see Stuart Macintyre and Anna Clark, *The History Wars*, Melbourne University Press, Carlton, 2003.

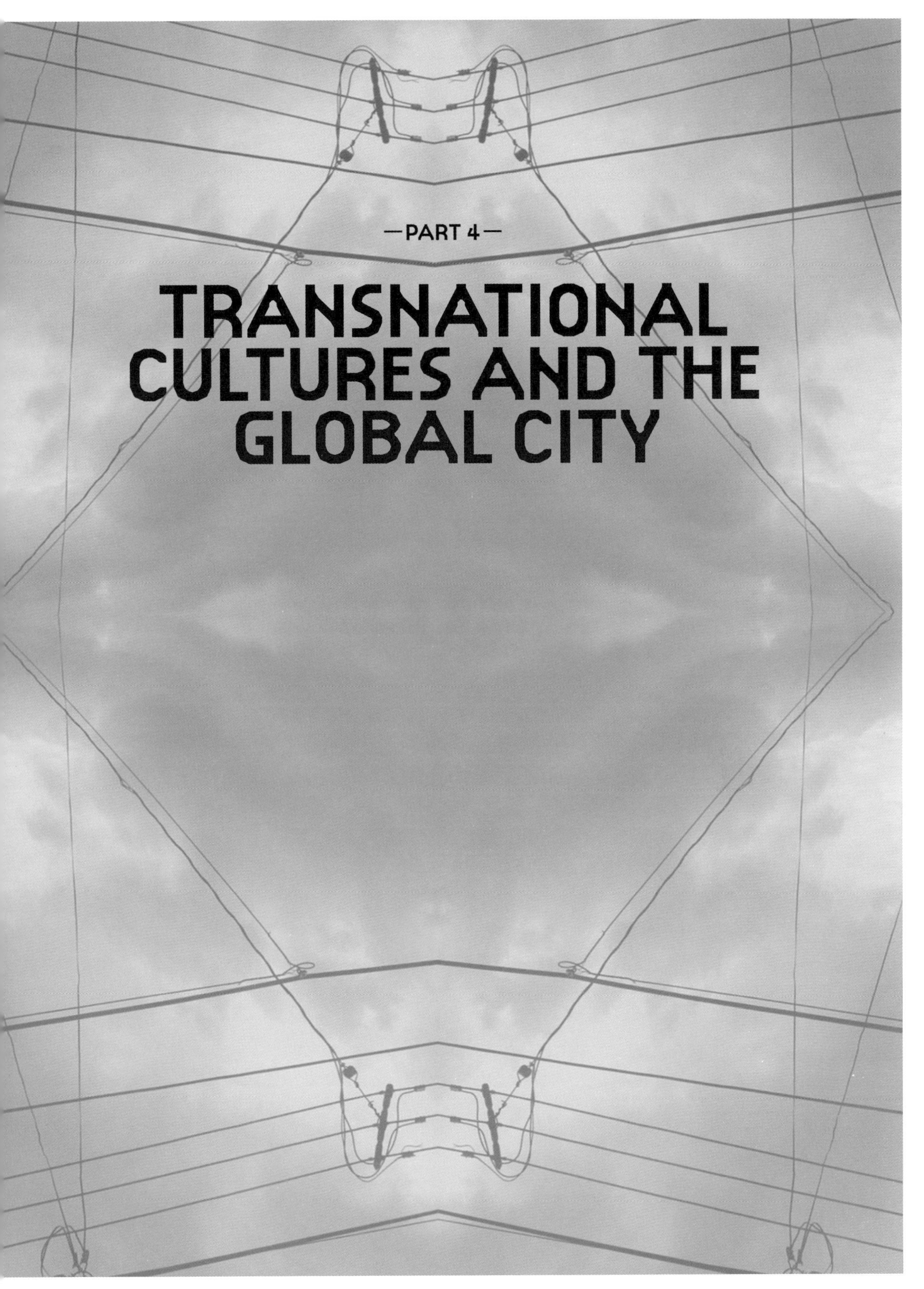

TRANSNATIONAL CULTURES AND THE GLOBAL CITY

Inroduction: The Burden of Culture in the Global City

SCOTT MCQUIRE

The emergence of the so-called network society in the 1990s was intimately connected to the rise of 'global cities'. As theorists such as Saskia Sassen[1] argued, the ascendancy of the global city was vital to the extension of the global economy. By dint of their 'hyper-concentration' of advanced information and communications infrastructure such as fibre optic networks, global cities assumed a command and control function necessary for running giant corporations across multiple countries, playing an increasingly important role in linking their national economies into global circuits.[2] In this context, the city experiences paradoxical spatial developments, as its traditional function as a 'centre' is subjected to enormous pressures, resulting in simultaneous concentration and dispersal. While global cities require a specific technological infrastructure materially housed in their central cores, this infrastructure is precisely what facilitates a new inter-city and interregional geography. The result is what Sassen terms a 'partial unbundling' of the nation, a movement which accentuates the unevenness of globalisation and underlines the fact that geography still plays a critical role in the network society. But it is a role played on a changed stage. Specific sectors of the global city are now more closely and routinely connected to similar parts of other global cities than they are to physically proximate neighbourhoods, which lack the necessary high-speed communications infrastructure and ancillary services.

In this context, a new hierarchy of cities has emerged. As older manufacturing-oriented city centres have been displaced by the new urban economic core of financial and service activities, cities such as Melbourne and Montreal have given way to Sydney and Toronto. A related consequence is the transformation of the *function* of the city centre. The *cultural* role of the city core assumes a new prominence, as cultural and educational institutions become increasingly important elements in the global competition for skilled workers, international students and tourists. This is the case for declining manufacturing centres such as Liverpool and Bilbao as much as for first-tier global cities such as London, Tokyo and New York. The cumulative force of these transformations has affected art at a number of levels, having an impact on its institutional location, the practice of contemporary artists and the nature of the artwork. Perhaps most significantly, the *structural* role of art is shifting.

The close connection between art and the city is not new. Modern art had an intimate relation to the emergence of the modern city. New perceptual experiences related to the mechanical environment of the industrial city—its dynamic forms of movement, segmented and systematised processes of work, novel architectural structures based on iron, steel and glass, its innovative practices of entertainment and modes of consumption—were central to the radical break initiated by cubism at the start of the twentieth century. If one strand of modernism, centred around Futurism, de Stijl, Constructivism and the Bauhaus, sought to give expression to the key modern experiences of speed, fragmentation and simultaneity, another strand exemplified by surrealism gave more attention to the ambivalent currents of technological progress. As Walter Benjamin pointed, this sensibility extended well beyond merely highlighting the 'irrationality' of instrumental reason, but involved the first explorations of the revolutionary potential of outmoded commodities and redundant areas of the industrial city. Duchamp's mining of the uncanny qualities of everyday objects, Schwitters' investigation of junk, refuse and industrial waste, and Aragon's poetic interrogation of decrepit and abandoned spaces stand as exemplars of this modern sensibility attuned to the built-in obsolescence of both objects and urban spaces in commodity-driven culture.

The modern industrial city was also the locus of an unprecedented influx of strangers, attracting migrants moving from country to city or travelling across national borders to new cultures. These quintessentially *metropolitan* experiences of cultural difference and cultural heterogeneity occurred in parallel with the expansion of new institutions for regulating cross-cultural exchange. Key examples were the anthropological exhibits from the South Pacific and Africa at the Trocadero Museum in Paris, which fascinated modern artists such as Picasso and helped to drive paradigmatic modernist shifts in visual form and perspective.

Given the centrality of the industrial city to the formation of modernism, it is not surprising, then, that its displacement presages fundamental changes in contemporary art and cultural exchange. There are a number of interrelated trajectories to such changes. New materials—so-called 'new media' beginning with video in the 1970s but rapidly extending to digital tools and networks—have assumed an increasingly important role in art and cultural production. One effect of this move towards art based around technological images rather than collections of material objects is that the 'white cube' of modernism is no longer the unquestioned model for institutions displaying art. New 'black box' art galleries based around technological images have opened around the world, at sites such as ZKM in Karlsruhe, ACMI in Melbourne, FACT in Liverpool, Kiasma in Helsinki and Sendai in Japan. Most significant is the fact that these institutions are not simply new venues for displaying art, but involve attempts to establish new resources for collaborative production.

Most of these institutions were conceived as the dotcom boom ramped up in velocity and the digital future seemed to be all blue skies. The 'new economy' promised by the digital threshold informed the significant shift in the prevailing discourse around art, as the concept of 'creative industries' assumed greater prominence. This shift was formalised in the UK in 1998 with the release of the Blair government's *Creative Industries Mapping Document*. In Liz Greenhalgh's breathlessly optimistic terms:

> The industries of the 'creative economy' are part of the second revolution defined by [Tony] Blair as the convergence between new technology and creativity. ... It goes beyond the tortuous definitions of what constitutes art or the cultural industries that obsessed arts administrators throughout the 1980s. In fact, it blows away the idea that there is a closed category called 'art'.[3]

Up to this point, Greenhalgh's argument bears some resemblance to the feminist and post-colonial critiques of mainstream art, which attacked the notion of a closed and ahistorical set of aesthetic standards by pointing out that they functioned to exclude a whole range of subjects and practitioners. However, her punch line strikes a quite different tone:

> Instead, it draws on new management theory. Notions of 'creativity' and creative capital, innovations and learning organisations, are now part of strategies for organisational change.

While Greenhalgh begins by presenting Creative Industries in terms of a populist critique of elite art, she quickly harnesses it to what turns out to be the overriding goal: generating and exploiting intellectual property.[4] If the strategic value of the rhetoric of 'creative industries' is to put contemporary art on the cultural agenda in new ways, its risk is the reduction of art to an R&D arm of the 'new economy'. The issue is not simply the supposed contamination of art by money—the romantic vision of the starving artist needs to go the same way as traditional defences of 'art for art's sake'. But, in the aftermath of the dotcom crash, the rhetoric of creative industries is far less seductive. Now the chips are being called in, revealing how problematic it is for art to be *required* to generate short-term returns on funding conceived of as 'subsidy' or 'seeding investment'.

This is the burden facing culture in the global city. Artists and arts institutions must be experimental and bold, but they must also attract private investment, put bums on seats, bring in tourist dollars and address multiple constituencies. Is it any wonder that the 'success' story of contemporary art institutions has become the touring blockbuster show where creativity lies in making alliances and securing star attractions which can be marketed along the lines of major movies?

Yet, as Vincent Mosco reminds us, it is not enough simply to puncture the myth of new technology; we must also seek to recover the desire for new forms of interconnectedness, which underwrote the colonisation of their utopian promise by dotcom speculators.[5] While the rhetoric of openness and transparency has to be tested against the reality of uneven access and the continuation of the imbalances in information flow, it is important to keep another eye open to the emergence of new regional flows. Key questions are still to be answered about the new networks of the 'network society' and what sort of cultural institutions and urban spaces they will support. What sorts of connections are enabled and disabled? How are they to be *articulated* with the traditional public spaces of cities, such as streets, boulevards, squares and gardens? How will new 'flows' and 'clusters' be fostered—ones which no longer depend on traditional affiliations and alignments, but enable the same sort of unpredictability that the public streets of the modern city once promised? What is the work of art in the context of the digital city? Who are the publics it addresses? And if the artwork is no longer an object or an image but a *process* of interaction with diverse publics, what kind of institution is required to house it?

NOTES

1　Saskia Sassen (ed.), *Global Networks, Linked Cities*, Routledge, New York & London, 2002.

2　In Sassen's usage command and control functions embrace all top-level financial, legal, accounting, managerial, executive and planning functions.

3　Liz Greenhalgh, 'From Arts Policy to Creative Economy', *Media International Australia*, vol. 87, May 1998, pp. 84–94.

4　See *Creative Industries Mapping Document* 2001, p. 3, available at <www.culture.gov.uk>.

5　Vincent Mosco, *The Digital Sublime: Myth, Power and Cyberspace*, MIT Press, Cambridge, Mass., 2004.

Does the Empire Really Rule?

VIRGINIA PÉREZ-RATTON

INTRODUCTION: WHO IS LISTENING?

This paper does not focus on a specific project. However, many of the ideas I will express are, rather than theoretical approaches, the result of my experience in public office and private artistic initiatives within the Central American context; of the confrontation of that background with the structures of international cultural agency; and of the recent radical shifts toward stronger control, growing censorship and an evident conservative wave in relation to cultural production. This region has been quite peripheral to the art world, to international cultural arenas, and to the main centres of thought-generation, but quite close to the doings and un-doings of the North American imperial power. A few facts might offer a different insight into how we deal with it and continue working, no matter what the odds.

The Central American isthmus runs from Guatemala to Panama. However, Panama was part of Colombia until 1903 and has had a somewhat different colonial past from the other five countries (Guatemala itself, Honduras, El Salvador, Nicaragua and Costa Rica), which were formerly states or provinces under the '*Capitanía General de Guatemala*' and dominated by Spain's political, economic and ecclesiastical power until independence in 1821.

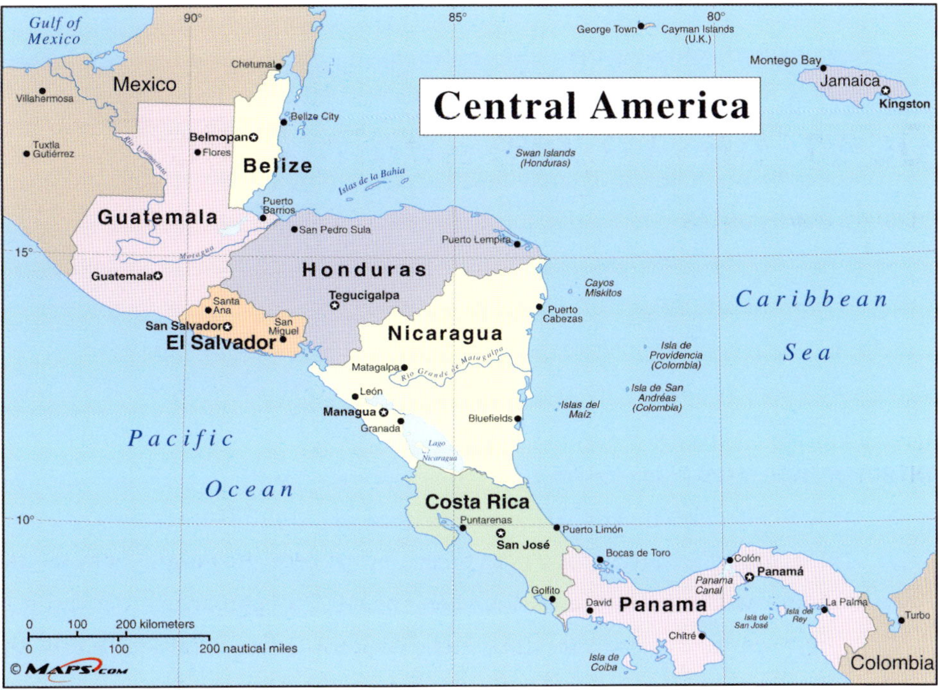

The Central American isthmus.

In 1903, US President Theodore Roosevelt declared to the United States Senate, 'I took the Isthmus.' No wonder we Central Americans define our identity not only in relation to a diverse pre-Columbian heritage and to the traditional colonial power, Spain, but in relation to the United States. From independence from Spain in 1821, which took place without the liberation movements that did happen in South America, imperialist intentions were always present, first on the part of Mexico, and then through William Walker, an American mercenary who was 'invited' by the Liberal Party of Nicaragua to fight the Conservatives, but was in fact trying to establish slavery states linked to the southern US. Walker was finally expelled in what is called the 'Campaign of 1856', in which Costa Rican troops and civilians marched to

Nicaragua. The presence of the United Fruit Company, the various railway companies, and the Panama Canal meant the virtual occupation of the region since the end of the nineteenth century. The US Marines disembarked in the 1930s in Nicaragua to combat Sandino, who had led the rebel movement against the Somoza dynasty since its beginnings. In 1954, the Americans once again intervened and ousted Jacobo Arbenz, the democratically elected Guatemalan president who had sought far-reaching changes in land owner-ship and education. This coup was the detonator for the guerrilla movements in Guatemala, with bloodshed that gradually spread to the rest of the region and finally exploded in an open armed conflict that lasted until the late 1980s. Only Costa Rica was exempt from the war, having abolished the army in 1948 and secured education, civil liberties and social welfare early on. However, the country was indeed affected in its trade relations to the region and by the massive influx of refugees and economic migrants, coinciding with one of the major economic crises in the country.

The peace process was initiated in 1989, just a couple of years before the 'Operation Just Cause', the American invasion that ousted the initially American-appointed Noriega from Panama, bombing a large, densely populated section of Panama City and killing around 5000 Panamanians. Each country had its own peace agreement between the guerrilla movements and the tradi-tional powers. The last agreement, between the right-wing Arena and the leftist Frente Farabundo Martí, took place in El Salvador in 1996. This new regional situation implied different relations between right- and left-wing factions, armies, paramilitaries, counter-revolutionaries and guerrillas in each country. The ensuing changes in Central America created new expecta-tions, not only political and economic, but also in relation to cultural production and networking, and the inclusion of Panama in regional discus-sions seemed essential.

The idea of this conference, in which notions of empire and ruins were addressed, and in which networking apparently functioned as a general framework, seemed very close to our own experience in these last years. Up to the early 1990s, Central America was a central issue: from the upheaval of the Sandinistas to the Iran–Contra scandal, we were constantly in the news. We had been the battleground for two imperial powers, and we were left with the ruins. Once the peace agreement was signed, and the reconstruction process started, we disappeared once more into the shadows of non-places. By then, the focus had shifted to Eastern Europe, and the Balkan conflict on the doorstep of the European Union.

In 2002, the Odense Klaedefabrik art centre in Denmark organised an exhibition including several Central American artists, titled *Who is talking? Towards a new internationalism*. I was asked to write the catalogue essay. I titled it 'They are talking, but who is listening?'.

RECONSTRUCTION

The cultural production strategies that followed during the 1990s, particularly in the visual arts, were implemented in a very basic and domestic way: trying to pull ourselves together in the first place, exorcising memory of the unspeakable, of the unforgivable, of the unrepeatable, trying to avoid going back to it, and reconstructing the internal broken links. Collaborative regional action from within started to take shape in various ways. Efforts were directed towards several aspects: solving the invisibility problem, counteracting the stereotypes associated with official and promoted images, and most of all, towards the creation of *Place.* It was necessary to re-create our image, to find and understand our own complex, changing and contradictory identities, and end the romantic connotations of the land of handsome macho guerrillas under volcanic landscapes, depart from the no less exotic images of untouched jungles, wild animals and piña-colada-sipping natives in their hammocks, and correct the much less attractive idea of uneducated indigenous masses incapable of mature political decisions. Emerging from decades of civil war and conflict,

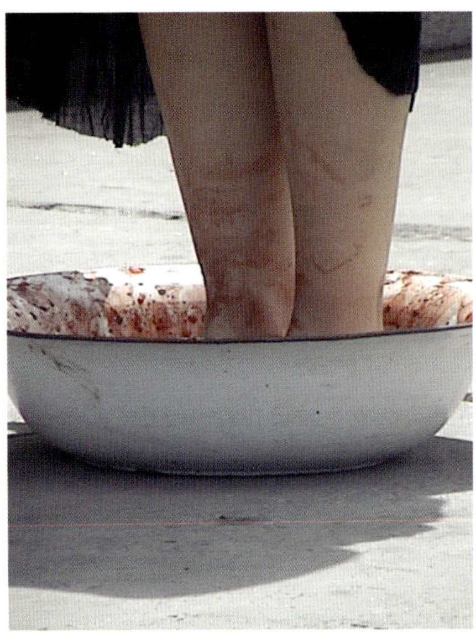

Regina Galindo, performance from the exhibition *To Live Here* (2003), curated by Rosina Cazali; courtesy of the artist.

the region, also battered by severe natural disasters, was trying to pick up the remains of itself. Building another society has proven difficult, and has only been partially successful at the economic and social levels, as poverty and unemployment are still at frightful levels in Nicaragua and Honduras, and even in Costa Rica the gap between rich and poor is much greater, street gangs plus drug-related crime have replaced the political violence everywhere, and corruption is rampant. However, slightly more democratic processes are in place instead of dynasties and dictators, the former guerrilla movements have become politically recognised parties, and some corrupt politicians have been brought to trial. At the cultural level, the perception of the area has definitely changed; a regional network has been successful in sharing projects and creating a mutual awareness of one another's production, and there has been a rise in our international visibility and presence. *We are talking, and trying to be heard.*

Costa Rica was to some degree a catalyst in this process, having had a more developed institutional structure since the mid 1970s, and a decade-long influx of intellectuals and cultural professionals from Latin America to an army-less country and land of asylum At this moment, economic migrants from Nicaragua still make up roughly 8 per cent of our population, and the influx of Colombians and Argentines is so strong that they are now required to have entrance visas.

Regional work has been possible mainly through local initiatives from the private, independent and nonprofit sector, implemented in the postwar context

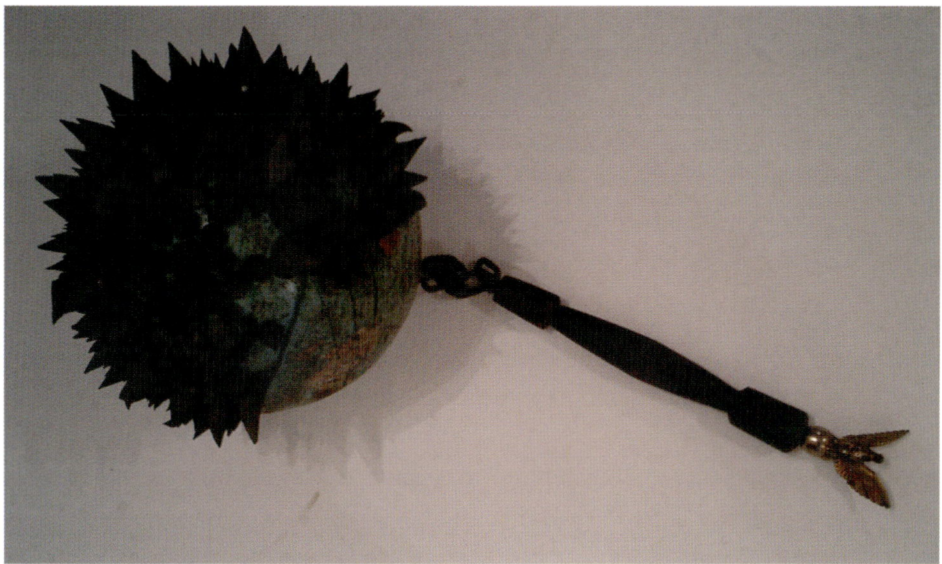

Raul Quintanilla, *New World Dis-order* (2003), object made of a
tin mapamundi half covered in tree thorns; courtesy of the artist.

with the support of some of the myriad NGOs that arrived in Central America
in the last years of the conflict and after the peace agreements. While many of
these organisations' effectiveness has been questioned, a few of them have had
an agenda of co-operation in cultural development that has indeed contributed
to the reconfiguration of the battered regional structures. With the dismember-
ing of the Soviet Union and the crisis of the left, these NGOs (both European and
North American) helped in recuperating certain socially oriented policies. Up to
now, this support has been decisive in the development, sustainability and
autonomy of projects, through moderate financing of fellowships, exhibitions,
publications, residencies and meetings throughout the region. Things seemed
to be shaping up and the regional network in the visual arts has been streng-
thened during the last six or seven years. A greater access to communication,
including the Internet, allowed us to work on a daily basis with colleagues, to

share projects, papers, and images constantly. Artists, particularly of the younger generation, are more connected, more informed and more aware of things happening 'out there' than ever before. Conditions for critical frameworks have been slowly appearing. Solidarity has been an essential aspect in this reconstruction, but there has also been a definite change in the direction of the cultural production: it seems to feel liberated from the burden of being either a revolutionary statement, or the voice and conscience of the people, of having to conform to the aesthetics of war or the aesthetics of 'tropicality' and exoticism. Political discourse is strong, maybe more than ever, because it is now envisioned within a larger scope than the adherence to a narrow ideology. This discourse stems more from an individual voice and position than a collective one, subtler and less direct than before, but in some cases extremely powerful.

NEW WORLD DISORDER

Then came September 11. Then came also the enforced polarisation of the world by the only superpower, wounded in its pride and might, its vulnerability exposed to the whole world. The unilateral and aggressive attitude in decision-making that was put into place, this time without having to consider the dissuasive presence of another power, clearly disclosed to the rest of the world the preferred tactics of the American government and its real identity. This identity is a very different one from the perception that Europeans, and I suppose Australians, have had of the United States as a stabilising power, a source of solutions and a guarantee for democracy and economic order, an image created after World War II with the reconstruction of Germany and Japan. The September 11 events and the present geopolitical conditions show another face, the one we know much better and have known for many years in Latin America: that of an interventionist power. Let's not forget that the US military bases in Panama were home to the School of the Americas, the training ground for

Latin American military forces, and whose curriculum included the arts of torture.

The consequences of the terrorist attacks and the ensuing North American misinformation campaign were immediately felt locally. Funding from US foundations was refused to non-US-based projects, visa procedures were tightened, higher fees required and extreme, humiliating security measures were imposed on every US-bound traveller, particularly anybody with ethnoracial characteristics or economic conditions that could turn him into a 'yellow' (suspicious) or 'red' (dangerous) traveller. Locally, the polarisation was also evident: economic interests linked to the US prevailed over dignity and critical positions on the Iraq invasion. Our governments acted once again like banana republics.

When reading the outline of this conference last year, I reflected how the new authoritarism was shaping our lives, not only due to September 11 and its direct sequels, or to the daily experience of extreme surveillance during my continuous travelling, but particularly due to the reversal in local official attitudes from the one assumed between 1986 and 1990 by our then president, Oscar Arias. One of the main figures in the peace process, he refused to allow the 'contras' to continue operating from our soil, enforced the neutrality status we had chosen, and tried to convince the US administration that an ally can have an individual opinion. The resulting tensions cost the country several months of no development aid, but finally, through intelligent and efficient diplomatic labour, Costa Rica finally had its way. Arias had also fought fiercely to get the five countries to sit down and negotiate peace without the presence of any external powers, and made regional presidents work until consensus was obtained and the promise of a series of treaties was signed. The Nobel Peace Prize he won made us believe the era of the banana republic had finally ended. But now, the emergence of a unipolar world, in which you are 'with them or against them', drove our incapable President Pacheco and his Foreign Affairs Minister to bow their heads before the 'empire's' designs, in an unacceptable regression, evidence of our 'back yard' complex, and

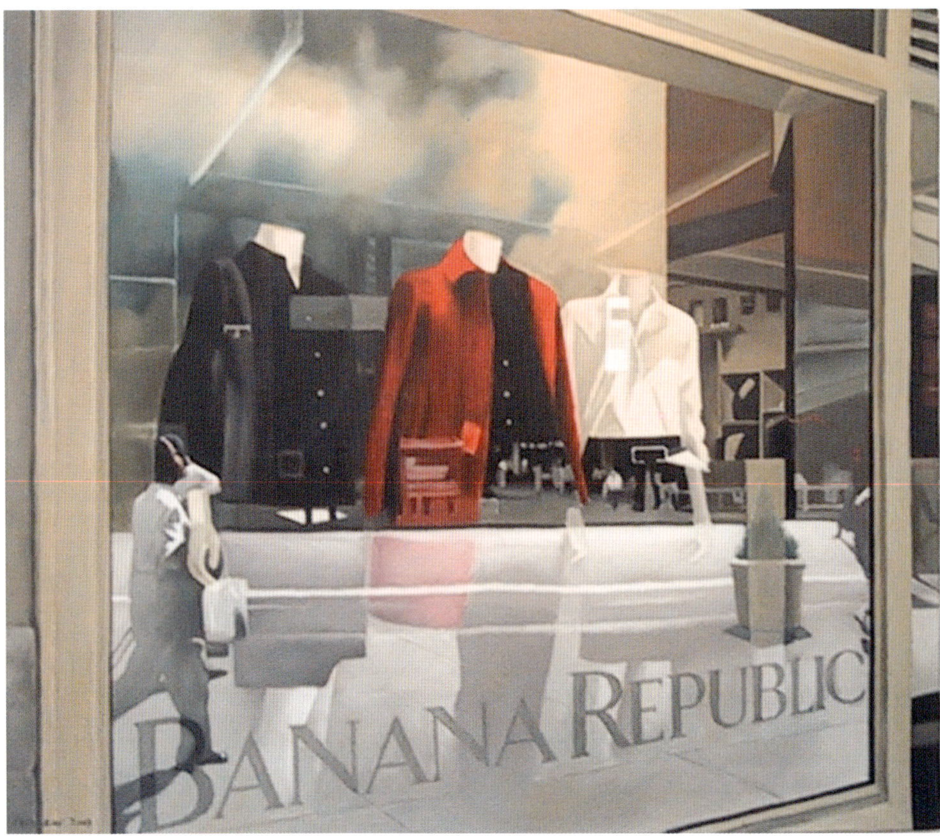

Moises Barrios, *Vitrina #2* (2003), Oleo, 150 × 130cm;
courtesy of the artist.

pledge support to the Coalition, appearing in *Fahrenheit 9/11* as one of the backward, weak governments supporting the Iraq invasion.[2]

This efficient construction of fear as a way of living, or surviving, progressively installed since 2001 (although we were not all fearing the same foe), this intentional implementation of a global terror regime, has its roots in the Cold War, when the 'Communist threat' was the justification each time the US decided to change a government here or there. However, we had not experienced it in the same way during the conflicts in Central America, dotted with

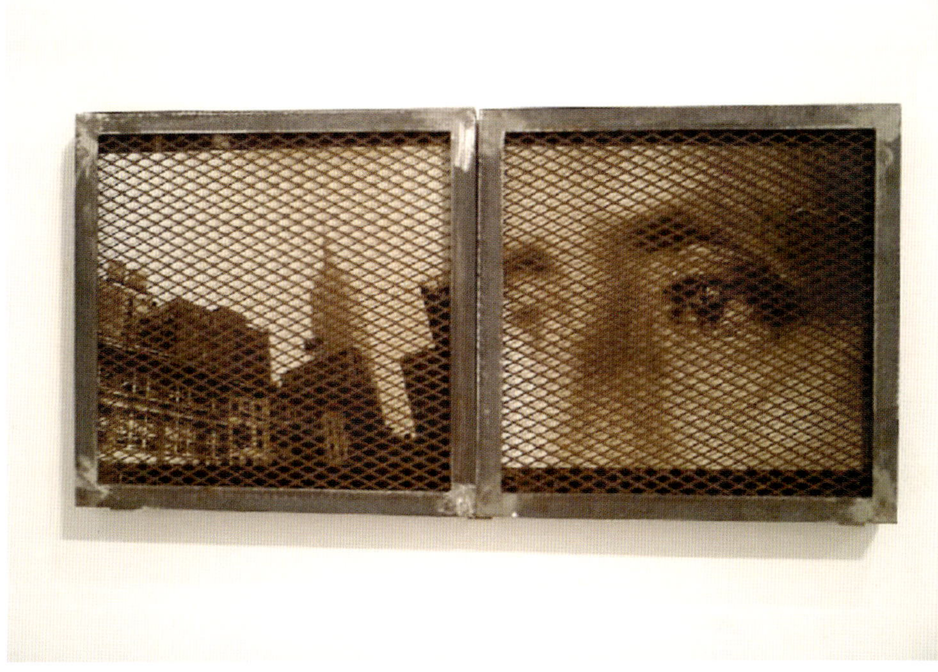

Luis González Palma, *Tensiones Herméticas* (1999), sepia-toned
silver gelatin print mounted under metal mesh, 50 × 50cm;
courtesy of the artist.

American interventions up to the late 1980s. This time, it was a new state of
affairs that seemed to cover the whole world with a dark shadow. Growing
mobility may have been one of the factors that multiplied the effects of this
policy. People who travel constantly, who migrate, who change their localities,
experience a completely different world from those who do not depend on
international movement or contacts for their daily work or routine. Considering that a large percentage of Central America's populations live in Chicago,
Los Angeles, New York, Miami or Washington, travelling back and forth, and
that the economies of countries like El Salvador are mostly sustained by the
expatriate workers' monthly remittances, one can imagine the effect of the
North American control policies.

THE CONVENIENCE OF WAR AND DIVISION

> The elevation of terrorism to the status of a universal force has institutionalised a permanent state of war on a planetary scale … Everything is happening as if the United States searched, for some obscure reason, to maintain a certain degree of international tension, a limited but endemic war situation.[3]

Fortunately, one can only go along with lies for so long, and maybe being Latin American, we are already negatively predisposed to the American information policies, as we are familiar with the short-sightedness of many of its governments and accustomed to its lack of respect for any Other. We are also painfully close to solving day-to-day local problems that are the real issues directly affecting our work and our liberty in the production of culture. So the imposition of fear, and the threat of being labelled an enemy of the USA, have not stopped people from believing in what they are doing and doing what they believe in. After some time one realises this global fear is really in the mind, and suddenly, it is the idea of ruins in relation to empire that starts to make more sense: in fact, we are witnessing what seems to be a serious crisis of the empire, and the emergence of a new state of world affairs. Writers like Emmanuel Todd even consider that the only superpower will, sooner or later, become just one more among others in the developed world. Although this can be considered wishful thinking, there are many factors that might lead to such a state of affairs. An imperial system does not only depend on its internal relations; it depends on a certain relation with the world, which must be dominated, absorbed and transformed, to maintain its power.

An empire must be economically powerful and productive. The United States has become a consuming society more than a productive one, and it depends on much of the world for its consumerism. However, we all seem to ignore this. As an example, we have been led to believe that not signing free trade agreements with the US is a death sentence for our economies. Instead of uniting many smaller forces to exert a greater leverage in negotiations, we have been giving in to pressures and preparing to lose, among other things, the little cultural development we have secured.

But if the rest of the world would start to envision the United States as a superpower in eventual decline, with its grip threatened by a global community that is much larger, developed, informed and populated than it was during the Cold War, its legitimacy as the ruling empire might be questioned. The whole world, and particularly the Islamic world, is going through a transition towards another kind of organisation, and the United States knows this. This is why the present US government is on a warpath to provoke fractures through extremism and fundamentalism, in order to maintain a power that they know can be endangered by the empowerment of others. We should be aware of this, as we are the ones who recognise and legitimate its power. If we were to understand that the empire needs the rest of the world, and begin to negotiate on other terms, learn to act collectively, then we might arrive at better outcomes. But if we do not solve our internal quarrels and disputes, we will continue in serfdom.

FEAR AND FREEDOM ARE IN OUR MINDS

In order to sustain our cultural production, it is first necessary to concentrate on solving the local problems and to consolidate projects internally. The creation of place, of a sense of belonging, is essential to this consolidation in a region like Central America, plagued with placelessness. It is possible to do this without constantly feeling threatened by the Patriot Act, for example, and it does happen in many countries. The greatest fear should not be the empire's will but the weak local politics that allow global authoritarism to overtake our societies. Considering also that much of the cultural development continues to depend on international support, ours is a very precarious situation that needs to construct an ideological project of internal understanding, support and responsibility. It is interesting to note that within the International Arts Festival to take place from 17–27 November in Costa Rica, and in connection with the Iberoamerican Summit during the same month, the National Council of University Rectors has organised a symposium titled 'Central America: a future is possible', in which there is no mention of the role of the United States; instead it is an introspective reflection on ourselves.

Fear is in our minds: *Bowling for Columbine,* Michael Moore's powerful documentary film, was indeed a lesson in how a state can manipulate public opinion and create a country-wide or even a world-wide paranoia. This awareness is only possible through education, through access to communication and information, through social justice. And that is a problem to be solved locally, through collective social responsibility.

Freedom is in the mind.[4] Freedom and lack of fear can be sought through several strategies or in several spaces, related to either a physical space or a spiritual one. Exile, marginalisation and mass attention may be three of these spaces, created by writers and artists who wish to continue their activity and need to find an alternative to a dangerous or impossible situation. These are possibilities through which suppressed art can seek refuge in order to continue passing on its message. But other locations for freedom can offer the hope of continuity in our own space, and we must continue to build Place. In this sense, we must also learn to access and permeate the spheres of power, to use it to our advantage if possible. The public, international space of recognition offers the necessary exposure that will eventually protect or legitimate the writer, the artist, the cultural agent or activist in his own context.

One of the tools that has been essential in the construction of spaces of freedom through education and communication is, paradoxically, a military device. The Internet was designed by the military defence as a network that would be independent and difficult to trace. The percentage of people with access to it must increase, and so will awareness, liberty and spaces of self-expression.

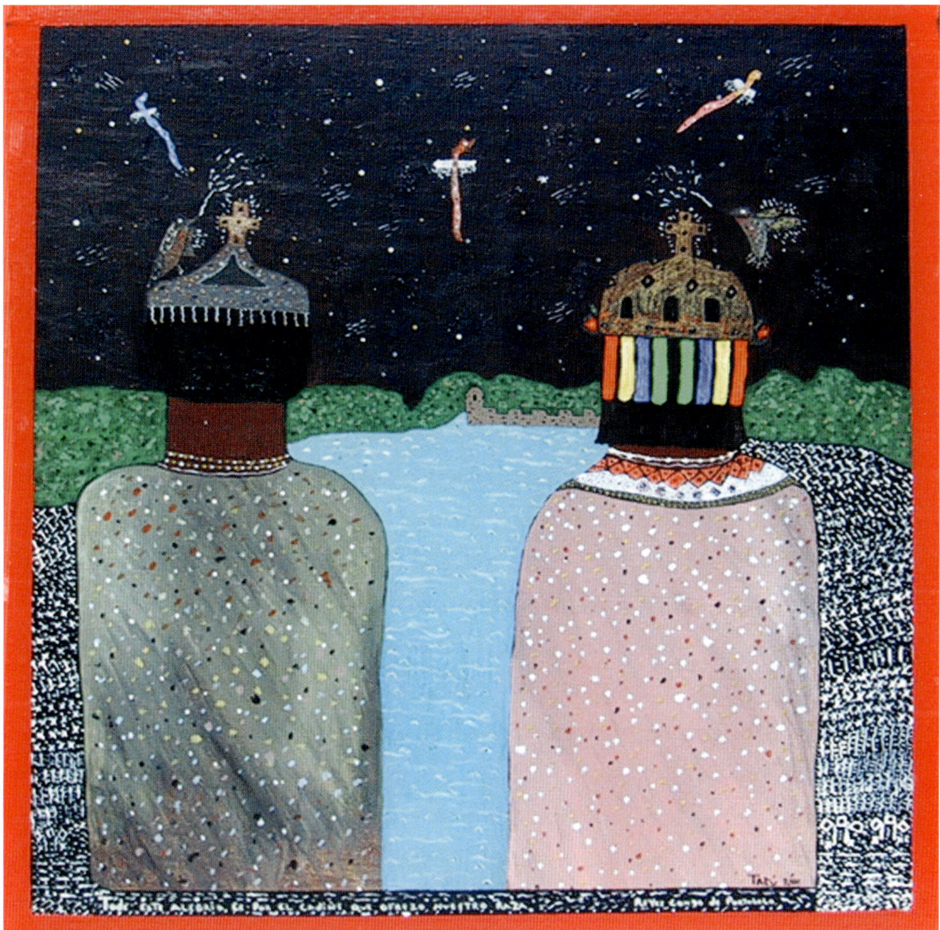

Tatú, *Los Reyes Congo* (2001), acrylic on canvas, 59.5 × 56.5cm;
courtesy of the artist.

This virtual space, which is used by millions, cannot be controlled and censored through traditional methods. The Internet is therefore the ultimate form of individual freedom for everyone who has access to a computer and a telephone.[5]

The projects and proposals that have sprung up in Central America as a reaction to the gaps in official initiatives would not be possible without the existence of the Internet. TEOR/éTica, the project I founded in 1999, started in one six-by-four-metre room with a telephone and a laptop, communicating its activities and attracting regional neighbours through the Internet. We constantly receive images and information from the region, and have built a digital and hard copy archive for researchers and students to consult. La Curanderia, a curatorial one-woman project, consists of Rosina Cazali and her computer. Cazali has organised powerful, controversial public space exhibitions including *To Live Here* and *Blue October* in Guatemala. TaJO, founded by Patricia Belli in Nicaragua, was a discussion and critical workshop that took place at the artist's studio in Managua, using her own computer for all communications. It has now evolved towards a project-generating space and has just finished *Articulaciones*, a series of actions and performances over a week, with a minimum budget and a maximum communication system directed to all colleagues in the area. Other, smaller projects take place in homes and public spaces, and we all receive enough information to be aware of what is happening throughout Central America, thus solving the isolation problems of the past. All of this has allowed us to create a solid network and to be able to work not as individual projects or people, but as a region with seven countries, each one with a different situation, sharing a more or less common colonial past. Each has evolved differently and the whole presents a mosaic of cultures, races and religions. It is a region open to continuous transit and exchange, a complex region still trying to decipher postwar history, but where things are happening every day, where cultural production is taking place, and where there is still hope, no matter what.

NOTES

1   However, massive immigration of non-qualified populations over the past 20
    years has led some right-wing politicians to present a new, tough Migratory
    Law, now being discussed in Congress.

2   Fortunately, a few months after this paper was presented, the Constitutional
    Court ruled against President Pacheco's support for the war as
    unconstitutional, and forced him to leave the coalition.

3   Emmanuel Todd, *Après l'empire: essai sur la décomposition du système américain,*
    Gallimard, Paris, 2002, p. 11. Todd had published 'The Final Fall' in 1976,
    announcing the end of the Soviet sphere, and in 1998, an essay on the
    stagnation of developed societies.

4   Els van der Plas, Malu Halasa, Marlous Willemsen (eds), *Creating Spaces of
    Freedom: Culture in Defiance,* Saqi Books, London and Prince Claus Fund Library,
    The Hague, 2002.

5   Ibid., p. 9.

Venture Culturalism, or
Tales of Culture and Commerce
in the City of Lost Empire

EDDIE BERG

This essay is about Liverpool, the city in which I was born and bred. It's about FACT (Foundation for Art and Creative Technology), the organisation that I developed and nurtured from scratch. It's about difference and distinctiveness, how an autonomous cultural tradition like that of Liverpool frames and informs its contemporary culture, its sense of self and its place in the world. It's about how that cultural tradition has been shaped and how its transgressive nature is now being contested as the city emerges from the profound and painful adjustment to the end of empire. It's about the relationship between culture and commerce, between enterprise and creativity, and how this has forged a particular form of cultural opportunism which some have termed 'venture culturalism'. It's about how contemporary cultural projects with a strong international emphasis, like FACT and the Liverpool Biennial, have emerged through this new tradition and not because of any initial civic or state cultural intervention—and why they would have no legitimacy if they did. It's about the role and place of art and artists in this context. It's about the burdens and expectations of culture in a city in which the negative impacts of globalisation, privatisation and the erosion of the public sphere are practically unparalleled in western Europe. It's about what might happen next …

In 1839, Herman Melville, aged 20 and then a sailor, first came to Liverpool. This is how he recalled his first experience of the city:

> In the evening, especially when the sailors are gathered in great numbers, these streets present a most singular spectacle, the entire population of the vicinity being seemingly turned into them. Hand-organ, fiddles and cymbals, plied by strolling-musicians, mix with the songs of the seaman, the babble of women and children and the whining of beggars. From the various boarding houses … proceeds the noise of revelry and dancing.

Ten years later his novel *Redburn* was first published. In it Melville paints a breathless, fantastical picture of Liverpool as vivid as the crowded brilliance of London in Dickens' work:

> Of all the sea ports in the world, Liverpool, perhaps, most abounds in all the variety of land-sharks, land-rats and other vermin, which make the hapless mariner their prey. In the shape of landlords, bar-keepers, clothiers, crimps, and boarding house loungers, the land-sharks devour him limb by limb, while the land-rats and mice constantly nibble at his purse.
>
> And yet sailors love this Liverpool, and upon long voyages to distant parts of the globe, will be continually dilating upon its charms and attractions, and extolling it above all other sea ports in the world.

Melville's great-great-grandnephew, the pop-star Moby, came to Liverpool 150 years after the publication of *Redburn*, in 1999. This is what Moby had to say:

> We went down to Cream last night and I was refused entry. Which was kind of ironic because they were playing one of my songs inside.

The streets outside were wild. People were singing, dancing, shouting, fighting. It was crazy, but really fascinating. It wasn't like anywhere else I'd been and I loved it. It was winter but people didn't seem to wear very much clothing. It all felt very promiscuous and exciting and edgy. It made me wonder about the culture of this beautiful, sad place. How did it get to be like this?

That's a very good question. So let me try to explain.

Liverpool's heyday as a transatlantic passenger port was well over by the time I was growing up there, but ships still sailed into the Mersey from places you could only find on a spinning globe. I remember lying in bed and listening to the sound of the foghorns on the river, and the only birdsong I recognised was that of seagulls. Liverpool's economic malaise was nearing its zenith as I approached my teenage years, but I grew up believing that this half-abandoned wreck of empire was a world-class city. But as much as I loved its spirit and character, I also grew up hating it for what it represented. I felt like I was sleeping with the dead.

Liverpool was famous the world over because the city, and everything in it, was connected with the sea. Almost everyone there had come from the sea. My dad was in the merchant navy for twenty years. So was his dad. When my dad came back from the sea he became a marine engineer on the docks. I spent a lot of my free time as a kid hanging out at the docks. They were practically empty then but I loved the sense of being immersed in the debris of history. But growing up in a city with a big, complex and dubious history—yet one in rapid decline—is confusing, disturbing and scary. I was surrounded by the historical evidence of Liverpool's profound place in the world, yet there were few traces of its future.

For a long period of time Liverpool was the second city of Empire. It was Europe's main port for trade with North America. For the century and a half of the Industrial Revolution, Liverpool was a hothouse of capitalist investment.

The canal system (1760s), the first commercial railway (1830s), and the Mersey Tunnel (1930s): these were unparalleled achievements. The city assumed it would always lead the way.

Liverpool's Irish population swelled during the second part of the nineteenth century after the famine and the promise of work on the railroads. By 1870 it was estimated that half of Liverpool's populace was first-generation Irish. Although commercial shipping declined, the city remained the primary point of embarkation for emigrants—especially refugees from fascism—from Europe to North America. Its continuous maritime links to all corners of the globe over the past three centuries have resulted in a markedly multicultural population. For instance, Liverpool has the oldest Chinese community in western Europe. Liverpool also established a culture of tolerance and acceptance rarely found elsewhere in Britain. Here is more from Melville's Redburn:

> Three or four times, I encountered our black steward, dressed very handsomely, and walking arm in arm with a good-looking English woman. In New York, such a couple would have been mobbed in three minutes ... owing to the friendly reception extended to them and the immunities they enjoy in Liverpool, the black cooks and stewards of American ships are very much attached to this place ...

Liverpool then was as stupefyingly poor as it was scandalously rich. The riches helped create the urban fabric of the city centre, mostly defined by a fine collection of Georgian buildings, which still retain a grandeur and are also a constant reminder of Liverpool's role and place in the formation of empire.

In 1933 Liverpool's population peaked at 1.1 million. After World War II Liverpool was effectively abandoned: by successive governments, by old commerce, by its own people. The macro-political context had changed. Liverpool was facing west; the new emerging state of Europe was facing east.

The port was in decline; poverty, already endemic, was now spiralling out of control. By the mid 1970s Liverpool's population was less than 460 000 and that decline has only been arrested in the last five years. It has left the urban fabric looking like a half-eaten pretzel, full of holes, where once there were businesses and communities.

The city centre has had no form of master planning since before World War II. Buildings just emerged—not very often, but when they did they emerged anywhere, often without consent, only to be knocked down again a few years later. Subsequently, in the last sixty years the city has been knocked down more than it has been built up.

One of the key outcomes of these conscious and unconscious political acts of desertion by the nation-state has been to harden the city's sense of identity and reinforce its resolve to forge an autonomous cultural tradition.

Liverpool stands outside the major narrative frameworks of modern British history. What works as social or economic policy elsewhere, seldom works in Liverpool. The rules for Liverpool are different. It sees itself, and others see it, as a place apart: definitely not English, ambivalent even about being British.

As if to underline this, MORI (Market & Opinion Research International) undertook a poll four years ago about how people in the ten largest British cities perceived themselves and others. One of the questions posed was this: What is Britain's second city? In London the majority answer was Birmingham (it has the second highest city population in the UK). In Birmingham the answer was Birmingham. In Manchester it was Manchester. In Glasgow, it was Glasgow. In Liverpool, the majority answer to what is Britain's second city, was—London.

This answer also signifies the city's spirit of mischief, its irreverence, its self-deprecating humour and its lucid purchase on its own potent powers of myth-making.

Liverpool is still very poor by British and western European standards; so poor, in fact, that in 1994 the European Commission awarded Liverpool

Objective One Status. The city was granted nearly a billion pounds to be spent over six years. In order to be eligible for this cash it had to prove that its regional GDP was less than 75 per cent of the European average. Which it was. When it was measured again it was still below the poverty line. This made it eligible for another tranche of European cash. In 2000 Liverpool received a further 950 million pounds.

Now this is both a burden and an opportunity. The burden is dependency. Decades of neglect have left a huge psychological scar on the human landscape. To be neglected is one thing, to be ignored is quite another. In the 1980s the British media branded the city and its people as whingeing recidivists. Liverpool was 'self-pity city', a 'basket case': best left alone, ignored. As the philosopher Alain De Botton has noted, 'To be ignored is not only unpleasant, it is also, from an evolutionary perspective, unsafe. We are programmed to sense how a community perceives us; to be saddened by its censure and pleased by its love. We are the descendants of people who kept a close eye on what others thought of them.' The effect of this trauma is profound and visible to any visitor to the city. It's partly what gives the city its edge. The land-sharks are still there, dependent on others. It's just that now they wear Lacoste and are popularly known as 'scallies'.

This is the opportunity. For the first time in almost a century the city has the power to make far-reaching decisions about the way in which people will experience the urban environment over the next fifty years and what kind of place they want it to be. Last year Liverpool was awarded the title of European Capital of Culture 2008. So it's also time to consider the cultural infrastructure, with competing and conflicting notions of building and planning cultural quarters seemingly at odds with strategies of permeability and proximity.

Before I talk about FACT, the Liverpool Biennial and the role of art and artists in the city, let me summarise some of the interesting characteristics of Liverpool which I think inform its contemporary cultural milieu.

1. NATIONAL MARGINALITY AND WORLD CENTRALITY

Liverpool has its back to the land literally and metaphorically, yet retains a distinct sense of its place in world history, hence the 'world in one city' slogan used in support of the 2008 European Capital of Culture bid.

2. AN AUTONOMOUS CULTURAL TRADITION

Liverpool has a very strong sense of its own cultural identity, its distinctiveness, and its uniqueness, shaped by its history as a port, the impact of immigration and particular religious and political traditions. It has cultivated this cultural distinctiveness as a response to political and economic defeat.

3. LICIT AND ILLICIT PLEASURES

Liverpool gives equal value to licit and illicit pleasures. Catholic traditions, red light districts, old established minority communities and popular religion are the essential ingredients. Liverpool is the gambling, drugs and vice capital of Britain.

4. NOTIONS OF POPULAR JUSTICE

Liverpool has a strong sense of popular justice but also a strong sense of being hard done by. Consequently it suffers from paranoia and victimisation.

5. IT'S UNIQUELY MISUNDERSTOOD

Liverpool feels uniquely misunderstood. This links to the particular quality of humour and also to the importance of international connections. It feels less victimised the more it's internationally recognised, further problematising its relationship with national culture and politics.

6. FAILURE TO TURN CREATIVITY INTO INNOVATION

Liverpool has a strong and well-established reputation for cultural talent and creativity but has traditionally been unable to turn this creativity into innovative and profitable services and products. This is one of the differences between Liverpool and Manchester.

7. NEGATIVE PERCEPTIONS

Liverpool suffers profoundly from negative perceptions by the outside world, investors and economic and political decision-makers, and has enormous difficulty in getting and retaining inward investment. Civic leaders would describe this as a major place marketing issue.

8. LOYALTY

Liverpool invokes a strong sense of loyalty, and outsiders often fall in love with it. Why? It's a combination of things: friendliness of people, sense of belonging, historical and cultural traditions, irreverent sense of humour, open-mindedness, vitality, creativity, colourfulness and for artists especially, the ever-present sense of edge and the knowledge that anarchy rests barely below the waterline.

9. LIVERPOOL AS CITY-STATE

Liverpool sees itself as a city-state, as an island within a national territory. It has a love–hate relationship with the metropolitan centre, on the one hand having a reputation for crime, disorder, unreliability and backwardness and on the other, a recognised special role in the cultural formation of national identity. Liverpool is like the noir or repressed side of national culture.

Under the pressure of time, conformism and fatalism coming from our collective sense of powerlessness, is it any wonder that artists and creative people find the antidote in the bloody-mindedness and irreverence of Liverpool?

Like me, FACT is from Liverpool. Not the Liverpool of old, but the Liverpool of now and the future. It cost £11 million to build and equip. It's the first purpose-built arts building in the city for more than sixty years. And it's the first arts building of any scale in the city which has not come about in one of the following ways:

— as a gift to the city from a rich benefactor;
— by the city council, as a gesture of civic pride or to meet a perceived gap in provision; or
— as part of central government strategies to address social ills.

This is important.

How so? Let me explain. FACT began life as Moviola in 1988. At that time it was just me, working out of a small office in central Liverpool. The idea was simple: to commission artists' film, video and new media projects and to work in partnership with galleries around the country in order to present this work. The primary vehicle for achieving this was the Video Positive Biennial, which was conceived by Moviola and first staged in 1989. There wasn't very much money to speak of at the time and little in the way of physical resources. But it proved to be the largest installation-based film and video event to be held in Britain to that point.

1988 was the year that Tate Liverpool opened in a converted Victorian warehouse on the Albert Dock and became one of the key venues for Video Positive. The Tate was the centrepiece of a regeneration project that had come about, in part, as a result of central government initiatives to combat the city's social ills, most starkly expressed—or repressed, depending on your perspective—in 1981 when the Toxteth uprisings inspired copycat riots across Britain.

Moviola grew and developed a number of national services, including the national exhibition technology support service (MITES). By 1995 the work we were doing and many of the international artists we were commissioning had, by and large, gone from the margins to the mainstream. Practice had evolved and diversified, technologies had developed, audience expectations were changing. This was the moment to conceive a new cultural enterprise and that's what we did.

But here's the rub. Everyone in Liverpool has a project. That's because, as Lewis Biggs pointed out in his essay in the Liverpool Biennial 2002 catalogue, everyone in Liverpool is ducking and diving, bobbing and weaving. Up to something. On the make. Everyone is engaged, no matter how obliquely, in a form of cultural production. Liverpool produces more than it consumes. It's as if everyone has swallowed a copy of Fred Hirsch's *Social Limits to Growth* and come to a tacit agreement that all consumption is positional, we are consequently trapped in self-defeating cycles of desire and dissatisfaction, and the only way to break out of this cycle is to become a producer.

So I had a new building project, but then again, so did everybody else. Neither the civic great and the good nor the city council gave much of a helping hand at first. The national Arts Council always supported it, but they were only one part of the funding package. The people who really saw its potential locally were in the private sector, and as the primary source of the city's new entrepreneurial energy they carried a lot of weight. So we were positioned as cultural entrepreneurs, or 'venture culturalists', alongside the new duckers and divers, bobbers and weavers of the city.

FACT is unique within the UK cultural landscape. No other cultural institution has the same mix of programs, spaces, resources and expertise. It's a centre for film, video and new and emerging media art. It has cinemas, galleries, flexible spaces, spaces for online projects, spaces to support production, creation and ideas. We produce as well as consume. It cost £11 million to build and equip. Ninety per cent of the monies came from three sources: the Arts Council, the European Commission and the Regional Economic Development Agency. There was no funding from the city, though it now cleverly claims FACT as its own, particularly since FACT was singled out by the judges who awarded the title of European Capital of Culture 2008 as one of the main reasons why Liverpool secured the title.

We commission a lot of work for the galleries by international artists, such as Isaac Julien's *Baltimore*, commissioned for the opening of the FACT building in February 2003. We also commission partnership projects between international artists and Liverpool communities. This effort, called the Collaboration Programme, is art made as a joint effort by artists and people who would never describe themselves as artists. Almost 100 projects have been commissioned in twelve years. This isn't an outreach/education program or simply projects which satisfy the fluffy polemics of Nicholas Bourriaud's *Relational Aesthetics*. On the whole, this is the real thing, where consumers become active producers and owners of their respective projects.

One example is Tenantspin. It started four years ago when Superflex, the Danish artists' collective, came, at our request, to work with a community of people who were mostly in their sixties, seventies and eighties and were based in the oldest high-rise tower block in Liverpool, another potent symbol of the city's contemporary ills. From that initial experiment the Tenantspin project has emerged. Dozens of tenants now inhabit the FACT building on a daily basis, preparing and producing webcasts, running training courses for other residents, or simply hanging out. Many artists come to hang out with them and sometimes do projects. The tenants now deliver 'workshops' across the world, and we are rolling out a series of mobile webcast projects with various communities across England's north-west.

In helping to develop Tenantspin, Superflex proposed a shift in attitudes and understanding of the space of art and the role of the artist. The pilot project asked us to consider a reframing of the artist's social role and of the relationship between artist, artwork and recipient, viewer or participant. This is a crucial point because they insist on their own studied neutrality in the face of demands to politicise their art or to suggest a kind of manifesto for their projects. Instead they speak about tools: the means to achieve objectives determined by others.

Projects like Tenantspin, and the Collaboration Programme, rely for their legitimacy on the principles of trust and shared values, and the construction of frameworks and networks for negotiation between artists, communities and other agencies. It's arguable that if FACT were a creation of the civic authorities, it would be unlikely to establish that legitimacy with either the artists or the communities that are now part of the production culture of the city.

Legitimacy is a key issue for James Moores. He is the single largest investor in the Liverpool Biennial. His contribution each year is more than the Arts Council's and the city's investment combined. James is the grandson of John Moores, who established the football pools and other businesses in the city and elsewhere around the world in the first decades of the last century. They are filthy rich. So is James. He's a practising artist and distrusts authority. For the Biennial to be legitimate for him, for artists, and for communities, it had to emerge out of need, unlike the Biennale in Valencia or Barcelona, which appeared to be established in order to attract tourists or to change the image of the city. And so the Liverpool Biennial began without the city even knowing about it. James believes in the power of art to change cities and to change people's lives, but that it has to come from some unofficial place for it to retain its value.

I was part of the curatorial team that worked on the 2002 edition of the Biennial. One of the projects which had a huge impact locally—as well as being a big hit with the critics—was *Villa Victoria* by Tatsurou Bashi.

When Bashi visited the city for the first time he stumbled upon this great edifice of the grandmother of empire. Until Bashi's intervention it had been notable for only two things:

— the volume of pigeon shit that often encased it; and
— the local perception that the sculptor had given Victoria a penis, as in side profile she appeared to possess an erect member.

The statue stands under a cupola on a grandiose plinth. Bashi encased it— surrounding columns and all—in a giant wooden structure held up on scaffolding, so that the Queen stood inside a large hotel bedroom. People booked to stay there every night for ten weeks.

Bashi's work was a very clever take on the fact that, after a while, public monuments and statues fade into the background in our cities. It was a work that said something specifically about Liverpool, about differences between human scale and the monumental, about material differences in the urban environment, about inside and outside, and about the value and iconography of public commemoration.

Victoria's shadow hangs heavy over Liverpool in any case, as a symbol of the empire that made the city. And it turned out to be a perfect metaphor for the city as it negotiates the painful adjustment to the end of empire.

So what next for the cultural entrepôt? Not to be outdone by Sydney or Bilbao, Liverpool is getting its very own architectural icon in the form of Will Alsop's 'Fourth Grace', at a cost of £200 million. Unlike the icons of Sydney and Bilbao, the function of the building has yet to be revealed!

But as the cold breath of the zeitgeist, in the form of global capital, ensures that the image and impact of empire fade from the city, we enter a period that is full of contested ideas, views and perspectives. Is Liverpool and its cultural milieu—with projects like FACT and Liverpool Biennial now being assimilated into the new mainstream—simply conforming to one of Richard Florida's notions of plug-and-play communities (liberal, urbane, tolerant)? Or, as Kate Oakley from Demos puts it in her critique of Florida, 'in his world places like Liverpool are reduced to nothing more than lifestyle amenities, which can very appealing if you're young, male and single—but what about the rest of us?' Exactly.

Perhaps now, as never before, Liverpool's civic leaders as well as FACT, the Liverpool Biennial and other agents of cultural change, share some particular challenges, which might be summarised as follows:

1. HOW TO RETAIN THE NOTION OF 'EDGE'?

How will it be possible to give value to the edgy quality of the city as cultural organisations and projects turn this into an asset? How can it be made into an urban countermodel to the dehumanised and bureaucratised globalised city?

2. WILL EXPLICIT RECOGNITION OF THE 'EDGINESS' OF LIVERPOOL UNDERMINE ITS DISTINCTIVENESS?

Should edginess become a *place marketing concept* or will it kill the golden goose? The danger of explicit 'official' promotion of dissidence or deviance is that it destroys it by normalising it. But can it be mobilised and supported so that it is renewed, enabling others and future generations to benefit from it?

3. HOW TO CELEBRATE LIVERPOOL'S 'UNRULY GENIUS'?

The historical dimension of Liverpool and this awkwardness, this 'unruly genius', relied on the global function of the port, which has changed. The future of the city's edginess relies on creating new international links, which will keep the city open and ensure an influx of alternative ideas and people.

4. HOW TO CELEBRATE AND REVIVE TRANSGRESSIVE AND SUBVERSIVE TRADITIONS?

The focus on edginess requires a bold approach which recognises the value of transgressive and subversive traditions—and the role of art and artists within these traditions—as well as their cost and difficulty, and also seeks to include outsiders—'those beyond the pale'—within this program.

In 1869 the English poet, literary critic and social commentator Matthew Arnold published *Culture and Anarchy*, his book-length defence of the purpose of art. In it, Arnold defined art as 'the criticism of life'. Empires may have come and gone, but 135 years later this assertion appears more important than ever. 'The criticism of life' is surely both the burden and a central function of culture in the global city.

Other Speak: The Poetics of Cultural Difference

PAUL CARTER

Allegories are, in the realm of thought, what ruins are in the realm of things.
—Walter Benjamin

Arguments for the recognition of cultural difference are usually couched in political terms. The enemies of diversity are attacked because they are powerful. If they were weak, as most fundamentalist sects are, their indifference to difference might be tolerated. But when different histories, geographies, cultures and life experiences are measured in terms of their exchange value in the global marketplace, it is, as it were, different. A future in which the ideal type of humanity is the white, middle-class American consumer is hardly liberating. But, as long as the political institutions traditionally associated with the promulgation of difference collude in the market's rhetoric—such as the claim that Society does not exist, only individuals—our power of collective self-determination is greatly weakened. Underlying the advocacy of cultural difference is often another motive: a lament for democracy's retreat from its historical project of securing freedom of speech. When the marketplace acquires the power to *auction* the right to speak differently, it is evident that democratic rights are eroded. In this climate, those who denounce the homogenisation that occurs when a globalised capitalist economy seeks to make consumers of us sublimate another frustration: the powerlessness of democracy to speak, the usurpation of its language of individual difference.

In fact, there is a double loss: discursive and spatial. Edward Said alluded to the first of these in his lecture, 'The Public Role of Writers and Intellectuals'. When '[t]he main goal of this dominant discourse [of global capitalism] is to fashion the merciless logic of corporate profit-making and political power into a normal state of affairs, "that is the way things are", in the process rendering rational resistance to these notions into something altogether and practically unrealistic, irrational, utopian',[1] the role of the engaged writer qua intellectual is obvious. It is, despite the devaluation of the language of reason, to speak eloquently and truthfully about the plight of the culturally different. But here is the rub. How is the language of resistance to differentiate itself from the language of the State Department? When Plain Speak has replaced parabolic modes of communication, what discursive authority remains to the writer? Said promises to consider later in the same lecture 'the possibility that there remains an area outside and untouched by the globalised one' he is examining, but that discussion never occurs. As a result, the place of writing, identified with the interests of the poor and oppressed, is assimilated to the public role of the intellectual. The implication is that writing—the full reach of literary expression—must be pared back to the bare stylistic minimum needed to combat globalisation on its own ground.

The *place* of writing cultural difference is similarly attenuated. If Said's stylistic rapprochement with power is not accepted, the writer is swept from the marketplace, the old agora of democratic discourse. Writing of the new global cities where no one 'lives', Jean-Francois Lyotard, who *does* champion an area outside the globalised one, tries to give that place a name. The megalopolis, he writes, 'does not permit writing, inscribing'.[2]

It follows that public space, *Öffentlichkeit*, in these conditions, stops being the space for experiencing, testing and affirming the state of a mind open to the event, and in which the mind seeks to elaborate an idea of that state itself, especially under the sign of the 'new'. Public space today is transformed into a market of cultural commodities, in which 'the new' has become an additional source of surplus value.[3]

Less sanguine about the survival of free thought in the new globalised marketplace, Lyotard concludes that the reduction of space and time to grids that furnish the smooth conditions of maximum capitalistic exchange means that 'thought and writing are isolated and placed in the ghetto, in the sense in which the work of Kafka deploys that theme'.[4] The Kafkaesque ghetto is both a physical location and a place in language. It resists the massive site clearance preliminary to the construction of the global city. Its indirect language, its habit of speaking in Kafkaesque parables, also resists Plain Speak's principle of instant translatability; hence, '[i]t must be exterminated because it constitutes an empty opacity for the programme of total mobilisation in view or transparency.'[5]

Here, the *practical* dilemma of writing cultural difference emerges: the politics of engagement demands one style, the poetics of resistance another. Ien Ang tries to overcome these difficulties when she locates the project of 'cultural translation in a globalised world' in a liminal zone. Arguing that 'the moment of translation, the very movement to and fro [should] acquire … primacy over the substance of the identities', she asserts that this moment 'establishes an intercultural borderzone': it is a 'liminal space', even a 'bor-derland'.[6] Hers is a model of communication that identifies the discourse of cultural difference with the production and practice of distinctive social and political identities, occupying equally distinctive crossover zones. Her zones of noisy multiplicity seem remote from the darker than dark cell in which Kafka secreted himself. Perhaps both have something in common with the 'other "other place"' called for in *Repressed Spaces*[7]: if the founding 'other place' of democracy has become a marketplace where prices are fixed but not values, the discourse that enables us to imagine our world differently must take flight to another place, one which, like public space, exists equally in language and in space. But the question remains: what is it about the communication of cultural difference that flight from the smooth plain of the dominant discourse is intended to preserve?

A response to this question begins by demurring from the assumption, which Said seems to make, that the 'dominant discourse', whether deployed by the State Department or by multinational economists, is 'transparent', its meanings presented without rhetorical investment. As Donald Levine points out, 'The institutions of modern society and culture require an enormous increase in resources of univocal communication.' Clear, unambiguous expression 'advances our capabilities for gaining cognitive [and we might add, operational] mastery of the world'.[8] This holds true whether the institutionalised writer is a left-wing intellectual or the President's speechwriter, but it does not render univocal communication value-free. Even when, for example, straightforward language is used to defend variety of choice, it presupposes an eradication. For choice, as Verene argues, is the product of living in 'a technological world ... a world without memory', where '[t]houghts are understood as instruments and persons as agents in a field of action and problem-solving.'[9] In this sense, other forms of expression (for example, the entire repertoire of persuasive or rhetorical figures of speech classically associated with publicly conducted politics) communicate difference, not because they are employed on behalf of the right cause, but because their parabolic character—the ambiguous relationship between tenor and vehicle, in I. A. Richards' terms—preserves the trace of difference.

But in any case Plain Speak is neither univocal nor transparent. The politicians of globalism do not use the abstract language of instrumental reason. They employ the homely language of the back verandah. The visual equivalent of their anecdotal, rhetorically deflationary mode is the TV commercial which businesses use to promote their products globally. Whatever its provenance, it is axiomatic that the 'dominant discourse' must give the global agenda a human face. A politician illustrates a discussion of the future of environmental biodiversity with the image of an unemployed forestry worker. A multinational producer of hamburgers makes acceptable the faceless consumption of environmental and human resources by zooming in on a satisfied mouth. Such techniques of representation may pose as an unassuming respect for the matter-of-fact, but their dissolution of the fates of entire societies into the tastes of a single, idealised consumer—a ploy that updates a rhetorical device classically known as prosopopoeia—serves, in effect, to privatise the public sphere. David Marquand amplifies this point in his recent book, *Decline of the Public*. Exit, as he calls the substitution of market relationships for political ones characterising the neo-liberal ascendancy in the 1980s, 'is, almost by definition, expressive, free and spontaneous. It is individualistic and, in a profound sense, private.' The convenient paradox is that this contraction of the world's value to an individual's self-interest keys in directly to global capitalism's agenda. 'Emotionally, perhaps even intellectually, those values [of authenticity, of direct experience, of all that was implied in the fashionable solipsism of "doing your own thing"] are first cousins to the values of market liberalism.'[10]

In this situation, it is not a question of critiquing the 'dominant discourse' on its own terms, using the unambiguous language of instrumental reason *more reasonably*. It is a matter, first, of recognising that the discourse likely to eliminate difference makes banal the figurative language traditionally associated with political expression in democratic societies. That is, the positivistic, univocal language of government and business is not an unequivocal and principled flight from the parabolic, but a careless corruption and banalisation of rhetorical resources. In reference to the prestige that the symbol enjoyed in Modernist literary theory and practice, J. Hillis Miller hazards this explanation:

Allegory—the word means to speak figuratively, or to speak in other terms, or to speak of other things in public, from the Greek *allegorein*, *allos*, other, plus *agoreuein*, to speak (in public), from *agora*, an assembly, but also the marketplace or customary place of assembly. If agoraphobia is a fear of open spaces, would allegoraphobia be the fear of that form of language which speaks otherwise?[11]

But the same might be said of the language of the 'privatist renaissance' Marquand describes: it is allegoraphobic. And, if we recall Aristotle's remark in the third book of the *Rhetoric*, that good prose style 'should have a "foreign" [*xenikos*] quality, that is, distinctive, away from the common',[12] it is easy to see that writing cultural difference *is* a matter of poetic style.

It should be clear, then, that what is needed in relation to the dominant discourse is not simply an ever-vigilant media criticism. This, however liberally motivated, is couched in the language of instrumental reason. Its univocal character may yield a kind of cognitive mastery, but its voice, lacking the immediate mask that power wears to broadcast its pronouncements, is unlikely to make much political difference. In Britain, at least, this reflects the historical fact that democracy has remained tied to the interests represented by the constitutional monarchy, and these easily mesh with economic dominance. The notion of a public with a collectively influential voice has never been welcomed or encouraged by the power elites. As David Marquand puts it, 'in the public domain, accountability can come only through the Voice—in other words through argument, discussion, debate and democratic engagement. But in nineteenth- and early twentieth-century Britain, accountability through Voice was lacking or attenuated; and the growth of the public domain did nothing to enhance it.' Indeed, at the core of the Gladstonian central state lay a tradition of autonomous executive power, a parliamentary monarchy which 'was not supposed to be democratic, still less participatory'.[13] In this context, vigorous public debate is doubly hindered; it is prone to the allegoraphobic

… [T]he true meaning of the Olympics to Australians as topography was a matter of retracing tracks, restaging the mobile experience of the race and the interval of the leap. It might have little or nothing to do with dates, times and distances, and everything to do with recapitulating the transcendent efforts of great athletes in the ordinary steps and site-pacings of spectators, those visitors to the stadia who, in between events, took the opportunity to visit Fig Grove, there to repose, to wander, and gradually to find themselves in a dense network of rhythmic threads taking part in a race of their own. Lewis and I symbolised this exchange between public history and private history in complementing the monumental writing of the vertical faces with graffiti clusters.

These clusters were inspired by handwriting and monograms contributed by Australian Olympic athletes, but we wanted them, in their scaled-up flourish and calligraphic excess, to suggest the 'I was fleetingly here' of the graffiti artist. Childlike in their freedom of gesture, we also thought of them like the chalked out figures children use, or used to use, in their endless repertoire of counting-out games. Inside these tiny arenas the youthful jumpers and chanters first rehearse future roles as athletes and spectators; and this too we wanted to acknowledge.

In contrast with the capital letters imperturbably striding left to right, suggesting mighty but remote events, these markings paid tribute to the democratic presence of the eye witness—without whose devotion the Olympics would have no audience …

—from Paul Carter, Trace, the Book of Relay,
    unpublished manuscript, 2001

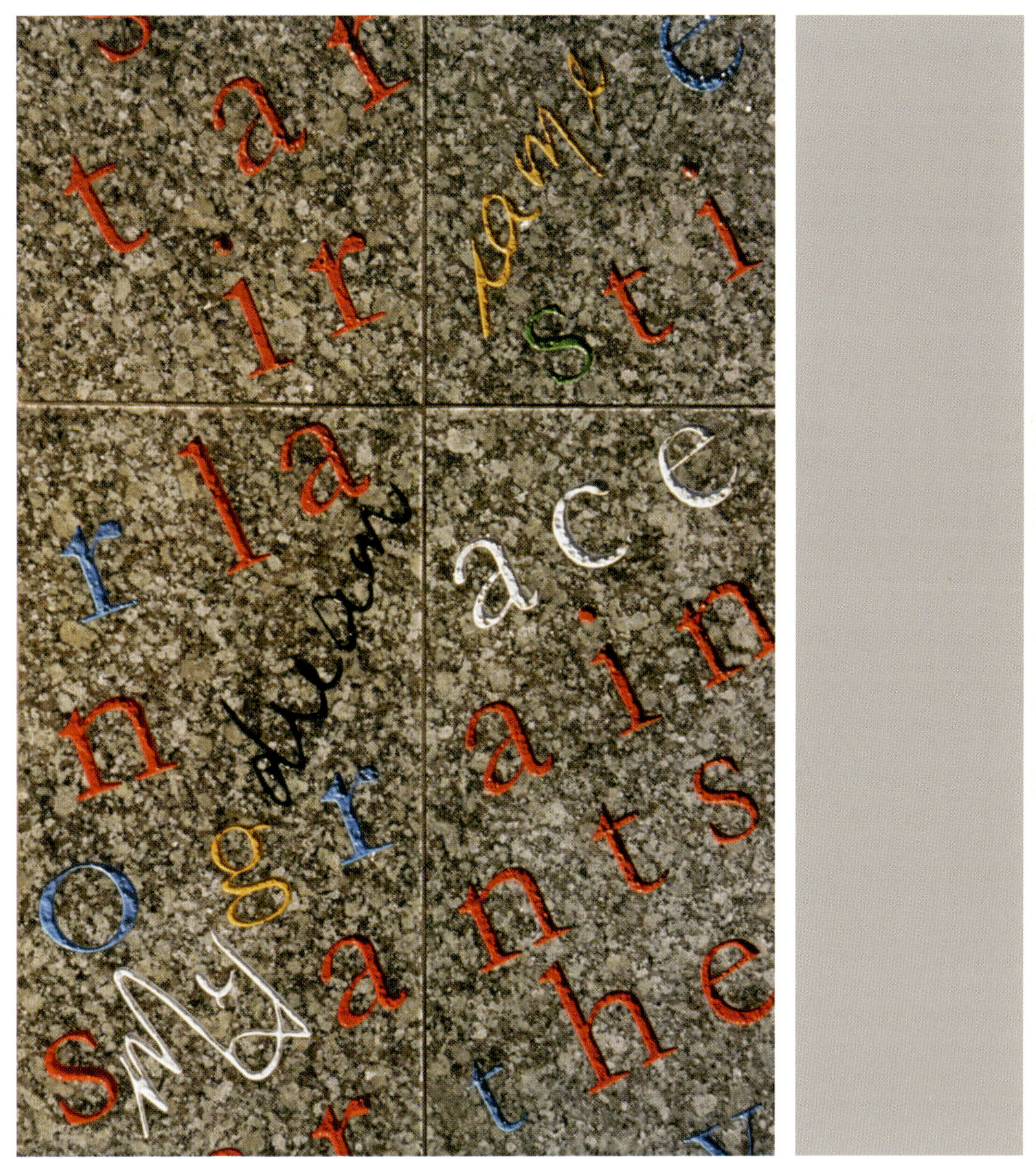

Paul Carter and Ruark Lewis, *Relay* (1999), detail of Graffiti Cluster
no. 27, Fig Tree Grove, Homebush Bay; courtesy of Paul Carter.

restriction on figurative speech, and its advocacy of cultural difference benignly neutralised.

The implication of this seems plain. Advocacy of cultural difference needs to overcome allegoraphobia. Marquand maintains that the reinvention of the public domain, with its respect for 'diversity, pluralism, *difference*',[14] turns on achieving 'accountability through Voice'.[15] Yet this prompts the question: what kind of Voice? Expressing its collective will in what way? As Marquand points out, 'Differences need protection. Pressures for centralisation are omnipresent; and they have been enhanced, not weakened, by the communications revolution.'[16] As already intimated, allegory, or Other Speak, has a long association with democracy's capacity to articulate the value of difference. Nevertheless, Marquand's point about centralisation oddly bears on allegory's diminished prestige as a bearer of public meanings. In another discussion about the difference between the symbolic and allegorical modes of figurative expression, philosopher Hans-Georg Gadamer argues that the difference between allegory and symbol is that the former makes the reference explicit, while the latter leaves it implicit: 'In the case of allegory, the reference must be known in advance. In the case of the symbol ... the particular represents itself as a fragment of being that promises to complete and make whole whatever corresponds to it.'[17] Allegory, therefore, 'is only possible for a poetry as long as there exists a secure common horizon of interpretation in which it can take place'.[18] On this definition, the centralisation that Marquand sees as the enemy of allegory should be its *friend*, as, in principle, it restores a common horizon, one that globalises the pursuit of individual satisfaction.

The flaw in the argument is easily detected. The 'common horizon' of the dominant discourse of global capitalism is not predicated on a negotiation between the visible and the invisible. Unlike absolute monarchs or papal incumbents, the captains of consumption assume the ends are plain to see—even if rhetorical sleight of hand is needed to lend them a face. With

Gadamer's figure in mind, perhaps this can be expressed by way of a geographical allegory. The common horizon of interpretation that underwrites the 'reference' of allegory is a boundary that marks the passage from the visible to the invisible realm. By contrast, the horizon global capitalism invokes is infinite. There is no translation between physical and metaphysical realms. The world, according to the promotors of boundless expansion, is flat. We who inhabit it, economic Cartesians, are Flat Earthers. The horizon does not signify finitude, and inculcate a sense of interdependence that draws individuals together. As a sign of always deferred arrival, retreating as we approach, the horizon embodies capitalism's Lacanian desire. It calibrates the need to go on, rendering graspable what cannot be grasped.

The ideological basis of this conception resides in the brute fact that, after all, the earth is round not flat. And it is likely that this is not only a figurative way of illustrating the irrationality of capitalism's adherence to a fantasy of infinite expansion: it may be literally the case that capitalists cannot abide the notion of inhabiting an allegorical surface whose topology binds them to return to the hidden meaning of what they have done.

The communications revolution may not favour discourses of difference, but this merely underlines the impracticability of advocating a return to unreconstructed allegorical modes of expression. There are good historical reasons why allegory became a threatened rhetorical species, and these need to be understood if a new allegoraphilia is to be cultivated. It is no accident that, on the historical seesaw of poetic taste, allegory's prestige went down as the value accorded to the symbol went up. The ascendancy of the symbol towards the end of the nineteenth century was symptomatic of the erosion of that common horizon of bourgeois realist values. The fact that allegory made explicit what it referred to seemed to Walter Benjamin to be a sign of its weakness as a poetic vehicle. In his aphorism, 'Allegories are, in the realm of thought, what ruins are in the realm of things', Benjamin means that they impede a Hegelian manifestation (or *Scheinen*) of the 'Idea' as such. Instead of

… Treating the letters as material objects enabled me to secrete the other meanings differently. Enigma resided in the physical fact that volumes of typography crossed through each other: letters were warped, hidden and disclosed by other letters; the common horizon of interpretation was set by the landscape of the letter field itself …

In relation to allegory (and Nearamnew) consider : 'Neoplatonic theorists emphasise the necessity of a text's hinting at the existence of its hidden meaning. The surface will point to added symbolic complications by means of, as Coulter felicitously puts it, the "suggestive incompleteness" of its literal text.' (Rollinson, 9). This Neoplatonic sense of allegory contradicts Benjamin's identification of allegory with ruin; instead, it is the breaking off of the surface meaning that suggests the inner beauty; it is the apostrophe that defines the eloquence of the appeal. Here it is the under-sense that is stressed—recalling the other Greek term, hyponoia.

This well captures the logic of the visual or sculptural rhetoric of Nearamnew …'

—from Paul Carter, Diary, September 2004.

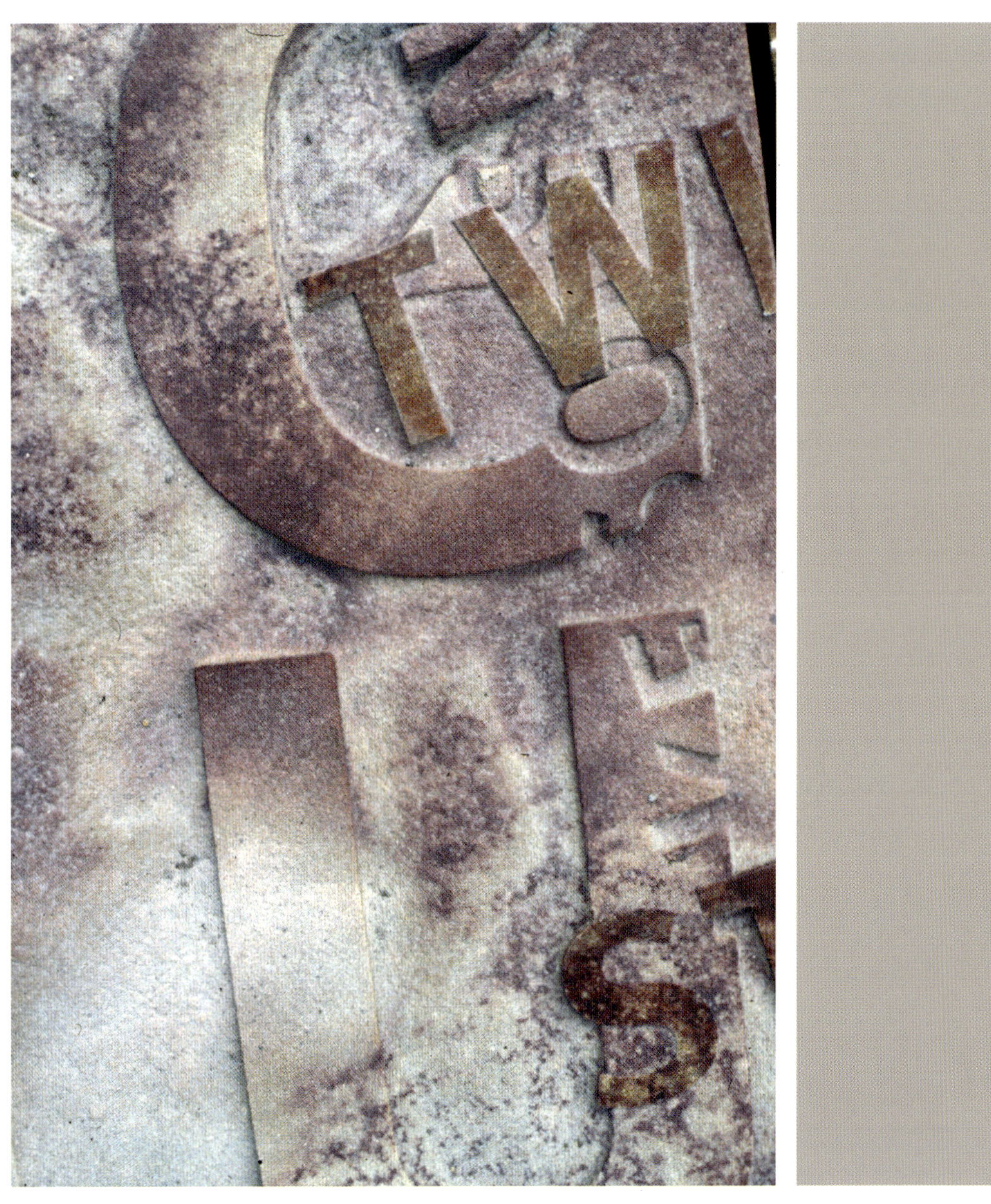

Paul Carter in collaboration with Lab architecture studio,
Nearamnew (2003), detail of Regional Ground Figure No. 1,
The Maker's Vision, Federation Square, Melbourne;
courtesy of Paul Carter.

contributing to the fusion of idea and matter, they insist on their disjunction. As Miller interprets Benjamin,

> In allegory, writing and personification reveal, bring out into the open as *Scheinen*, the eternal disjunction between the inscribed sign and its material embodiment. It is writing, the characters written on nature as features are written on a face, which devastates it … In allegory naked matter shines through. It shines through as the failure of the idea to transform nature or thought. In this sense allegories are, in the realm of thought, what ruins are in the realm of things.[19]

The aesthetic corollary is obvious: as Murray Krieger writes of allegory, to overcome 'the dualistic character of the signifier looking helplessly across the chasm of time at an unreachable signified'[20], a figure of speech is preferable that fuses idea and matter, making here and there, past and present simultaneously present. This is precisely the function of the symbol in Symbolist theory. To return to Miller: a symbol 'is a physical sign in preordained correspondence with a certain metaphysical reality. Material sign, subjective emotion, and supernatural originating power come together in the symbol.'[21] In a way, the Modernist project of purifying the tongue of the tribe took the form of privatising allegory, and, by re-presenting its overarching figures of speech as broken fragments, symbolically intimating a larger form that could no longer be built, it aimed at shoring up the strangeness of poetry in a time when the common horizon of interpretation had withdrawn. This was therapeutic. It seemed to confront the fragmentation directly and preserved at least the relics of poetic reason. But the effect of this was to cede the public domain to an expository form of prose that had little to do with allegory: Eliot's split of sensibility, which he attributed to the Metaphysicals, applied in reality to his own experience of the crisis of reference.

Formally, any initiative to restore allegory's lost dignity would need to begin with a distinction between two commonly received meanings of the term. Reductively described, allegory is, as Coleridge dismissively put it, the 'translation of abstract notions into a picture-language which is itself nothing but an abstraction from objects of the senses'.[22] The imagery of TV commercials is allegorical in this sense, and as Coleridge indicates, in putting a face to abstractions, it doubly deceives—the face selected misrepresents not only an intellectual object but the evidence of the senses as well. However, allegory can also refer to figurative language in general. In this application, it includes metaphor, the use of irony, riddles or enigmas, fables, parables and prosopopoeia (or personification)—in short, the full gamut of rhetorical devices the classical orator employed when called upon to speak persuasively in public. In this second definition, it is not the forceful clarity of allegory that amazes, but its suggestiveness, its intriguing strangeness. This quality arises from the fact that speaking (and writing) as 'other' always implies a horizon beyond which language cannot go. Translated into phenomenological (but also political) terms, this horizon is the place from which the speaker's own speech comes, the common horizon of a shared language but for which communication would be impossible. The fact that, despite this commonality, communication is necessary proves that inscribed into language as it were, is difference, the fact that a shared horizon of interpretation presupposes separateness, strangeness and the always imminent lapse into silence and barbarism.

On this argument, the fact that allegory allows naked matter to show through is a strength rather than a weakness. As Paul de Man put it in an influential re-evaluation, allegorical writing embodies a suspicion of symbols precisely because their magical presencing disguises the reality of temporal and spatial disjunction. 'Whereas the symbol postulates the possibility of an identity or identification', allegory, viewed positively, 'designates primarily a distance in relation to its own origin, and, renouncing the nostalgia and the desire to coincide, it establishes its language in the void of this temporal difference.'[23] On this reading, differentiated from metaphor, symbol and conventional prosopopoeia, allegory recovers its privileged role as the discourse of the other place, that other place being understood now as 'other' to the 'market of cultural commodities'. If public space is understood as creating the distance that allows an approach to the other that does *not* lead to enslavement, the collapse of cultural difference, then allegory's recognition of the limits of what can be represented and communicated becomes its greatest political and poetic virtue.[24]

Evidently—to pursue the literary implications of this—the new allegory operates without a 'common horizon'. As a poetic device that foregrounds experiences of finitude, it nevertheless has to construct a meaning that is, culturally speaking, horizonless. In Kafka, as in Beckett, the horizonless experience is, in effect, the crisis of reference itself, the existential intuition that nothing makes sense, that the symbols, absorbed into the discourse of authority, have ceased to have any metaphysical meaning beyond their power to confine our freedom. Hence Gadamer finds that the 'apparently familiar world' Kafka describes

> is accompanied by a mysterious feeling of strangeness which creates the impression that everything in it actually points beyond itself to something else. At the same time, we cannot interpret all this as allegory, precisely because the principal event that this masterly example of narrative art presents to us is the dissolution of any shared horizon of interpretation ... The text evokes poetically the mere semblance of allegory and opens out onto the realm of ambiguity.[25]

Suspending identification, allegorical discourse is the speech 'in other words' that characterises public speech when the ideology of the free market has privatised the traditional domain of public speech. Far from depending upon a shared horizon of belief, it appeals to what cannot be known, the ever-present horizon of unknowing. In this sense, the revivified allegory recapitulates the origins of civil society, in which communication is necessarily open, incomplete and renewed. We experience this individually whenever we open to ourselves to who is clearly not self-same (but 'other' by definition). Merleau-Ponty argues that the first 'other' is 'a primordial relation between me and my speech … Through this relation, the other myself can become other … The common language which we speak is something like the anonymous corporeality which we share with other organisms.'[26] Yet the language is 'common' by virtue of a certain figurative, gestural invitation:

> [I]n speech we realise the impossible agreement between two totalities not because speech forces us back upon ourselves to discover some unique spirit in which we participate but because speech concerns us, catches us indirectly, seduces us, trails us along, transforms us into the other and him into us, abolishes the limit between mine and not-mine.[27]

In a related spirit, Emmanuel Levinas also revivifies the allegorical mode. In place of the worn-out figure of personification or prosopopoeia, which all too easily renders the strange familiar, he defines the face as that which cannot be alienated, referring to 'the "beyond" from which the face comes'.[28] In place of the horizon as the vanishing point and limit of representation, he conceives of the other approaching us from beyond the horizon.[29] In this reformulation, allegory preserves rather than tames the finitude of all communication, its double register reflecting the inevitable difference written into all relations between things. The difference is not merely spatial but temporal. Hence, Levinas can speak of the face 'as the very mortality of the other man'.[30] In this context what Levinas calls an 'ethical agoraphobia' occurs when the face of the other is withdrawn, to be replaced instead by a multiplicity of egos competing for attention. Levinas associated this anxiety with the way in which capitalism structures social relations: 'Ethical agoraphobia is a response not to an open space, but to a space where words and money are exchanged.'[31] In this situation, 'the space of the world, incessantly expanding though it may be, remains a place in which I am incessantly immured'.[32] That is, the horizonless ego-projection of capitalism is a 'ghetto', and the 'ghetto' of Lyotard is, by contrast, the allegorical condition that frees man into his personal responsibility.[33]

It is not only these allegorical interpretations of the allegorical mode that suggest that the writing of cultural difference is likely to be allegorically inflected. From a more technical point of view it may also be true. According to Paxson, Levinas's far-reaching meditation on the face of the other is prefigured in the sense in which prosopopoeia was classically understood. Personification did not necessarily mean the reduction of an idea to an image remarkably mirroring one's own interests: it could be 'the apostrophic "making present" of a dead ancestor'.[34] And this observation rapidly advances us towards a technical question of our own—one to which our preceding remarks have all been leading: how, in the commodified public space of globalising capitalism—where, as Lyotard asserts, democracy's capacity of self-renewal is banished—can the discourse of cultural difference make its mark? For the insight that Paxson offers us is this: that allegory, as the figuring forth of what is absent—the *Rhetorica* author says 'personification consists in representing an absent person as present, or in making a mute thing or one lacking form articulate'[35]—is not simply a mode of expression but a technique of representation. *Allegory is like writing*, for writing is precisely the technique for making present someone who is absent.

In other words, a revivified allegorical mode might take seriously the otherness of writing itself. Writing, in our system at least, is not picture-writing; there is no one-to-one correspondence between the letter and an object of the senses. The relationship is more subtle, as the double sense of the Greek word 'character' intimates. A character is both a letter of the alphabet and a persona or mask. It is this ambiguity that embodies the work writing does—for, as Paxson points out, a writer who uses personification is involved in more work than one who does not because 'it involves the portrayal of the emotions of children, women, nations, and even of voiceless things, all of which require to represented in character'.[36] Allegory as writing does its work of articulating cultural difference, not because of what it represents, but because of the way it represents it: obliquely, in character. As an inscriptive, sculptural or calligraphic practice, writing draws the line, producing meanings comparable to those furnished by a drawing or other significant pattern. In giving voice to dumb things, allegory does not necessarily assimilate their difference to discourse: embedded in the materiality of writing, an anonymous corporeality is given a face that remains strange.

This, then, is my proposition: that a revivified allegorical mode capable of making its mark in an agora whose surfaces have been smoothed away so as to leave no trace of democratic activity has to be a material practice of writing and speaking, and not simply a voice from the ghetto. And yet, as a site for the production of cultural difference, perhaps the contemporary ghetto should not be disparaged: for, according to Lyotard's allegory, it is in the ghetto that the kind of public space writing I am advocating as typifying the new allegorically inflected art practice emerges. The 'ghetto' is not 'an area outside and untouched by the globalised one': formed from the 'ruin of the *domus*', it is the place where the experience of cultural difference is inscribed—and inscribed differently:

> To inhabit the uninhabitable is the condition of the ghetto. The ghetto is the impossibility of the domus. Thought is not in the ghetto. Every work to which prodigal thought resolves itself secretes the wall of its ghetto, serves to neutralise its thought. It can only leave its trace upon the brick. Making media graffiti, ultimate prodigality, last homage to the lost frugality.[37]

… The urge to scribble 'over' walls stems from a desire to materialise their existence. The symbolic walls that physically isolate us yield to real walls that are places in their own right. As writing places, they are sites of secret performance (writing, reading, passing by). The wall has its thematics (the fantasy of the other side), but it also has its own eidetic reservoir. Graffiti 'unconsciously' transgress the official ornamentation of the surface. They build up visual blocks of colour. They substitute giant letters for columns, doors and windows. They create reading prospects, which they render enigmatic. There is a fantasy of the man in the wall: the Tacheles hunting party, for example, is formally similar to the 'line of power' derived from the 1860s staged corroboree photograph. One is to imagine the wall as the home of ghosts, puppets and doubles. The wall is also the edge of the tomb, the original locus of dramatic representation. Again, I can imagine that WIYN is entirely reconceived as a wall drama, dispersed and located around the walls of any city. Via the meditation on graffiti, its migration from a non-theatrical radio work to a 'nontheatrical' theatre work occurs …

—from Paul Carter, What is Your Name Production Diary, 18–23 May 2004

This is gnomically expressed, but the loss of public space that it invokes is clear enough. The quality of public space that has been lost in the era of global capitalism is its impressionability, its receptivity to thinking, its function as a writing surface. Public space can no longer be incised or inscribed; it has grown hard, smooth and surfaceless. Under these conditions, 'design', the drawing of lines, is also dematerialised. As an intellectual practice of remaking, re-marking and rethinking place, design

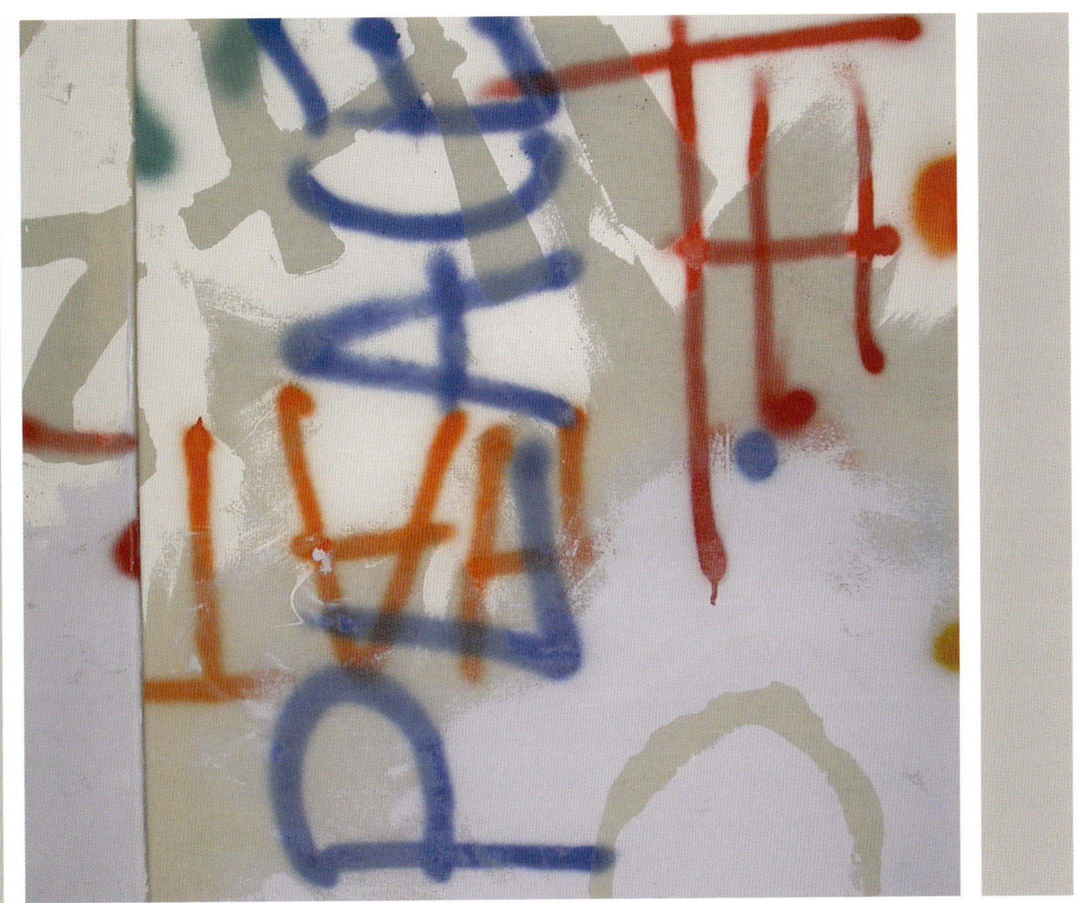

Paul Carter, *What Is Your Name* (2004), detail of moveable
grafitti panel designed by Hagen, Theaterdiscounter, Berlin,
June. Production by Prompt! Berlin (Director: Marieke Zwilling);
courtesy of Paul Carter.

has to abandon its material connection with the make-up of the place. The
lines it draws (its writing) are drawn over the place, but enjoy no choreo-
graphic relation. There is no friction: no suffering, no incision, no bleeding.
According to Lyotard, who maintains 'that any and all thought … should
require and involve inscription',

we think in a world of inscriptions already there. Call this culture if you like. And if we think, this is because there's still something missing in this plenitude and room has to be made for this lack by making the mind a blank which allows the something else remaining to be thought to happen. But this can only 'emerge' as already inscribed in its turn.[38]

If this genealogy of loss is correct, it justifies an even more surprising proposition. Not only is the allegory of the agora manifest in its physical design; the origin of public space is cognate with writing. Public space is the place of inscription. But for its prior inscription, the reinscription represented by thought could not occur. Such a statement does not imply a repetition of what has already been laid down. The *chôra* of public space is a potential space, a plastic arrangement, like language, that allows the continuous transformation and re-formation of what can be said, imagined and done. The *chôra* stands in relation to Cartesian space and time as discourse stands in relation to the grammarian's ideally fixed language. In this sense public space also stages its own insufficiency: it bears the mark of the absence it came to fill. Public space is always unfulfilled: this is why it incubates the promise of change. However, constitutionally open, public space does not ask to be filled up: the plenitude it solicits is not measured in terms of a quantity and density of buildings, monuments and 'outlets', but in the collective rhythmos of social relations. Public space incubates a desire that cannot be satisfied, the same desire that keeps the space 'public', open to the prospect of better times.

Another way to say this is that as the place of inscription—the place whose figure is the 'undistinguishable blot' of many inscriptions—public space continually cancels out what has been written. The place—the 'other "other place"' of democracy—is not a place at all in any static sense, but the setting of a mass mobility made sociable; and the art of inscription proper to its well-being is one alive to placing. The writing alive to its own placing is one that can contemplate its own disappearance, bear witness to its own erasure; in a time and place where the different (the untameable) is denied, any other kind of writing would fail to meet its responsibility. In this context, the moral function of graffiti emerges. If, in the present state, the writer must write from the ghetto, then, Lyotard concludes, 'Let us at least bear witness, and again, and for no one, to thinking as disaster, nomadism, difference and redundancy. Let's write our graffiti since we can't engrave. That seems to be a matter of real gravity.'[39]

NOTES

1   Edward Said, 'The Public Role of Writers and Intellectuals', *The Alfred Deakin Lectures: Ideas for the Future of a Civil Society*, ABC Books, Sydney, 2001, p. 475.

2   Jean-Francois Lyotard, 'Domus and the Megalopolis', in Lyotard, *The Inhuman: Reflections on Time* (trans. G. Bennington & R. Bowlby), Stanford University Press, Stanford, California, 1991, p. 202.

3   Ibid.

4   Jean-Francois Lyotard, 'Time Today', in *The Inhuman: Reflections on Time*, p. 76.

5   Ibid.

6   Ien Ang, 'Cultural Translation in a Globalised World', in N. Papastergiadis (ed.), *Complex Entanglements*, Rivers Oram Press, London and Boston, 2003, pp. 34–5.

7   Paul Carter, *Repressed Spaces: The Poetics of Agoraphobia*, Reaktion, London, 2002.

8   Donald Levine, *The Flight from Ambiguity: Essays in Social and Cultural Theory*, University of Chicago Press, Chicago, 1985, p. 8.

9   Donald Verene, *Philosophy and the Return to Self-Knowledge*, Yale University Press, New Haven, Connecticut, 1997, p. 35.

10   David Marquand, *Decline of the Public*, Polity Press, London, 2004, pp. 92–3.

11   J. Hillis Miller, 'The Two Allegories', in M. W. Bloomfield (ed.), *Allegory, Myth, and Symbol*, Harvard University Press, Cambridge, Massachusetts, 1981, p. 356.

12   Philip Rollinson, *Classical Theories of Allegory and Christian Culture*, Duquesne University Press, Pittsburgh, 1985, p. 131.

13   Marquand, p. 61.

14   Ibid., p. 141.

15   Ibid., p. 139.

16   Ibid., p. 141.

17   Hans-Georg Gadamer, *The Relevance of the Beautiful and Other Essays* (trans. N. Walker), Cambridge University Press, Cambridge, 1986, p. 32.

18   Ibid., p. 70.

19   Miller, p. 365.

20   Murray Krieger, '"A Waking Dream": The Symbolic Alternative to Allegory', in M. W. Bloomfield (ed.), *Allegory, Myth, and Symbol*, Harvard University Press, Cambridge, Massachusetts, 1981, p. 4.

21   Miller, p. 367.

22   Krieger, p. 5.

23   Krieger, pp. 14–15.

24   Maurice Merleau-Ponty, *The Visible and the Invisible* (ed. C. Lefort, trans. A. Lingis), Northwestern University Press, Evanston, Illinois, 1968. Merleau-Ponty describes the distance between the seer and the thing thus: 'it is not an obstacle between them, it is their means of communication'.

25   Gadamer, p. 71.

26   Maurice Merleau-Ponty, *The Prose of the World* (trans. John O'Neill), Northwestern University Press, Evanston, Illinois, 1973, p. 140.

27   Ibid., p. 145.

28   Emmanual Levinas, *Basic Philosophical Writings*, Indiana University Press, Bloomington, Indiana, 1996, p. 59.

29   Thus, 'I set the signifying of the face in opposition to understanding and meaning grasped on the basis of the horizon': Emmanuel Levinas, *On Thinking of the Other: Entre-Nous* (trans. M. B. Smith and B. Harshav), Athlone Press, London, 1998, p. 10.

30   Levinas, *On Thinking of the Other: Entre-Nous*, p. 186.

31   Ibid.

32   Ibid.

33   John Llewelyn, *Emmanuel Levinas: The Genealogy of Ethics*, Routledge, London, 1995, pp. 204–5.

34   James J. Paxson, *The Poetics of Personification*, Cambridge University Press, Cambridge, 1994, p. 12.

35   Ibid., p. 13.

36   Ibid., p. 19.

37   Lyotard, 'Domus and the Megalopolis', pp. 200–201.

38   Jean-Francois Lyotard, 'Can thought go on without a Body?' in *The Inhuman: Reflections on Time* (trans. G. Bennington & R. Bowlby), Stanford University Press, Stanford, California, 1991, p. 20.

39   Lyotard, 'Domus and the Megalopolis', p. 203.

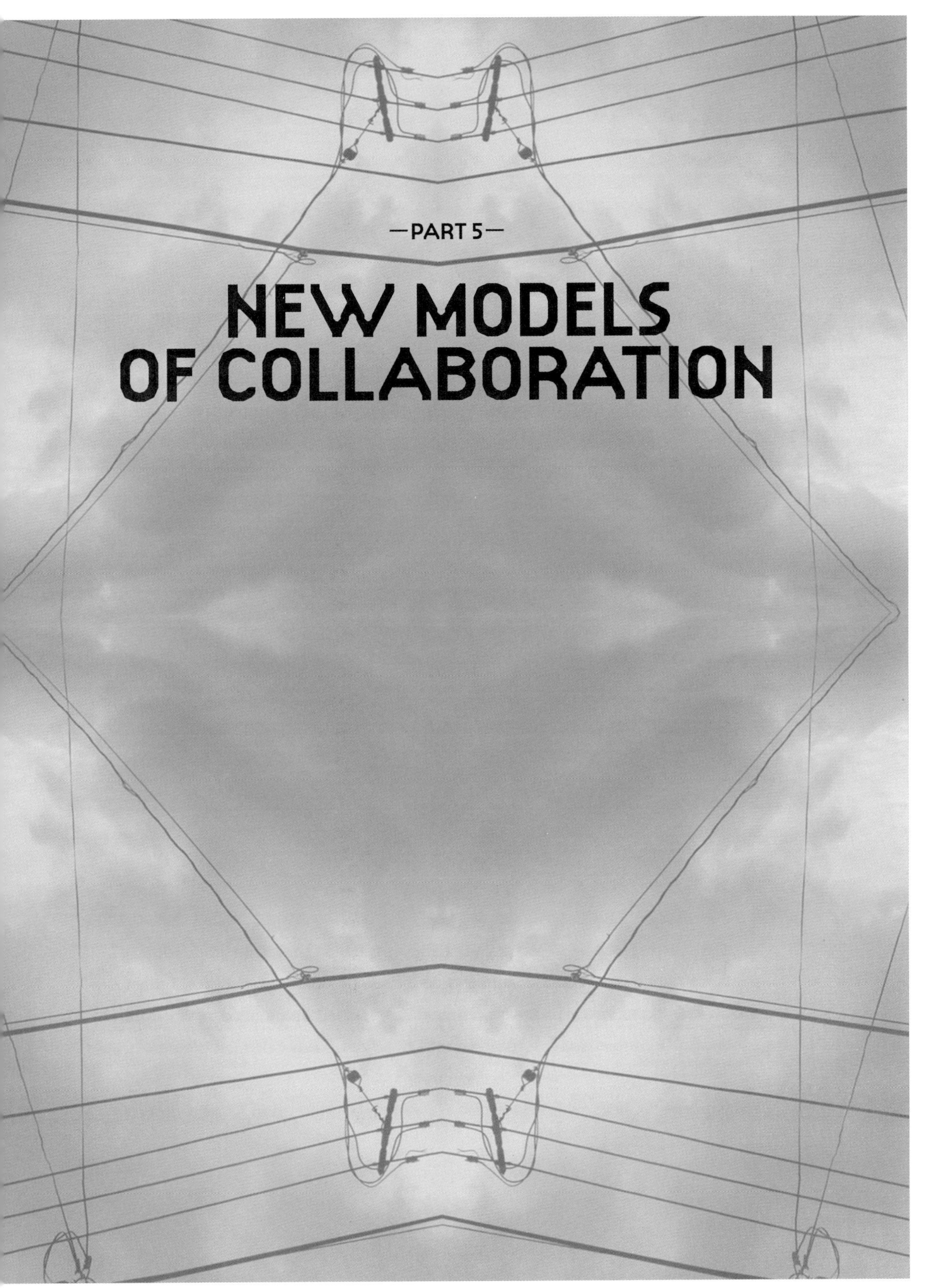
—PART 5—
NEW MODELS
OF COLLABORATION

Introduction:
New Models of Collaboration

VICTORIA LYNN

It could be argued that the challenge for cultural collaboration is more pressing now than at any other time in history. This is due in part to the fact that cultural institutions are increasingly in competition with one another, and with an expanding home and virtual entertainment industry. Pressure is such that our museums and art galleries tread a fine line between the multiple roles of cultural preservation and entertainment. Cultural organisations have a number of choices. They can persevere with the nineteenth-century notion of the museum as a pinnacle of high taste, which has a civilising role within the community. At the other extreme, museums can (and do) become entertainment venues where the cultural artefact is subservient to the marketing plan. More challenging, and more interesting, is the opportunity for cultural institutions to collaborate with one another in order to both demonstrate and stimulate artistic challenge and surprise, and further, to maintain a level of internal research and development that leads to the production of collaborative events from within. (This was a vision being developed in the early years at Melbourne's Australian Centre for the Moving Image, which has since been superseded by a bid for the entertainment dollar.)

The increasing affordability and lure of digital technologies provides a platform for such collaborations. While the technical opportunities have increased enormously, so too has the amount of work and range of expertise required: technical advice, software development, sound components, technical installation assistance, film crews, the manufacture of design components or screens. Behind every pixel is a large mainframe. In this environment, artists and curators can and do work with, and through, other fields of endeavour, such as biotechnology, cinema, architecture, music and design. They do so, however, not to 'entertain', but to expand an understanding of creativity—be it an aesthetic principle, a statement about place, an interdisciplinary event or a virtual environment. In recent years the relationship between commercialisation and creativity has been prematurely forced, to such an extent that art engaging with technology is often justified in terms of its potential contribution to employment figures in the 'creative industries'.

No collaboration will work unless there is a shared understanding of the complexity of how we move through and communicate in our contemporary world. We live in an era of the simultaneous coexistence of different spatial sensibilities—in two parallel universes that more often than not meld into one another: the physical and the virtual. The Japanese architect Toyo Ito has written that 'each of us today possesses two bodies: the body that a human being has always possessed and the virtual body that has come into being with the spread of the media. The former seeks the beautiful light and fresh breeze found in nature.' The other body, which responds to the electronic environment, might be called 'a media-like body in search of information'.[1] The relationship between these two bodies is constantly shifting. Ito argues that we connect to architecture and the city through both of them. We don't just have architects now; we also have information architects.

Collaboration cannot be forced. It has to arise from shared goals, which more often than not have a sense of urgency. Some of history's most notable collaborations have evolved at a time of political instability and human suffering. Often, the spirit of collaboration is the first sentiment to fade when an organisation is under financial stress; when the competition for funds is at its most potent. It has been my experience that the most enduring and memorable collaborations are the small gestures of co-operation between friends. Such collaborators are drawn to work together like a magnetic force, clustering around a place or principle that drives the artist to forgo individualistic goals and participate in a shared field of endeavour.

NOTE

1   Toyo Ito, 'The Transparent Urban Forest', *The Japanese Architect*, issue 19, 1995, pp. 77–8.

Attunement and Agility

ROSS GIBSON

'Globalisation' and 'crisis'. The words chime throughout this book. And rightly so. My contribution adds some notions that are complementary but not identical, namely 'complex parochialism' and 'definitive instability'. The former exists in the shadow of globalisation; the latter is noise in the atmosphere of any persistent crisis. These terms will take us to the phenomena advertised in the title of this essay: 'attunement' and 'agility'. So, I'll bring four items to the scholarly glossary. We'll see if they're useful.

First, 'complex parochialism'. Let me start with half the puzzle, with 'parochialism'. It has ecclesiastical or reactionary connotations, but it doesn't need to be like that. Parochialism can be a technical and secular term too, which is how I want to use it here. 'Parochialism' can describe a practice whereby one attends to a 'parish', a small administrative district that one knows intimately.

It sounds simple enough. But we know such simplicity is an illusion nowadays. Parishes were once presumed to be singular, their concerns known and shared by the parishioners. But consider any modern locality. We know our places are infused with all manner of belief systems and power systems, all manner of dialects, needs, fears and suspicions. We know that everyday life is stippled with contentions and incommensurabilities. We know this, but we also simultaneously try to ignore it in order to get something done. Amid the volatility there is usually a countermanding desire to be 'grounded' and coherent. It's the chorus each of us sings with good and bad faith about what we know. Even if one tries to operate parochially and is committed to knowing and fostering coherence in a place, one knows too that the issues enlivening any place worth living in are unstable, unsettling, *complex*.

'Complexity' is a good step on the way to analysing definitive instability. The word derives from the Latin *plectare*, 'to braid'. In a complex circumstance, new elements are constantly being introduced to the instance at hand. A complex system is not exclusively bounded or stable. Now, doesn't this sound like everyday life in our various communities as globalisation and networked communications burgeon? We still aspire to partake of something as functional as *society*; but we know too that we are on the edge of chaos where new elements get added, existing influences wane or wax or mutate under the influence of internal and external forces.

With this *changefulness* understood, I hope it's clearer why parochialism is still important: even as we need global connectivity in order to brace ourselves against the vicissitudes of contemporary economies, we know that a network holds together only as long as its local *nodes*—its secular parishes—are as strong as its outreaching tendrils. We know that sociability is simultaneously intensive and extensive.

We know too that we live in *dynamic systems* rather than in *fixed structures* or durational inevitabilities. Each moment is contingent on variable and unpredictable factors. Each moment has import and meaning depending on how we conduct ourselves within an ever-extending panoply of semantic and social negotiations. Each moment is *situated*, therefore, even though it is also shifty. In this respect we know that we are in a *post-structuralist* circumstance, that from moment to moment we can conjure some systematic sense but also that the system tends away from stability, toward alteration.

'Alteration' is a startling word when examined closely. It's the process of experiencing alterity or *otherness*, the process whereby you move through otherness and have it move through you, until you alter as a result of your encounter with difference, your encounter with products and progenitors of instability.

Now, I need to remind myself that my task is to consider how *collaboration* might best occur in contemporary social systems. With all the above-mentioned alteration and quickness in view, I shall consider what knowledge and what capabilities might be needed so we can collaborate (that is, *work together*) despite all our differences, despite our definitive instability.

So now we come to *attunement* and *agility*. Instead of glossing these terms etymologically as I've done with the other key words, let me exemplify them by describing a scenario where attunement and agility must prevail if the scene is to have any meaning. Let's imagine a project requiring collaboration.

The fact that we'll need to *imagine* the project is important: in a changeful world, the things that we create are to some degree without precedent. In a changeful world, imagining or *conjuring a possible scene* is the first collaborative action performed when people gather to bring about an outcome. To start a collaboration, some achievement, some thing or event or process needs to be held in one's mind and shared with other minds in a 'zone' of possibility, in an encounter with strangeness, an encounter with something that does not really exist. This is the gas that has to get bottled: otherness, uncertainty, alteration: the difference between received reality and real possibility.

I promised a particular example. Let's imagine a project that is possible because of computational technologies and communication networks. Let's consider a landscape, something extensive and complex, with a river system in its midst. This is a natural, social, sensory system. It has all kinds of smells, stories, actors, pictures, elements and urges in it, exiting it and entering it. It has social and historical patterns persisting through decades. It has batches of data gathered daily, gathered hourly, in real time. Sounds, texts, measurements, images get captured, represented, transmitted continuously. Inside this system, communities contend and combine.

Imagine the plethora of data associated with all this activity. Imagine this data in its various formats, all held as caches in different databases that are updating and sometimes breaking down or freezing up, minute by minute. Imagine how geographically and institutionally dispersed and isolated these various databases are likely to be. Now imagine what might happen if we found ways to aggregate these differentiated caches, all their different discourses, speculations, visualisations, descriptions and sonifications. Imagine too that such a system does not simply transmit or broadcast as one-way communication to consumers, but that it invites contribution from several different constituencies, which are aware of their role as contributors, a role that is not merely receptive.

Imagine trying to set the conditions that would enable this system to come together. (The Multiplicity projects that are described elsewhere in this book must grapple daily with these issues, I suspect.) In such a project, one would need to broker combinations of the cultural, cognitive, aesthetic and political factors; to mesh a profusion of genres, individuals, communities; to braid different strands of government and systems of power, different valencies of allowance and impediment. One would commence this brokerage based on a *hunch* (which is a shared imagining, actually): a hunch that if we can amalgamate these factors, then we might start to discern unforeseen patterns and sets of relationships in our environments and our polity. And this might help us to know better how to behave, how to act and react in our dynamic systems when strange weather booms in, say, or when unexpected political actions occur, for good and for bad.

So how would such a project come together in a situation where the amount of information, the array of protocols and the babble of languages are too profuse for any one mentality to contain it all?

One answer: collaboration through *attunement* and *agility*.

By attunement I mean a patient and experimental process of listening and signalling, listening and altering. I mean the ability that we ought to have learned by now in the aftermath of colonialism. I mean the ability for all constituents to be in place through time with each other, amid the different belief systems, habits and acknowledged variations of power, knowing all the while that there might be real mutual benefit in forming hybrid knowledge rather than inscribing one knowledge at the obliterative expense of another. Attunement is an ability to arrive at an effective frequency of transmission of information. Think of what happens in ham radio sessions:

signal ... signal ... response ... poor response ... signal ... adjustment ... better response ... adjustment ...

stronger signal ... stronger response ... adjustment ... attuned shared signal.

A common frequency is an alteration established via a wilful drift away from one's initial, known frequency.

Let me reiterate that I don't think this attunement is an innocent or value-free process. Our colonialism teaches us that there is always a dominant key and that it's rare for anything like equity to occur when a powerful entity chooses to cede a little autonomy to underlings.

But this is where agility comes in. Amid the negotiations and alterations, one needs to ask how readily, how frequently and how *knowingly* can all the operatives *move* to a shared level of possibility? Never denying that there are different degrees of freedom and 'purchase' in any particular collaborative opportunity, how might one still enact something creative and mutually beneficial?

The benefits come with the ability to improvise when change looms. And partly they come through *consciousness*, through acknowledging that there are imbalances and that agility is needed if the differences are not to paralyse our systems. Such consciousness can prompt us to practise attunement *for the benefit of the project* rather that for the benefit of any separate entity or group within the putative collaboration. It follows that if the project is delivered well and if the responsibility and credit for delivery are distributed truly, then the benefits are distributed too. The world and its participants get something good that was not there before. Utopian? Yes. Naïve? Not necessarily.

To show how complexity demands agility in the real world of management and finance, consider this typical scenario from information systems design:

> In the creation of complex databases or elaborate communication and storage networks, it used to be standard procedure to deploy 'software engineering'. This might be summarised as the 'blueprint approach'. Typically, with the blueprint approach, an organisation recognises that it has a challenging set of needs in relation to its databases and communication networks. It hires a specialist team to take care of the problem. The board of the commissioning company is nervous, because plenty of money is about to be spent and competitive performance is at stake. So the board, taking its governance obligations very seriously, insists that a detailed brief must be developed, with itemised 'deliverables', and that the progress of the project will be rigorously cross-checked against the brief and any departures from the brief will be penalised as variations or failures of delivery.
>
> The consultant team spends a few expensive months moving through the organisation, asking everyone what they want from the new system. The people being asked don't necessarily know, nor do they know how the outside world is changing or what alternative information technology systems are soon to show up in the marketplace, so they ask for everything they can think of. Eventually a system is synthesised out of this process. More precisely, it gets described and budgeted on paper, ahead of its creation. And the consultants set about delivering the thing that's detailed on paper.

Now, if everyone behaves diligently and satisfies the requirements of the board, the project will almost certainly be an expensive failure. For the world and the company will have altered markedly in the time between the drafting of the brief and the delivery of the system. And besides, the brief was founded in contradiction, ignorance, anxiety and wild desire. A complex and dynamic system was serviced by a structured mentality with faith in solid-state mechanisms, with expectations of social and moral fixity. The accountability applied during the development and delivery might have momentarily comforted the traditional anxieties of overseers, but these rigours were not aligned to the quickness of everyday reality.

This is why the blueprint process has always been properly described as *engineering*. It serves machinery. Instead, something like *fluid dynamics* would be more appropriate.

In response to this 'crisis', other good-governance approaches have recently emerged, processes more attuned to complexity and volatility. For example, consider the 'Agile Programming' and 'Extreme Programming' movements, which treat information technology design as an iterative regime that constantly evolves while it continuously performs.[1] According to Agile Programming protocols, the design team is accountable to a *planned* pattern of immediate needs and imminently useful developments. Or as the Agile Alliance explains its priorities, they seek 'to satisfy the customer through early and continuous delivery of valuable software'. If the two-step between immediacy and imminence can be achieved, then the system survives and even thrives because it is a dynamic process of evolution through action and reaction, rather like a robust ecosystem. Accountability is then is a question of how well you have set the conditions for the continuing 'health' of your system.

Agile–collaborative technique is by no means restricted to the information and communications technology sector. For example, historians of architecture (and of governance!) might see how the Sydney Opera House started with Jorn Utzon attempting agility with his Scandinavian workshop methods of research and deployment. Historians might also see how the project eventually collided with the solid-state, blueprint thinking of Davis Hughes and his New South Wales state government officers who took over and botched the finish of the Opera House.

If you work in a dynamic context—be it architecture, activism, or a family—you probably already know intuitively if not explicitly that your work proceeds best when attunement allows agility as well as accountability. As with many common sense realisations, it takes some real diligence to draw this knowledge out of its implicit state and to communicate it as analysis and theory.

One way to embolden ourselves for this task is to see how these newly minted ideas have precursors, and are therefore comprehensible because their precepts are already second nature to some people in our midst. For example, I see agility and attunement in the educational techniques known as 'heuristics', or discovery-based learning.[2] I see them in Polynesian way-finding,[3] and in land management regimes too, whether they be peasant, indigenous or ecologically scientific. I see them in many of the interpretive techniques of post-structuralist linguistics and textual analysis.[4] And just to prove that such thinking is available to all political affiliations, I see agility and attunement in much of the corporate research and wealth-creation philosophies propounded by marketeers like Michael Schrage and Richard Florida.[5] Ditto for the 'just in time' design-and-build protocols that now organise much transnational merchandising.[6] I see them in the 'adaptive deployment' and 'swarm-formation' manoeuvres being researched by military labs all over the world.[7]

As cracker-barrel philosophers everywhere would insist: there's nothing new under the sun. True perhaps, but each new moment in history makes every next option strange and in need of creativity, and strangely the best advice sometimes comes from the one you'd prefer to know only as the enemy. After all, there's no telling where the next revelation might come from. For the sun has never shone *exactly like this* before, not right here, right now.

NOTES

1   See <http://www.agilealliance.com/home> or <http://agilemanifesto.org>
    or <http://www.extremeprogramming.org> (all accessed May 2005). These
    approaches to software design are to some extent informed, of course, by
    many of the ethical and intellectual tenets of 'open source' computing cultures
    all around the world.

2   See Zbigniew Michalewicz and David B. Fogel, *How to Solve It: Modern Heuristics,*
    Springer, Berlin and New York, 2000.

3   See Will Kyselka, *An Ocean in Mind,* University of Hawaii Press, Honolulu, 1987.

4   See Paul Cilliers, *Complexity and Postmodernism: Understanding Complex Systems,*
    Routledge, London, 1998.

5   See Michael Schrage, *Serious Play: How the World's Best Companies Simulate to
    Innovate,* Harvard Business School Press, Boston, 1999. See Richard Florida,
    *The Rise of the Creative Class: And How It's Transforming Work, Leisure, Community
    and Everyday Life,* Basic Books, New York, 2002.

6   See <http://en.wikipedia.org/wiki/Just_in_time> (accessed May 2005).

7   See <http://icosystem.com/releases/release_310502.htm> (accessed May 2005).

The Site as a Textile of Paths and Relations: Netting the Egnatia

A DIALOGUE BETWEEN MARINA FOKIDIS (OXYMORON) AND LORENZO ROMITO (STALKER)

The Balkans, a rich mosaic of different cultures and religions in south-eastern Europe, have resembled, for some time now, a volcano in post-eruption state. Almost all of the borders are in a state of extreme tension. The Balkans are a neglected part of Europe that has been excluded from mainstream European Union debates until very recently.

The history of the Balkans has been framed by cultural collisions between East and West, uneven processes of modernisation, antagonistic structures for national integration, the forceful exchange of populations, territorial conflicts and shifting national borders. Despite the existence of a geological entity known as the Balkan Land, it is composed of peoples with diverse cultural characteristics. The unification under one single Balkan identity (during the Iron Curtain period) and the very character of the 'Balkan blood' have contributed to a geopolitical situation in the Balkan peninsula that goes beyond financial and territorial claims. The untranslatability of the present racism, the hostility and the conflicting relations, together with the very tight bonds between the inhabitants of that territory, have led to a unique type of semi-local immigration within the Balkan area. This in turn has led to an immigration that is not just a quest for a 'better future' in a foreign land, but also a 'homecoming'.

In the wake of the stereotypes of this old 'powder keg of Europe' it is necessary to invent new kinds of geopolitical and cultural identities. What seems quite obvious is that the solution to these concerns lies in a new synthesis of East and West, a healthy coexistence of occidental and eastern thought, within the realm of Europe in the twenty-first century. History proved that the answer is not to be found in a common being, but as the French philosopher Jean-Luc Nancy has stated, in 'being in common'. It is not about choosing sides; rather, it is about understanding the contradictory desires that shape social relations.

EGNATIA—A Journey of Migrating Memories is a interdisciplinary project that was initiated by Stalker, a group of artists, architects and theoreticians from Rome, in collaboration with Oxymoron, a nonprofit cultural organisation based in Athens and dedicated to the promotion of public contemporary art, and of which I am a founding member.

Our (Oxymoron's) invitation to the Stalker group to present another work of theirs (*Flying Carpet*) in Thessaloniki, Greece in 2001 prompted a team of Italian, Greek and Albanian artists to conduct an experimental road trip to the Balkan area, following the path of the old Egnatia road. There has not been a more effective way to understand that this road, which covers less than 1500 kilometres, for some people still constitutes a matter of life and death.

Egnatia is an ancient Roman road which was built in order to connect Rome and Constantinople: the western and eastern capitals of the divided Roman Empire. It passed through the south of Italy, Albania, Macedonia and Thrace. From the last decades of the Ottoman Empire in the nineteenth and early twentieth centuries, to the current movement of refugees, this road has been the site for the dramatic displacement of millions of Albanians, Armenians, Bulgarians, Greeks, Jews, Slavs, Turks, Kurds, Afghanis, and Iraqis. Notable was the Greek–Turkish population exchange agreed to in the Treaty of Lausanne in 1923. This forced one and a half million people to move from their homeland.

The project seeks to collect stories of displacement, recording real accounts from those who were moved or have been forced to move along the Egnatia 'bridge' on the fragmented border between East and West.

MARINA FOKIDIS: Site, in this project, is no longer a point in the map but a journey. It is a sequence of events and actions that occur in the spaces of the road. It is developed through the meetings of the participants: producers and receivers, artists and audiences. A particular goal for this project is for it to become an archive of memories and transform Egnatia road to what you have been calling an 'Actual Territory'. Through this perception of site as a political or theoretical concept, as a particular community, architects and artists have been redefining their role as constructors of a net of human relations extended outside the world of contemporary production.

How can these new sites of cultural production be studied in terms of their visual language, and their communication of knowledge?

LORENZO ROMITO: Each site is itself a complex system of relations. Each attempt to observe it is already an interference in this system of relations. It is the very process of observing that produces the reality itself. This means that there is no other way to comprehend than being a participant in the reality we'd like to observe. Its complexity in terms of relations is not objective evidence, but depends on the capability of the observer himself, especially in unplanned and self-produced realities. We think that the reason why these relations don't exist is because we, as observers, are not capable of interpreting them. We simply look at it as chaotic reality; as something that does not make sense to us. But when our process of observing is empathetic with the environment, even if this is extraneous to our patterns of comprehension, then we are becoming part of its emerging relation, part of the site itself. At the same time, being outsiders and therefore detached from the observed reality, we can attempt to interpret those emergencies and to communicate them.

Such situations are difficult to render intelligible because they lack connections to the present. They are to be physically witnessed rather than represented. The archive of experiences is the only possible form of mapping for these 'Actual Territories'. Here we are beginning to define new tools and methods to develop the self-representation of those realities that are producing paths and relationships.

MARINA FOKIDIS: I remember that when we invited you to present another work entitled *Flying Carpet* in Thessaloniki, Greece in 2001, you did not accept our invitation simply as such. You were not happy to show your work in Greece unless we could allocate a percentage of the budget to be used towards organising a road trip to the Balkan area, following the path of the Egnatia road. While the work was being transported from Albania to Greece we were physically on the road. This trip started in Rome and passed through different places in Albania, and as it arrived in Greece it provided the opportunity to some people to come in close touch with and be influenced by the changing environment to which they were exposed—in short, to give birth to new ideas for interconnected actions and creations. The phantom of Egnatia road, a mythic unity under which it is possible to gather a wide range of particular people and experiences, served in that case as a zone of mutual interest for fertile collaboration. The discovery of the contemporary development along the path, the very conditions of this journey, the interpersonal relations that have been developed 'on the road', as well as the deep involvement with the particular localities, constituted the basis for the creation of a multicultural laboratory, which is currently in process. It is true that these kinds of cultural productions still cannot be executed outside institutional circumstances, but they are no longer determined by them. A process of working that probably derives from the necessity to survive in an absurd reality has developed into a kind of public art that engages matters found in the core of real life outside the contemporary art system. Various kind of collaborations emerge in diverse locations, simultaneously involving the initiators, the public (which is usually the observed communities), the post-production team and the institution in a horizontal hierarchy. And although such endeavours often do not survive the pressures for commercialisation that frame the contemporary art market, their value resides both in an object and in the interaction among all the participants.

How could one define the nature of collaboration in such ephemeral situations? Do receivers and producers adopt truly interchangeable roles?

LORENZO ROMITO: It's a process where the producers and receivers play a common game. That's the reason why we have never conceived Stalker as a group but as an interrelated and open system that is growing and emerging, through its actions and through all the individuals that operate with (for and among) Stalker. It is a reality without one physical body, not even the one of the persons who gave life to it. 'We' have always been an entity that comprises 'others', who, without pretending to be us, participate in the activities of becoming 'us' in their/our actions.

This way Stalker could be anyone. Stalker is a desiring community where no one belongs and where individuals encounter each other. It is an unstable entity, a temporary community that is founded on possibilities, on desire, on intention, on promise and waiting.

Such desiring power is Stalker's hypothesis: 'transgressive excitement, tension in motion, energetic investment in the future'. Stalker will always generate the dissipation of energies by drawing on a dynamic vital geometry. In order to make this power come to life it is necessary to proceed without any fixed schema.

By 'coming to life' it generates a space, which is an ethical, political and aesthetic space; a real, autonomous, living space; a territory made up of environments, situations and places which have been taken away from chaos, finding its way away from destruction and destroyers, re-establishing a creative circularity which has been taken away from us by the transformation of life into merchandise. This is Stalker's necessary ethical, political and aesthetic approach. Without these premises, Stalker's games run the risk of turning out to be fixed games.

MARINA FOKIDIS: An issue that may arise in relation to these activities is their sustainability: how to maintain the net of relations formed without the permanent co-ordination of the initiators. How can these collaborations be realised as a variety of beginnings and not as a dead end? They are certainly actions that cannot be consumed within the presentation of a fixed project, even in its best scenario, and art historians, critics and curators may need to start learning how to facilitate and evaluate them beyond their cutting-edge quality.

LORENZO ROMITO: How we affirm these insurgent practices inside political and theoretical contexts is the very critical point. It occurs at the intersection between formal and informal, and in between emerging and defined rules. This question has to be faced by crossing the terrain of the misunderstanding, of the translation, of the compromise sometimes, and of the political confrontation with others. After years of activities we had the urge to create what we called Osservatorio Nomade (ON). This is a wider international network that operates on different levels and is intended to implement and sustain the Stalker activities. It responded to three needs that we realised were urgent.

One, as I said, is to be able to interact with social, cultural and political institutions, reaching higher levels of communication and organisation, and formulating strategies for financing the activities without having to compromise our attitude. Another was to co-operate with a wider net of researchers. The third was to open an educational program on Stalker and ON practices that could address the needs of both the young searchers and the communities. These three strategies would lead to a process of transferring the responsibility for the endeavour, thereby allowing us to leave but not to abandon those realities, and to connect them into an operating network. This is actually the biggest bet in our engagement with the enacted environments.

For the Stalker group this way of working is the result of a process that has been going on for several years. Since 1995, they have been engaging research and actions within abandoned areas or regions under transformation. And each project of theirs has been created in direct partnership with people, a community. Their commodity is in that case a kind of social service. It will lead to a visual library of records based on a network of close encounters. The aim is for these records to articulate and contemplate conflicts and differences, providing in that way a more informal 'space' for the representation of the views of different minority groups that have been oppressed due to territorial conflicts and religious beliefs.

EGNATIA—A Journey of Migrating Memories has just received funding from the European Union. The stories are being collected through 'agencies' that opened in some of the major European cities that have become destinations for the displaced, such as Athens, Berlin, Istanbul, Paris and Rome, as well as along the Egnatia Road in Otranto and Thessaloniki. All the oral testimonies are being translated to visual language and all the produced artistic works will be presented in common exhibitions. At a later stage, each story will be transferred to a paving stone and will serve as testimony. The storyteller will determine where his or her personalised paving stone will be placed along the Egnatia Road, creating veritable 'milestones' of memories. Almost every story leads us to a new reality, a new situation that has always been waiting to be discovered. The placement of the first two stones, one down by the sea in the city of Duress in Albania, and the other at a big refugee camp in the city of Lavrio, 55 kilometres outside Athens, follows the wishes of an Albanian immigrant and a Kurdish refugee. These directions provide a strange kind of

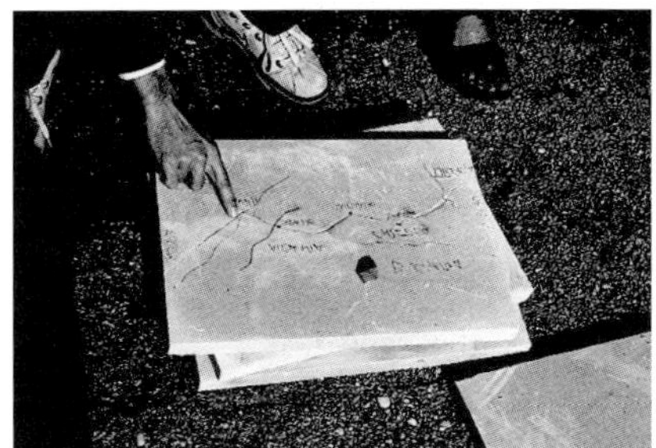
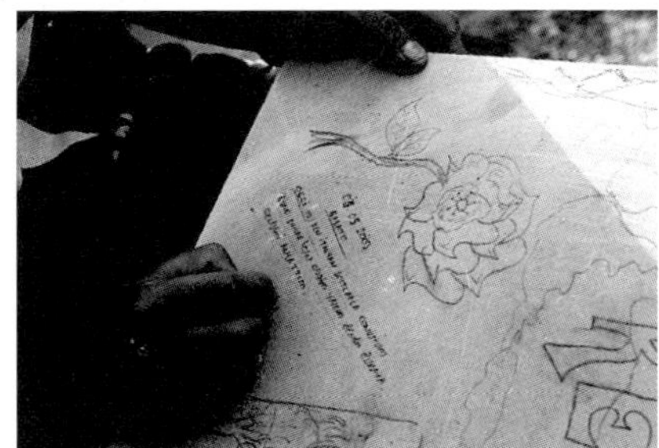
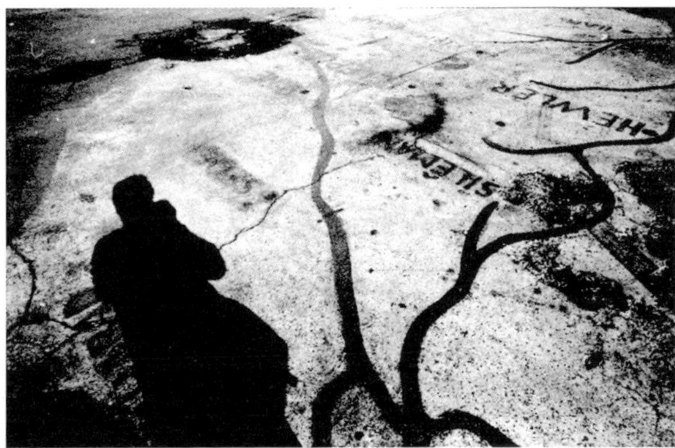
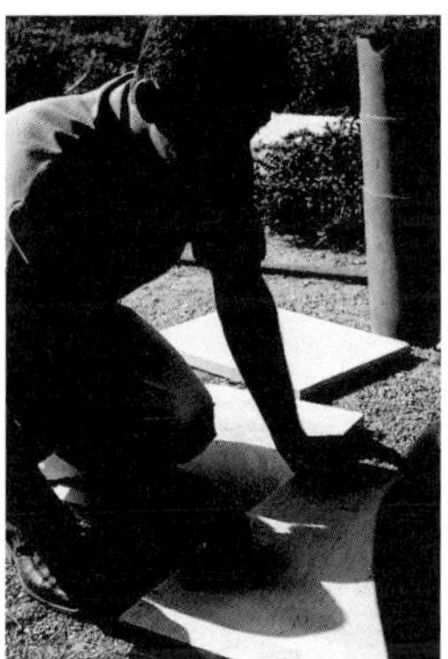

Images of the construction of the transnational monument for
the project *EGNATIA—A Journey of Migrating Memories*. Photographs
taken by Andrea Rocco; courtesy Osservatorio Nomade.

homecoming for all of us. The aim is to build a transnational monument on
the path of Egnatia road.

This method of working is not new. Lately, though, it has been re-embraced
by many curators, artists and critics so as to resist the rising art market,
which tends to commodify even the more critical practices. Rather than one
more multimedia installation, *EGNATIA—A Journey of Migrating Memories* seems
to be more a device for collecting testimonies and remapping a turbulent area
through personal stories. Although it exists symbolically as an idea for an
aesthetic art object for the moment, it could never be marketed, since the project
will be completed only when this sculpture is scattered—in a way, undone!

Engaging the displaced in the very process of creating could be understood not only as an artistic practice but also as a strategy of political importance.

The intention is to begin paving the Egnatia road, with its forgotten memories.

Small Gestures in Specific Places: On Collaboration and the Politics of Art

NIKOS PAPASTERGIADIS

I do not want to express myself any more; as an artist I want to connect myself with other people.

—Alicia Framis[1]

… what we suffer from these days is an excess of domesticity and a nostalgia for mobility.

—Guillermo Santamarina[2]

Today the movement of ideas, capital and people is faster and wilder than at any point in history. Globalisation has made the world more interconnected. The flows of traffic in this new network have not only accelerated to new speed levels, but the directions of movement have multiplied and leapt across the well-worn paths. In this massive race to pass on information, to circulate symbols, to move from one place to another, languages collide violently and enfold creatively within each other. The cultural dynamics of globalisation have presented new challenges to the existing models for explaining the forms of belonging and the patterns of exchange that are occurring in the world. Culture is no longer understood as the discrete and unique expression of activities and ideas that occur in particular places. No culture can exist in isolation. More people are on the move today than ever before in history, and paradoxically nation-states, while welcoming the advance of capital and new technology, are increasingly fortifying their borders against migrants. The contradictions and tensions in the deterritorialisation of cultures and peoples are compelling artists and intellectuals to rethink their methods.

The jagged contradictions of globalisation demand new theories of flow and resistance to reveal the turbulent patterns of movement occurring across the world. Cultural critics and curators are also in need of new conceptual frameworks. There is an urgent need for a new vocabulary in art discourse that is able to make sense of the complex forms of representation that simultaneously incorporate images from different locations and activate signs that contain within them a multiplicity of other signs, each embodying a series of contrary or competing codes. It is simply insufficient to categorise this work as merely hybrid or postmodern. To do justice to the complexity of the art work we need to develop frameworks that can address both these signs *of* difference and the process by which signs are made out of the artists' plays *with* difference.

Artists with more than one sense of home also present difficult questions about the status of their art. This 'pidgin' modality in the interaction between signs from diverse locations has implications not only for the experience of art, but also for the position of the artist. The conventional models of the artist as outsider or stranger, which recur throughout the discourse on modernism, are also in need of qualification. The radical model of the artist as opponent and the liberal benevolent schema of the artist as saviour are both underpinned by spatial models that place the artist outside the sphere of everyday life. First, there is a presumed correlation between the objectivity of the outsider and his or her critical distance from the host group. This is usually accompanied by the assumption that the artist as stranger may be a bearer of a benefit that can compensate for the visual short-sightedness and cultural lack of the dominant social order. Hal Foster has also recently argued that the significance of art is often tied to both the cultural location of the artist and his or her ability to move between different locales.[3] This form of mobility and dual position is often described as a form of shuttling. However, this metaphor also needs to be tested against the broader processes of global turbulence. Within this field cultural flows circulate in asymmetrical patterns; their complexity is marked by feedback loops and enfolding tactics that can have unintentional consequences, resulting in the dispersal and restructuring of symbols and codes.

What sort of place does art connote if it is constantly evoking a shuttling between places? In which language can the artist articulate the recognition that translations fail as often as they succeed? How does a bilingual or bicultural person simultaneously speak his or her mother tongue and see the world, which operates in a different or hybrid language? Every person who is bilingual will recognise this tension. However, this is not to say that this experience of the disjuncture between words is revealed only when we seek their equivalent in other languages or even in other places. This experience is not unique to migrants, exiles, artists and translators. As Nestor Garcia Canclini noted in relation to class and cross-cultural transformation: 'the whole field translates'.[4] We are all negotiating difference in our everyday lives; this process is a central and constitutive feature of modernity. Whether it is recognised as such is another matter.

The shift between the spiritual and the real, and from the ideal of a primal home to the journey towards the elusive modern home, there is now the added polarity of possibility—the click from the actual to the virtual. As McKenzie Wark has noted in 'A Hacker Manifesto'[5], while the progress of modernity leads us to the 'becoming concrete of virtuality itself', the idea of the double still 'spooks' the world. Our sense of place in the world, our knowledge of which direction to follow, our recognition of the identity that contains our 'selves', our belonging to a culture that gives form to all this knowledge of place and identity—these quests are still haunted by both the loss of some earlier fragment and the gnawing lack of completion in the present.

I am struck by the unending need to rethink the parameters of place and the spectres of identity in the contemporary relationship between art and politics, and between the aesthetic and the ethical, and the role of everyday life in cultural production. In the past there was a tendency to explain these relationships in terms of binary oppositions or vertical hierarchies. That is, for artists to become political, it was assumed that they should oppose the dominant institutions from an external position. Similarly, the 'pool' of everyday life was seen as a source from which the artist would draw inspiration. Everyday life was the raw matter that was transformed by the artist into a higher level of imagery. These oppositional and hierarchical categories were seen as the means both to invigorate the traditions of art, and to elevate the artist to an objective vantage point.

My interest lies in the practice of artists who explicitly refute such dichotomies. New, complex forms of aesthetic and political practice are visible in the contemporary art world. My interest is drawn towards artists who do not use art merely to advance a political ideology, but who instead utilise all the available institutional resources to articulate new ideas and create new spheres of possibility. This entails a new understanding of the interconnectedness between place and art. Not only have the places for art multiplied, but the act of placing has become an integral part of art. This relationship not only heightens the dynamic exchange that occurs between identity and history within a given place, but also recognises the constitutive role of place. Concepts like territory and site often connote either a natural or neutral setting for the performance of external events. Drawing from theorists like Marc Auge, I would argue that place is an active and internal part of the relational and historical formation of identity.[6] Places both acquire and grant meaning through the engagements of cultural practice and agency. It is from this perspective that place is now perceived in more fluid terms, and as the artist Gair Dunlop has suggested, it is now time to forge new community projects by having 'an idea in residence'. Putting an idea in place, or finding a place for an idea, may liberate the artist from the onerous if not ludicrous task of socioeconomic regeneration, and focus attention on the human value of creative cultural practices.

The most radical gestures in contemporary art are no longer positioned outside the dominant institutions of art or on the moral high ground from which the artist can pour scorn on the foibles of everyday life. Collaborative artists like Lucy Orta, artist collectives like Superflex, and curatorial projects like *If I Ruled the World* work with and within the institutions of art in order to create connections with social groups and develop new political strategies of expressive resistance. Their engagement with everyday life, especially the codes and symbols of popular media culture, is not confined to invigorating the discourses of art, but is an admission that art belongs in the same time–space continuum of popular culture. Art is no longer aiming to be an elevated or belated response to events already staged in the sphere of everyday life. On the contrary, there is a dual level of commitment to the aesthetic and the political. In the past decade, there has been an emergence of project forms of artistic practice that work across diverse community networks. These projects offer a rare insight into alternative modes of social engagement. Charles Esche goes so far as to claim that the logic of creative exchange has the potential to contest the hegemony of economic rationalism. It is this combination of pragmatic modelling and cultural experimentation that has led Esche to argue that the place of art is now 'positioned in the territory between active political engagement and autonomous experimentation'.[7]

The story of contemporary art practice can no longer be told exclusively in the form of the historical survey, or as a mere cultural effect of socioeconomic changes. There are many parallel stories and competing genres that are constituted out of a shuttling between the discourse of art and the cultural politics of everyday life. To try to explain art in purely formal terms or to assume that the highest purpose of art is to deliver a new political agenda is, as Jacques Ranciere noted, 'somewhat beside the point'.[8] Art cannot be explained as a social activity that fulfils the stated goals of a national agenda or an economic order. The specific place of art is now increasingly located in networks that are both above and below the reach of the nation-state. Through the process of collaborating with community networks in local places, there is the opportunity for artists to uncover countercultural pockets and forge new transnational diasporas that defy the hegemonic order of the nation-state. Ranciere is correct to argue that the 'life of art' is found in the shuttling between the extremes of autonomy and heteronomy. Art cannot exist in its own discursive ghetto—it would inevitably spiral down to entropy. Similarly, if art is bound to serve other laws and conform to a given political order, it will also divest itself of any distinctive identity. To confine art to either extreme is a death sentence. The academic and the activist approaches to art are, in Ranciere's terms, the negation of the life of art.

The collaborative strategies employed by these artists and collectives are twofold. Following the example of an earlier generation of artists like Helio Oiticica, Lygia Clarke, Joseph Beuys and David Medalla, they seek to reach new audiences and include their participation as part of the construction and experience of the work. The work therefore finds its completion in the active experience of the public. However, their collaborative techniques also operate on a second level. As complexity in society has led to increasing atomisation, these projects have recognised the need to create new forms of exchange between intellectuals, professionals and community groups. Lucy Orta claims that her work can only bring a certain problem to a point of clarity when there is an open debate among different people. In these collaborations the function of the museum has taken on a new focus:

> I don't see museums as spaces any longer; I see them as part of a larger management team which help co-ordinate the various collaborations

of the artistic process ... I have found that an exhibition can form a role to both reflect upon a subject and raise concerns to another level of debate.[9]

In a recent project called *Fluid Architecture*, Orta occupied the former Army Drill Hall at the edges of Melbourne's Central Business District.[10] The specificity of this site is crucial to the relations that were established as work was executed. For over a decade the army had chosen to conduct its marching and shooting exercises away from the gaze of the city. The old art deco building fell into disuse and its absurd decorative motifs began to crumble and peel. Its decay was compounded by the fading status of the neighbourhood. Next to the Drill Hall lay the forlorn headquarters of a collapsed national airline, and beside it is the redundant bluestone building of a brewery that has gone global. On this site, and at a time when the world was becoming increasingly callous toward the plight of refugees, Orta proposed a project with the heart as a symbol for hospitality. Her aim was not to lead a protest against the civic authorities, or to present herself in a morally superior position, but rather to organise a diverse network of individuals and groups to develop its own sense of how an artistic situation could give and gain a heart from collective action.

The politics in this practice is situational. Clusters form with no specific structure. The form is found in the responsive process of working through the issues and interacting with the other participants. During the project the musician Tim O'Dwyer created a pulsing ambience of found sounds and improvised rhythms, while the architect James Legge worked with a design team led by Michael Douglas and a community of activists and artists from local tower blocks and art schools. The project culminated in performances in new body suits, and sculptural installations that stretched the concept of mutual support and collective movement. A comment made by Paul Virilio on Orta's practice served as the theme of this project: 'One individual depends on the warmth of another. The warmth of one gives warmth to the other. The physical link weaves the social link.'

A crucial feature of this collaborative practice is the dynamic incorporation of all elements of the museum and gallery structures. It cuts against the hierarchical master roles of the artist and curator, and mobilises a horizontal integration of the so-called technical and educational 'support staff'. Ideas are developed simultaneously in a horizontal manner, rather than being defined from above and then executed down a vertical and sequential chain of command. The realisation, fabrication and public dissemination of the work occur in the process of actualising the idea, rather than being compartmentalised and distributed under the exclusive categories of creativity, production and promotion. The artist collective Superflex also works in the cross-disciplinary mode. Whether it is in the *Biogas* project for recycling waste in third-world farming communities, or the *Superchannel* project for empowering residents in marginalised tower blocks, their goal is to create processes that not only offer a critique of socioeconomic conditions, but also generate a utility with clear aesthetic and political relevance.[11] Pierre Restany, a critic who has witnessed both the collaborative strategies of the earlier generations and Orta's most recent projects, had the perspicacity to define these multidisciplinary practices as a form of 'relational aesthetics'.

What transpires within such seemingly small gestures is the bigger expression of a desire for connection. These are unlikely reference points for cultural and aesthetic revolutions. If anything, they could be little reminders of things past. They are certainly not the manifestos for the future. They are far too light and slender to withstand such applied functions. What could be significant in such small gestures in specific places? At one level, alienation begins with the shutdown of communication and ends with the trivialisation of all exchanges. The power of the poetic gesture in art is revolutionary in that it acts as a circuit-breaker in the closed system of equivalence between signs, to which we are habituated. The twentieth-century discourse on art was littered with big claims about small gestures. Elaborate narratives have been articulated to expose the hidden signs, to uncover the buried processes and reveal the intended messages. At times these stories served no other function than the hyperbolic repetition of romantic myths; in other instances, such as the most recent work of T. J. Clark, there is a melancholic review of both the ruins that lurked within the grid of modernity and the ruination of the revolutionary promises of modernism.[12]

According to Paul Virilio, there is another dimension to the destruction of our sense of place. The battle is not confined to the competing ideologies of capitalism and socialism, but also threatens to arise due to the technologies of tele-presence which have displaced culture from their specific links to a given place and created chaotic feedback effects among people dispersed across the globe. In mournful tones he declares that once global corporatism has captured the media flows that criss-cross our spatial environment, then our agency will be crushed by new repressive regimes.

> The *real city*, which is situated in a precise place and which gave its name to the politics of nations, is giving way to the *virtual city*, that deterritorialized meta-city which is hence to become the site of that *metropolitics*, the totalitarian or rather globalitarian character of which will be plain for all to see.[13]

The curator Isobel Carlos is also conscious of the collapse of ideological models; however, she is not so pessimistic about the spaces for defining collective action and expressing a personal vision. The excesses of the new communication technologies and contradictory patterns of dispersed communities have conjoined to disturb the foundations of modernism. Globalisation has intensified interconnectedness but also heightened the sense of disorientation. In this turbulent context Carlos maintains that art still has a 'fundamental role in the quest for sense'. However, the position from which the artist speaks is neither the superior role of authority nor the mystic voice of the prophet offering a 'panacea for the world's problems'. Today, Carlos argues, the artist adopts a more modest tone, utilising personal, self-representative modes that can connect with the experiences of other people in local communities. Contemporary artists not only appropriate objects from everyday life, as did the early avant-garde, but they also use familiar techniques such as home video presentations. The style of contemporary art is thus often blurred with what Carlos calls the 'non-artistic' practices of mass media and domestic self-representation. This blurring not only undermines the hierarchical divisions of culture, but also heightens the realm of subjective experience in the public domain. Carlos declares that 'nowadays art is a field in which we encounter life: a fictionalised life'.[14] This practice can also be witnessed in numerous projects that were staged in *Documenta XI*, ranging from Chohrey Feyzdjou's obsessive cataloguing of burnt materials in eponymously named trunks and containers, Sanja Ivekovic's ongoing documentation of the process of soliciting and reconstructing her mother's official records, to Destiny Deacon's journey to her motherland in order to construct imaginary scenes of an absent postcard communication.[15]

My attention to the relationship between art and place was originally provoked by the way artists located their studios in the abandoned and derelict sectors of the city. I was attracted to these places because the high level of improvisation made them feel more 'homely' than domestic space I had seen in the suburbs. I was aware that this decision for re-utilisation was often driven by economic imperatives, but even successful artists tended to maintain studios in these places. They stayed not just for sentimental reasons, but perhaps because they obtained inspiration from the possibility that forgotten histories and alternative ways of being could still be found within the contradictions of these abandoned zones. It is also possible that these zones offered an even more general space: a location for contemplation and reflection. I imagine that these spaces prompted other unconscious connections, enabling artists to think though the un-thought thoughts of our time. These were breathing spaces in which attention was allowed to wander.

At the beginning of the twentieth century, artists responded to the changes in the modern city with a mixed sense of awe and excitement. Modernity was ushered in by the power of new industrial technologies. The sweeping socio-economic changes pushed many earlier forms of culture to the side. The damage was often justified by the promise of a higher level of liberation and emancipation. Many remained sceptical of such a blind faith in progress, but even artists who had been critical of capitalism's impact on society still believed that the machine age could be harnessed to produce a new utopia. For instance, in the postwar period, Constant Nieuwenhuys constructed images, models and maps for his imaginary city 'New Babylon'.[16] By the end of the twentieth century the glow of modernity was tarnished and contaminated. The promise of lifting ordinary people above the ground and onto higher levels sank into the filthy mud of accumulated waste and pollution. The radical task of the artist shifted from dreaming the new utopia to dealing with the dystopia that surrounded urban life. Artists like Bargmann and Levy began their practice in the form of a 'clean-up' operation. Yona Friedman also stressed that the task of the artist shifted from invention to recycling, from expressing a new vision for the future to developing new ethical collaborations to deal with the legacies of the machine age:

All living beings together produce an enormous amount of refuse. This mass is larger than the total mass of all living beings. Refuse produced by one species might be a resource for another species. Human technology starts with the conversion of things found into things useful. Architecture emerges since the original fallout of agriculture. Our present civilisation produces more fallout than all previous civilisations together. Much of that fallout can be recycled, for example, by artists who turn junk into works of art. A large part of industrial fallout becomes converted by the poorest people into objects for their own use: shelter, mobiles. The huge shanty towns all around the globe are but an example of reconversion. Shanty towns are at the scale of the city, what the *merzbau* was at the scale of the sculpture: both are works of art out of mainstream aesthetics.[17]

This process of reconversion also brings to the surface the complex layering of history and memories that lurk within the city. What do artists uncover when they excavate objects from the remains of the post-industrial landscape? What sorts of mental maps are made when artists wander through the streets of the city? Can artists reveal the real 'face' of the city? Since the founding of Rome, the city has thrived on multiplicity.[18] The stories we find create more stories, each stratum revealing another, every journey unfolding a new route. Even ruins defy the cliché that, at last, here is a place where time and things have stood still. For ruins are like way stations, where convergence and departure operate according to a slower and rougher schedule.

To contemplate the meaning of these places is neither an opportunity for nostalgia, nor an exercise in sighing at the cruelty of fate. The visual power of ruins runs deeper in our modern unconscious. It is no coincidence that Freud often used archaeological metaphors to depict the processes of the mind. The image of layers of earlier cities buried under every city was, for Freud, a powerful metaphor for describing the dynamic of change and repetition, waste and accumulation, desire and memory that also occurred in the mind. Hubert Damisch observed that Freud struggled with his own metaphor. For Freud, the traces left in cities were not just an analogy for the process of the mind, but also a common place. Knowing that Freud recognised the limits of the archaeological metaphor but refused to renounce it, Damisch speculates:

But why did he find it necessary to evoke visual images, figuration, in this connection if not because the mind itself must, at one time or another, have passed the same way, have found its place in them?[19]

From this perspective, or rather from this sense of place, we can revisit the debates on the place of art in the global city. The particularist claims that the place of art could be defined by its relationship to specific civic functions or bound to primordial forms of communal attachments have been displaced by a new discourse that stresses a new kind of universalism. I am suspicious of these broad claims and would prefer to direct my thoughts to the way art participates in the understanding of the hybrid forms of urban life. The turbulent patterns of global migration and the complex formations in new urban conurbations have catapulted the social questions in art to new levels of urgency. The forms of exile and displacement in the contemporary city have taken more hard twists and found new jagged edges. There is a growing need to address the questions of how we belong in the city and what can be done in the name of art.

If we consider the ways in which artists have not just inhabited buildings abandoned by commerce and citizens, but have also staged their events in these parts of the city, we can also gain a new perspective on the relationship between the available spaces in the post-industrial urban landscape and the conception, production and display of art. However, the edges of the city that were previously occupied by artists have now become the new focal points of the real estate market. The new middle-class penchant for loft living, the adoption of studio spaces by new media industries, and the pathos of art galleries like the Tate Modern are forces that have now combined to expand the reach of the heritage sector and accelerate the colonisation of the spaces of artistic production. A new blind spot has now emerged in the crossfire between gentrification and the aestheticisation of our urban landscape: the studio is no longer the privileged space for the production of art. If the institutions of art are to have any ambition other than being the mausoleum of art, then they must also confront these new forces. Today the gallery is not just a place for the display of complete works of art, but also the mechanism for its production and the platform for further forms of spatial engagement.

The gallery needs to be involved in the unfinished processes of art. It can facilitate the realisation of working processes and the conception of new engagements, rather than simply accumulating the products that have survived the tests of taste and opportunity.

Artists like Lucy Orta recognise that the institutions of contemporary art are demanding homes. However, Orta also considers that the political process of negotiation about the modes of engagement between place and perception is a central part of her artistic practice. Social issues such as poverty and homelessness have become common features of urban life in global cities. The growing expression of a blasé attitude by citizens and civic authorities has compelled artists to develop new critical strategies and to locate their practice in different sites. Orta has also dragged the institutional apparatus of the museum into transitional zones, such as train stations and abandoned buildings, in order to create new 'vehicles' and temporary 'laboratories' for connecting political and artistic ideas. Orta sees her role as forging links between the hopes and the fears of everyday life: 'I wish to be present in the social arena as a catalyst between utopia and reality—I call this Instigator Sculpture.'[20] These forms of artistic and social collaboration can revitalise the old debates on the politics of representation as they return us to the difference between *topos* and *tropos*.

Art is never outside or above the dynamic field of social change; it never develops in a purely autonomous manner. I would also stress that art is never entirely determined by its social context, for while it appropriates symbols from across the cultural spectrum it remains a critical vector in the representation of contemporary society. However, the manner of its engagement within this field needs further clarification. The central contention of this paper is that art is neither the simulated mask which conceals, nor the rhetorical arm which reveals the political struggle: its function is not confined to dramatising the repressive or reflecting the inequitable forces of social life. This does not mean that art is not involved in the struggles against the dominant order, or is dissociated from the representation of utopian visions. Rather, it implies that the recruitment of art in the politics of opposition does not fall into a pre-set position. Such a robust view on the relationship between art and politics is often lacking in contemporary critical theory. It is now fashionable to complain about the absence of 'heroic' artists, dwell on the impossibility of politics, or ponder the resistance of the sublime to representation in art. For instance, while lamenting the limited political utility of art, the philosopher J. M. Bernstein also sought to redefine its social contribution in terms of an 'ethical commitment'. However, this attempt to redeem the social value of art depends on the false assumption that art, politics and ethics are already external to each other. Bernstein's view might not be so melancholic if it were not for the assumption that the 'bridge' between art and politics has been lost.[21] There is no bridge that connects art and politics. Bridging is part of the politics of art.

NOTES

1   Quoted by Isobel Carlos, 'Non-Style and Self Refenciality', Lecture at the Art Gallery of New South Wales, Sydney Biennale, 2002.

2   Guillermo Santamarina, 'Recodifying a Non-existent Field', in Jean Fisher (ed.), *Global Visions*, Kala Press, London, 1994, p. 23.

3   Hal Foster, 'The Artist as Ethnographer', in Jean Fisher (ed.), *Global Visions*, Kala Press, London, 1994.

4   Nestor Garcia Canclini, *Hybrid Cultures*, University of Minnesota Press, Minneapolis, 1995.

5   McKenzie Wark, 'A Hacker Manifesto', Lecture at the Art Gallery of NSW, Sydney Biennale, 2002.

6   Marc Auge, *Non-Places*, Verso, London, 1995, p. 77.

7   Charles Esche, 'Modest Proposals', Catalogue Essay for Berlin Biennale, 2001.

8   Jacques Ranciere, 'The Aesthetic Revolution', *New Left Review*, No. 14, March/April 2002, p. 151.

9   Lucy Orta, interview with Hou Hanru, June 1999.

10   Lucy Orta, *Fluid Architecture,* Melbourne, 2002.

11   Superflex, *Biogas,* Artspace, Sydney, 1998, and *Superchannel,* Liverpool Biennale, Liverpool, 1999.

12   T. J. Clark, *Farewell to an Idea,* Yale University Press, New Haven, 1999.

13   Paul Virilio, *The Information Bomb* (trans. Chris Turner), Verso, London, 2000, pp. 10–11.

14   Isobel Carlos, 'Non-Style and Self Referentiality', Lecture at the Art Gallery of NSW, Sydney Biennale, 2002.

15   Chohrey Feyzdjou, 'Boutique Product of Chohrey Feyzdjou', 1973–1993; Sanja Ivekovic, 'Searching for My Mother's Number', 2002; Destiny Deacon, 'Postcards from Mummy', 1998; all from *Documenta XI,* curated by Okwui Enwezor, Kassel, 2002.

16   This juxtaposition between the modernist vision of utopia and the dystopic spaces of post-industrial landscapes was powerfully staged in *Documenta XI.*

17   Yona Friedman, Wall panel text, *Documenta XI,* Kassel, 2002.

18   Michel Serres, *Rome: The Book of Foundations,* Stanford University Press, Palo Alto, California, 1991.

19   Hubert Damisch, *Skyline: The Narcissistic City,* Stanford University Press, Palo Alto, California, 2001, p. 114.

20   Lucy Orta, interview with Andrew Bolton, 'The Super Modern Wardrobe', September 2001.

21   J. M. Bernstein, *The Fate of Art: Aesthetic Alienation from Kant to Derrida and Adorno,* Polity Press, Cambridge, 1992.

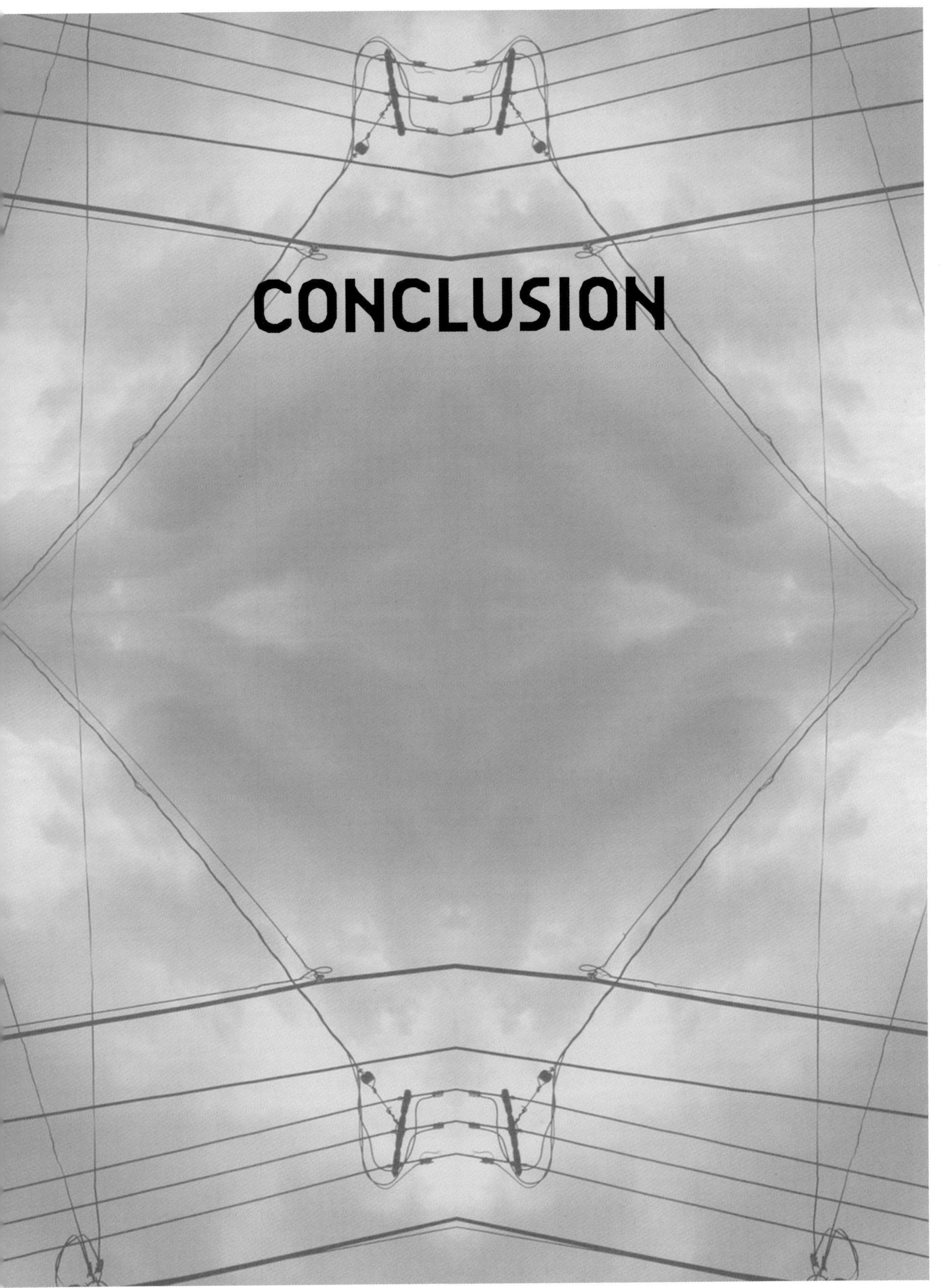

CONCLUSION

Citizens, Consumers
and Migrants

SEAN CUBITT

THE TROUBLE WITH IDENTITY

In June 2004, two events threw into question some dearly held beliefs about the nature of the global process in the early twentieth century. First, negotiations at the Doha round having struck a rock on farm subsidies, the World Trade Organisation (WTO) issued a judgement against the subsidies paid to US cotton farmers; potentially the crack in the wall that will bring down the export subsidy regime in the USA and Europe. Secondly, the USA's United Nations negotiators dropped their claims to the exemption of US citizens from the jurisdiction of the International Criminal Court. Neither decision ends US hegemony in the period since the fall of the Berlin Wall, but both indicate that the US is not able to act exclusively on the world stage. Robert Cooper captures the unusual situation of the USA:

> The USA is the more doubtful case since it is not clear that the US government or Congress accepts either the necessity or desirability of interdependence, or its corollaries of openness, mutual surveillance and mutual interference, to the same extent as most European governments now do.[1]

Cooper's concern is to make the case for a postmodern, neo-liberal imperialism grounded in the duty of 'postmodern' states—those matching the criteria so problematic for the USA—to enforce order on 'pre-modern' states which are incapable of securing peace and prosperity within their borders. In some respects, his arguments are a blueprint for a transition from national to supranational interests, converging with emergent instruments of global governance such as the WTO. Peculiarities of the US Constitution—notably the division of powers that makes a presidential signature on a treaty subject to complex negotiations between constitutional bodies—keep the USA apart from the rest of Cooper's postmodern states. This exclusion has frequently appeared as US imperialism. The case, as the events of June 2004 suggest, is more complex.

Cooper's concept of benevolent imperialism is not without its adumbrations of Hardt and Negri's important work, *Empire*.[2] Core to their argument is an analysis of US constitutionalism as a model for global sovereignty. The balance of powers between the institutions of the USA constitutes a networked sovereignty, differing from older republicanisms because rule is immanent to the network; not displaced to a divine exterior. This networked sovereignty, they argue, has become the grounds for a new global order, Empire, characterised by its ubiquity. Unlike older regimes, Empire appears to be a smooth, undifferentiated space, one notably bereft of any distinction between inside and outside. Everyone is welcomed into the new, global republic. Difference is encouraged on the basis of cultural and historical identities. And Empire undertakes to manage difference through a plethora of micro-conflicts and negotiations. Older institutions, the sources of subjectivity in their Foucauldian–Althusserian analysis, share the loss of the inside–outside distinction, bringing about an 'omni-crisis' in which the core terms of institutions—family values, prison discipline—spread throughout societies in criss-crossing conflicts which Empire must manage. This process they characterise as 'corruption', which means 'on the one hand, that Empire is impure or hybrid and, on the other, that imperial rule functions by breaking down… Empire requires that all relations be accidental'.[3] At the same time, in a parallel movement, production quits its location in the factories and is generalised across all social relations: 'The universality of human creation, the synthesis of freedom, desire, and living labour, is what takes place in the non-place of the postmodern relations of production'.[4] And yet, oppression and exploitation are also ubiquitous. This concept of Empire as a pervasive, dispersed, de-institutionalised and immanent sovereignty requires a new mode of political radicalism, one that is as global as Empire itself.

It is easy enough to hear in Hardt and Negri's account echoes of a utopian modernism which is at once immensely powerful in the art world. As de Duve argues, the development of an art of anything goes (*n'importe quoi*) in Duchamp's *Fountain* grounded a universalist ethos that not only whatever can be art but whoever can make it.[5] Through to the work of Beuys, and in the street, pop and interactive media arts, that thesis has been a hallmark of a modernist project in crisis; a democratisation that is also a devaluation. In Flusser's vocabulary, any artist then becomes a functionary, 'a person who plays with an apparatus and acts as a function of apparatus'.[6] The 'whoever' of imperial democracy is only different as a function of the apparatus of their identity, and their art entirely a product of the functioning of that apparatus in conjunction with the apparatus of art. This is the same function as that analysed by Hardt and Negri: the repositioning of production as a generalised and de-localised creativity perpetually managed in the process of omni-crisis in the interests of Empire.

In this context, it is worth noting a subtle drift in discussions of globalisation. Through the 1990s, one critical term was 'identity', and identity politics was placed counter to the operations of a globally homogenising capitalism. Though in more sophisticated analyses, identity was always understood as an effect rather than a given; nonetheless, as de Duve observes in another context:

Relativism is endemic, and when the claim to the universality of aesthetic judgement (which is to aesthetics what Kant's categorical imperative is to ethics, and thus the contrary of the pretention to universalism of values) is relinquished, we are left with, at best, commercial competition among cultural values and, at worst, ethnic warfare.[7]

In their response to the question of subjectivity and identity, Hardt and Negri draw on Etienne Balibar's influential concept of neo-racism. For Balibar, the old racism was biologically based, a matter of inheritance that excluded certain differences from civilisation, and encouraged their subordination or eradication (women, first nations). But the new racism is cultural. It specifies not the genetic but the cultural formation of the individual, assimilating those differences whole into a hybrid republic, but nonetheless discriminating on the basis that one cultural formation is more fitted for better-paid, higher-status jobs, and another for low pay and low status. Similarly, Deleuze and Guattari's construct 'White-man face' has no exterior, and therefore no excluded other. Instead, 'Racism operates by the determination of degrees of difference in relation to the White-man face, which endeavours to integrate non-conforming traits into increasingly eccentric and backward waves'.[8] Like Barthes' emblematic *Paris–Match* photo of the young black soldier saluting the French flag, postmodern imperialism colonises by assimilating, managing and exploiting difference. As de Duve argues, this is therefore no basis for a cultural politics, and as Rasheed Araeen has observed, assessing the growing capacity, even cupidity of the metropolitan art world to assimilate third-world artists, 'The victim is important for the liberal gaze, it is the way the powerful prove their humanism, and thus deflect the critical gaze of the deprived from its source of power.'[9] Identity politics is the politics of managerial imperialism, the unpaid research and development wing of the global exploitation of creativity wherever and whenever it occurs.

THE DISTRIBUTION PROBLEM

Among my notes on questions left over after the Empires, Ruins + Networks event in Melbourne, I find the following:

Is creativity a right or a goal? Or is it a property of labour, perhaps the most valuable in contemporary capital? How can global networks create non-exploitative avenues for creativity?

Is 'culture' an instrument of rule, of self-exploitation, and the last bastion of the legitimation of states? Does multiculturalism deny the validity of any one culture, local or global?

Is an alternate civil society possible, one that's capable of linking multi-locally, as opposed to globally? Is the bureaucracy the only service left that's genuinely civil, protecting plural voices against globalism? Is some supra-national protection possible? Desirable?

What is the status of the past in this? Can we shirk our duty to be responsible for all the past? How do we recognise both the guilt and the achievements of the past? Are we right to distinguish culturally between what our own people did and what others achieved? What responsibilities do we who are alive owe to the dead, and to the non-human environment, to the places and the times among which we live?

What ethical obligations are proper to teachers, writers, curators, artists? Is it proper for one profession to luxuriate in despair and another to proliferate naïve optimism?

How to reconcile the claims of the renewal of tradition and the celebration of hybridity?

A number of these questions share a common theme: the question of distribution, not only in space but in time. The critical literature on art tends to focus on production and on textuality, with some beginnings of work on the audience for art. But, in common with other cultural critique, art history largely ignores the question of circulation and its management outside museum studies and applied courses in curation. Given that artists will make work whatever the circumstances, and that the evidence is that other people will come and find it, who wants to change the distributive regimes of the art world? Emergent technologies in the twentieth century have struggled to find new modes of distribution—artists' film and video, broadcast interventions, mail and fax art, graffiti, recorded music and most recently the World Wide Web have battled to secure corners of an otherwise commercial universe for alternative uses. The sad truth is that the galleries and museums have been deeply reluctant to alter the terms of distribution on which they thrive, or to buck the collectively normative discourse of the art press.

To a great extent, the contradictions and paradoxes noted in these questions can be resolved in a single term: commodification. Labour and creativity, the past and the environment, professional services, the future of the state and of global networks can easily be put to the test of the market. The cold logic of neo-liberal economics exists precisely to answer such questions, to manage the unmanageable differences that constitute culture, and by naming them 'culture'; to make them objects, lifestyles and services that can be assimilated into the cracked but fluid smoothness of Empire. Commodification has a second benefit: it brings all these issues within the deliberative regime of the law, notably of civil and contractual law and the discourse of rights. All these ethical 'goods' can also be situated as economic goods, and their trade understood as a set of contractual relationships in which satisfactions advertised should be delivered once purchased. If I buy a piece of tribal art, I expect to purchase authenticity. If authenticity isn't delivered, I have legal grounds for complaint. As civil servants or employees of corporations and trusts, curators are obliged to work within the commodity structure of contemporary capital, as are the publishers of journals, the owners of commercial galleries and ultimately any artist striving to make a profession and a living from her/his art. The existence of alternative networks for the distribution of under-recognised or marginal creative production is proof that the market is capable of innovation; and any innovation worth its salt will reach a commercial equilibrium state when it finds the scale of activity that the market will bear. These observations are not intended ironically. They outline the existing state of affairs through which the kinds of question that arise from the kinds of discussion established, in great good faith, in Melbourne in 2004 are actually answered on a day-to-day basis.

Yet, it is precisely this day-to-day business of art that creates the sense of exclusion, oppression and exploitation that the 'Empires, Ruins + Networks' conference was intended to address. The question of distribution raises issues of ethical and political responsibility, which the commodity response cannot contain. The rights accumulating around the commodity are neither ethical nor political. Instead, in their legality, they are consumer rights (and in some degree mirrored as the rights of workers in the art world, rights severely curtailed by habits of self-exploitation). Like the rights claimed in some historical variants of identity politics, notably in their first great flowering during the 1960s civil rights, Black Power, feminist and gay liberation movements, such rights take the form of cultural contracts. In the society of the spectacle identified in those years by Guy Debord,[10] however, these rights already reveal themselves as consumer goods, spectacularised alongside the 'right to party'. Consumption and production of cultural identities, once the initial shock of the sheer novelty was granted the status of a value, were rapidly cross-fertilised. For Marx, consumption was a particular moment in the cycle of production; by the later 1960s, and certainly today, just-in-time production of micro-market specific goods is indistinguishable from consumption, or distinguishable only as a moment in the cycle of consumption. This is a typical deterritorialisation of sovereignty in the new imperialism: the consumer is king. Only consumers have the power to make things change, and they have the right to do so by the statutory rights enshrined in trades description acts and contractual law. The UN's Universal Declaration of Human Rights declares, in Article 6, 'Everyone has the right to recognition everywhere as a person before the law',[11] an expression that has as its obverse the truth that everyone is everywhere subject to the law that guarantees them security, health services, education, freedom of expression and religion and those other rights which, in the developed economies and increasingly elsewhere, are traded as commodities. The key figure in the commodification of art, therefore, is not the artist, nor the art institution, but the consumer, just as the consumer is key to the free play of the market in everything else—in the end, the market for de Duve's art of the whatever.

As Rosemary Coombe argues, Native Title or Aboriginal Title—the claims to legal status for the rights of first peoples to be recognised in national legislatures and judiciaries—may allow us 'to better understand the properties of culture(s) and the politics of possessing identity in a contemporary world'.[12] The terms are used knowingly: cultural identity, whatever else it may be, can be laid claim to as a possession whose ownership confers certain control over its uses: intellectual property rights significant among them. The example of Aboriginal Title suggests further that though the commodity and consumerism are largely dirty words in the critical vocabulary, there is a job of work to be done among them. 'Civil society is also the society of consumption and spectacle', in the words of George Yudicé,[13] to such an extent that it may no longer be possible to discuss either culture or citizenship without comprehending their implication in the cycle of consumption. Working within the system may be not only a noble calling; it may be unavoidable. Yet, to work critically within the commodity system, it is essential to be able to gain some kind of critical perspective; to stand outside on some other ground.

CITIZENS AND MIGRANTS

The last question among my conference notes was this:

What are the special responsibilities of migrants and hosts to themselves and each other?

The question has special meaning for me. The child of Irish emigrants, I live now in Aotearoa New Zealand. Like many of my generation and my profession, I have never lived at home in any sense that my Maori friends and neighbours would recognise. What marks even this voluntary and privileged mode of migration as distinct from those who are at home here is in part at least the status of citizenship. Maori, the first people of Aotearoa, are my first hosts, and second the other citizens of the country. The activity of hosting is not one of those regularly associated with citizenship, but it is intrinsic to citizenship in the contemporary world. The citizen is distinguished from the consumer in that the consumer has rights but the citizen has duties. The consumer's last recourse is to litigation; that of the citizen to deliberation. Consumer rights, however, are far closer to universality than citizen obligations; unsurprisingly, given the ubiquity of the commodity form in the early twenty-first century.

A citizen's rights are anchored in space by the borders of her/his country and in time by the duration of citizenship in the case of people moving to a new country or those whose citizenship is revoked. Consumer rights, however, are enshrined in law, including international law, and therefore have the eternity and ubiquity of law. Consumer rights in this sense are physical: they concern matter and energy, goods and services. Citizen duties, however, are bound by dimensionality: by the spaces and times during which they hold good. While citizenship is a phenomenon of nationality, and therefore is as mobile as the national concept (for example, in national sovereignty over diplomatic enclaves), it is also bound to a country—a territory. Metaphorically, citizenship provides the dimensionality that the physical flows of consumption lack. In the eyes of the citizen, such flows of matter and energy take on the shape of things, more specifically of objects that are external to the duties of citizenship. So the citizen not only can, but is obliged to, assess the value of these newly segmented flows, to assess them from beyond the de-differentiating management of difference that marks the commodity flows of Empire.

One of the tasks of citizenship is cultural legitimation. From the standpoint of the consumer, cultural legitimacy is only secured by matching cultural production to cultural consumption on a market basis. But from the standpoint of the citizen, legitimacy is constantly sought and constantly reconstructed in a the dynamic equilibrium of hegemonic negotiation and dialogue. Here, the claims of residual and emergent formations have far stronger claims than simply market share: they are also capable of legitimating specific practices and products, and may pass on some other benefits in order to secure those that most interest their fractional profiles. As well as internal subsidies for validated cultural activities (cinema, not games; opera, not comic books), a critical function of citizenship in the state is exercised at the border. For the citizen, the border is not only a cultural marker: it is the site of a membrane separating the country from the world. It serves, for example, as an epidemiological boundary; as the border marking the security that is such a crucial legitimating factor of the state; and as the limit point of cultural policy. In this last guise, the national boundary (with some exceptions, notably Kurdistan) flags not only the limit of the state, but also the limit of indigeneity, especially in Aotearoa New Zealand and in Australia. As Daniel Salée argues, globalisation of indigenous struggles actually increases local commitment: indigenous struggles are taken to global forums, not in order to transcend national boundaries, but rather to exercise additional pressures on national governments.[14]

Citizenship is perhaps a shallower experience than indigeneity but it is inseparable from the space–time of the traditional, land-based cultures that precede, nourish and in the end legitimate it. It is the indigenous that turns space into place: place is contingent on indigeneity. And citizenship is contingent on place. This dependent relation is deeply satisfying, but it is also deeply entrenched in the discourse of exception that separates the citizen and the citizen's country from the world. This is the paradox of Kantian cosmopolitanism: the phrase 'citizen of the world' is an oxymoron. Citizenship that gives dimension to its patch of earth cannot be reconciled with the place-lessness of the global consumer. The consumer, integral to the flows of production and consumption, is 'unfree' because she/he is incapable of self-reflexive critique. Citizenship is a prisoner in the space and time it constructs. Worse still, the instant gratifications of consumption's flows cannot be matched in the slower cycles of citizenship's construction of history and place. The economy of a nation would happily consume as many migrants as it needed, if only it could guarantee getting rid of them in a downturn. But given the historical task of citizenship, the possibility of instant turnaround is not available. Immigration control is not only a major legitimating function of the state, not only the most significant cultural policy aspect of its work, but a critical task for making history, the task not only of the state but of its citizens. This job is not only incommensurable with the timescales of consumption: it inhabits a wholly different world, a world of space–time that is literally imperceptible to the two-dimensional world of the consumer. The citizen's world is a world of artificial and natural objects, notably the bounded space of the country and its history, on which they are dependent. What kind of liberation then is possible? Vilém Flusser:

> But humans are not completely contingent. There is in their sur-roundings one place without things … This place that is free of things may be called the ironic. When we take an ironic stance, we are afforded a clearer view of our contingence.[15]

Foucault's politics depends on the existence of boundaries at which the constructions of subjectivity are in the balance. Flusser, however, is concerned with the transactions and transmissions that cross boundaries, and specifically with the experience of migration. The freedom of the migrant is the fruit of an existential crisis, of the forced or willed abandonment of home, but its result is the unexpected gift of freedom—from habitual horizons of reference, from unexamined traditions, from the dimensions specific, to every national and cultural formation. Although Flusser does not stipulate it, I believe this first moment of freedom, this moment of irony, is the moment elected by Nietzsche, whom Wyndham Lewis once described as 'the archetype of the vulgarizer… he set out to vulgarize… the notion of aristocracy'.[16] Nietzsche's freedom is the freedom of the elect, an ironic gaze from the mountaintop onto the miserable dupes below. For Flusser, however, this is only the first moment of freedom. The second, far more difficult, comes not from departure but from arrival. The exile arrives in the new home as something new, something different. Such difference is information; Bateson's 'difference that makes a difference'. The exile 'becomes the catalyst for the synthesis of new information' in an external dialogue with those that now surround him/her. At the same time, however, in an internal dialogue, the migrant compares the old home with the new, making with luck some creative novum out of their disparities.

> When such internal and external dialogues resonate with each other, not only the world but the settled inhabitants and the expellees as well are transformed creatively … the freedom of the expellee consists in remaining foreign, different from the others. It is the freedom to change oneself and others.[17]

Flusser, exiled from Czechoslovakia as a Jew and from Brazil by the military dictatorship, is not starry-eyed. He knows that the dialogue with the foreigner is as often angry, even murderous, as it is invigorating and open. No one said freedom would be easy. Critical to my argument is the insight that the migrant brings to the physics of consumption and dimensionality of citizenship the possibility of information.

In his enquiry into the origins of sovereignty, Giorgio Agamben lights upon the ancient Roman figure of *homo sacer*, the outcast who is at once the property of the gods and excluded from the normal prohibition against killing. Here,

Agamben discovers what he takes to be an original asymmetry: 'the sovereign is the one with respect to whom all men are potentially *homines sacri*, and *homo sacer* is the one with respect to whom all men act as sovereigns'.[18] Seated at the border between order and violence, the *homo sacer* defines both; the arbiter, in information theory's terms, of what it is to be information. The migrant is always prepared to discover that both the world and he/she is devoid of meaning: it is an abyss into which every exile has peered. Nonetheless, the migrant's freedom depends upon the existence of a citizenship from which it departs and another citizenship into which it arrives. There is, in other words, no pure externality, save only the tragic solipsism of Nietzsche's superman, an ironic freedom perpetually indebted to the oppression and toil of others. Migration is a moment in a process that embraces even as it is divided from the homely dimensions of citizenship, the geographies and traditions that make place and incite responsibilities. The migrant longs for responsibility, the obligations that create community, but her/his task is always to be different, and thence to signify.

Rather than answer my own questions—the logic of this argument suggests that the answers will in any case be social, not individual—I have tried in these pages to suggest the grounds on which they may be answered. Incorporating the moments of production, distribution and consumption, the cycle of consumer, citizen and migrant suggests a different mediation between the moments of a material existence; all that we have left to us in the immanent sovereignty of Empire. The human polis of the twenty-first century is already global. In the figure of the migrant, we can descry someone akin to Agamben's 'bare life': a different and therefore significant character whose rights and obligations are perpetually in question and perpetually having to be remade, suspended in a perpetual moment of arrival, only ever partially recognised as human, vulnerable, sacred. The cosmopolitan polis is in process of building now. It includes Kant's Eighth Thesis from the 'Idea for a Universal History with a Cosmopolitan Intent'.

> One can regard the history of the human species, in the large, as the
> realisation of a hidden plan of nature to bring about an internally, and for
> this purpose, also an externally perfect national constitution, as the sole
> state in which all of humanity's natural capacities can be developed.[19]

Although, as Hardt and Negri adduce, nature is no longer the repository of sovereignty, the developing international political regime, in all its ecological complexity of treaties, courts, alliances and pacts, is gradually forming a political unity, however contradictorily fragmentary as well as integrationist. For all its faults, the United Nations and other international bodies make it increasingly difficult (albeit still possible) for nations to go to war with each other. Equally successful, in its own terms, are the GATT and GATS agreements, in place now for more than fifty years and increasingly throwing open world markets to the interests of capital. What is missing from this scenario is the free movement of people, and the freedom of others to stay where they wish to be. In the rarified language of philosophy, we are all of us migrants, but by the same token we are all of us hosts, citizens whose obligations may yet extend to the social creativity of that challenging, dangerous, violent interface with the carrier of difference. As the migrant must surrender the pleasures of irony, the host must surrender the comforts of familiarity to achieve the freedom of being at home.

NOTES

1   Robert Cooper, 'The New Liberal Imperialism', *Observer Worldview*, 7 April 2002, <http://www.observer.co.uk/worldview/story/0,11581,680095,00.html>; also published as 'The Post-Modern State' in *Reordering the World: The Long Term Implications of September 11*, The Foreign Policy Centre, London, <http://www/fpc.org.uk>.

2   Michael Hardt and Antono Negri, *Empire*, Cambridge, MA, Harvard University Press, 2000.

3   Ibid., p. 202.

4   Ibid., p. 210.

5   Thierry de Duve, *Nominalisme picturale: Marcel Duchamp, la peinture et la modernité*, Paris, Editions de Minuit, 1984, trans. here by the author.

6   Vilém Flusser, *Towards a Philosophy of Photography*, trans. Anthony Matthews, intro. Hubertus Von Amelunxen, London, Reaktion Books, 2000, p.83.

7   Thierry de Duve, 'Postmodernism, Ethics and Aesthetics in the Age of Global Markets' in Jody Berland and Shelley Hornstein (eds), *Capital Culture: A Reader on Modernist Legacies, State Institutions, and the Value(s) of Art*, Montréal, McGill-Queen's University Press, 2000, p. 62.

8   Gilles Deleuze and Félix Guattari, *A Thousand Plateaus: Capitalism and Schizophrenia*, trans. Brian Massumi, Minneapolis, University of Minnesota Press, 1987, p. 178.

9   Rasheed Araeen, 'A New Beginning: Beyond Post-colonial Cultural Theory and Identity Politics', *Third Text*, 50, Spring, 2000, p. 17.

10   Guy Debord, *The Society of the Spectacle*, revised trans. [no trans. credit], Detroit, Black & Red, 1977.

11   United Nations, *Universal Declaration of Human Rights*, 1948, <http://www.un.org/Overview/rights.html>, accessed 12 May 2004.

12   Rosemary Coombe, *The Cultural Life of Intellectual Properties: Authorship, Appropriation and the Law*, Durham NC, Duke University Press, 1998, p. 247.

13   George Yudicé, 'Civil Society, Consumption and Governmentality in an Age of Global Restructuring', *Social Text*, 45, 1995, p. 5.

14   Daniel Salée, '*De la coupe aux lèvres : l'action politique des peuples autochtones sur la scène internationale et la reconfiguration des paramètres de la citoyenneté au Canada*', in M. Labelle, F. Rocher et A. M. Field (eds), *Contestation transnationale, diversité*

et citoyenneté dans l'espace québécois, Montréal, Presses de l'Université du Québec, 2004, pp. 156–207, trans. here by the author.

15   Vilém Flusser, *The Freedom of the Migrant: Objections to Nationalism*, trans. Kenneth Kronenberg, intro. Anke K. Finger (ed.), Urbana, University of Illinois Press, 2003, p. 20.

16   Wyndham Lewis, 'The Art of Being Ruled' [1926] in E. W. F. Tomlin (ed.), *Wyndham Lewis: An Anthology of his Prose*, London, Methuen, 1968, p. 114.

17   Vilém Flusser, *The Freedom of the Migrant*, p. 86.

18   Giorgio Agamben, *Homo Sacer: Sovereign Power and Bare Life,* trans. Daniel Heller-Roazen, Stanford, CA, Stanford University Press, 1998, p. 84.

19   Immanuel Kant, *Perpetual Peace and Other Essays on Politics, History and Morals,* trans. Ted Humphrey, Indianapolis IN, Hackett Publishing, 1983, p. 36.